# *Prom* NIGHT

# Prom NIGHT

## Youth, Schools, and Popular Culture

### Amy L. Best

ROUTLEDGE
A member of the Taylor & Francis Group
*New York & London*

Published in 2000 by
Routledge
29 West 35th Street
New York, NY 10001

Published in Great Britain by
Routledge
11 New Fetter Lane
London EC4P 4EE

*Routledge is an imprint of the Taylor & Francis Group.*

Printed in the United States of America on acid-free paper.

10 9 8 7 6 5 4 3 2 1

Library of Congress Cataloging-in-Publication Data

Best, Amy L., 1970–
    Prom night : youth, schools, and popular culture / Amy L. Best.
    p. cm.
    ISBN 0-415-92427-8 — ISBN 0-415-92428-6 (pbk.)
    1. Proms—Social Aspects—United States. 2. Proms—
United States—History—20th century. 3. High school
students—United States—Social life and customs—20th
century. I. Title.

GV1746.B49 2000
394'.3—dc21                                    00-041505

*For my grandmother*
*Helene Delano Holland*

Popular culture is made by the people, not produced by the culture industry. All the culture industries can do is produce a repertoire of texts or cultural resources for the various formations of the people to use or reject in the ongoing process of producing their popular culture.

—John Fiske, *Reading the Popular*

# Contents

# Acknowledgments

Attending high school as a white middle-class girl in a predominately white, largely upper-middle-class suburban community, I experienced a strange blending of privilege and powerlessness. My being white and middle-class resolutely gave me certain advantages and a sense of power that now as an adult often make me feel more than a little uneasy. Yet, it is unlikely that as a teenage girl I would ever have felt the sense of mightiness I felt had I not had a group of girlfriends who always inspired me by their collective sense of possibility. For friendships that have carried me into my adulthood I am grateful to MaryBeth Ihnken, Jodi (Cohen) Vince, Doc (Kriegsmann) Leddy, Jill Garner, Jiffy (Kriegsmann) Cassolini, Abby Chickering, Lisa (Brady) Maurer, and Karin (Helland) Farrell. You have shaped this book in ways that I could never fully explain. I also feel extraordinarily indebted to my family, particularly my parents, Natalie Best and Gary Best, and my sister, Christine Best, for believing in this project and, most importantly, in me.

This book is based on research I began as a graduate student. As such, many thanks are due to those who helped shape this project and my development as a sociologist. Thank you to Judith Barker, Jim Rothenberg, and Mike Yarrow, professors at Ithaca College, who challenged me in ways that changed my life. The environment at Syracuse University, where I studied as a graduate student, was also an intellectually supportive one. Especially, I would like to thank Judy Long, Sari Knopp Biklen, Marj DeVault, Julia Loughlin, and Rosaria Champagne, without whom this project would have never gotten off the ground or grown in the way it did. Without the critical push from Sari Knopp Biklen, it is unlikely I would ever have taken up such a project as a theoretical one. Her careful reading of this manuscript as it neared its completion provided me with much insight. Marj DeVault shaped my understanding of the methodological possibilities in countless ways. I feel especially lucky for having worked with Judy Long, my friend and thesis advisor, whose lifelong work as a feminist scholar helped carve out a space for a feminist sociologist like me to be institutionally supported. I am without words to express the extent of my gratitude, inspiration, and admiration.

To Leslie Bogad, whose critical insights contributed centrally to this becoming a book, and to the Popular Culture Institute at Syracuse University for its members' spirited and lively conversation, I am deeply indebted. Ian Lapp, Robin Riley, and Brenda Solomon, among so many others, were three with whom I always relished the chance to talk. Additionally

I would like to extend my thanks to Michelle Fine, for her comments on this project in its early stages, and to Amy Holzgang for her reading in its final stages. The sociology department at San Jose State University was particularly supportive as I worked to finish this book. A debt of gratitude goes to the School of Social Sciences at San Jose State University for their support during the last legs of this project. I am most grateful for the extensive comments from my editor, Ilene Kalish. Her suggestions were so critical and significant, I shall never underestimate the depths of her knowing, and her uncompromising sense of staying "true" to this project. I would be remiss if I were not to thank the kids I interviewed, for rearranging their schedules and letting me listen to what they had to say so that I could complete this project. A special thank you to Erika Lovette for providing me with much-needed photographs.

The loving support I received daily from my partner, Chris McCauley, was priceless. I am especially beholden for the various ways he believed in me and my work, and for his exhaustive efforts to create a space in which I could work. For helping me along the way for what has seemed a lifetime, what can I say?

# *One*

⁓

# *Introduction*

## A Night to Remember

While I was researching this project, a student gave birth in a bathroom stall at her high school prom. News coverage reported that after delivery she dropped the newborn into a garbage can and returned to the prom for one last dance.[1] This became a major story headlining televised and print news reports. Yet the media fury was quickly followed by a succession of public judgments decrying that the character of our nation's youth had plummeted to the irretrievable depths of moral degeneracy. The irony of this event was difficult to miss. An event often upheld as a last preserve of adolescent innocence, the prom, collided with a morally charged and tension-laden issue, teenage pregnancy—one celebrated, the other reviled. Further, the death of a newborn gave greater fuel to one of our nation's most recent media obsessions: senseless teen violence.

I first learned of this story not from the news, but from someone I worked with while living in New York City. It was such a bizarre story, fantastic in the true sense of the word, that I couldn't really believe it. But sure enough, when I returned home from work and turned on the news, there it was. For the next several days every time I turned on the television, updates of this story, termed the story of the "prom mom" in the popular press, were broadcast. That this girl was white, middle-class, and living in a suburb rather than urban, poor, or of color seems particularly relevant for understanding why this incident received so much attention. Since their development, the suburbs have been seen as spaces of shelter for white middle-class youth, insulating them from a changing world.[2] Just as suburbia is constructed as a safe space, so is the suburban school. Perhaps there is no event that epitomizes this safety more than the prom. The prom traditionally has been thought of as a domain of frivolous adolescent fun: an event at which kids dress up, have their pictures taken, and dance the night away. We are constantly presented with images of the prom in which teenagers, usually white and middle-class, are engaged in such examples of good-natured fun.

This story seemed to shatter the mythic image of suburban life, of white middle-class girlhood, of the "typical teen." Mobilized by fear of a generation out of control, the message was striking: our youth are in trouble.[3] That a baby could be killed at the high school prom seemed to further signal a complete collapse of all that was considered good and safe about adolescent life and schooling in white suburban America.

The prom is an iconic event in American culture, one that is consistently drawn upon in contemporary media to show the triumphs and travails of youth. Along with high school graduation, the prom is often heralded as one of the most important experiences in high school, perhaps even of all adolescence. Images of the prom as a coming-of-age rite permeate our culture. Yet, if we were to presume that the prom is a rite of passage, to what precisely would it be a rite of passage?

Perhaps, at some other moment in U.S. adolescent history, the prom may have been occasion for a young woman to stay out past eleven o'clock for the first time, or to wear brightly colored lipstick instead of a more discreet shade; it may have also been the first time a young man's parents permitted him to drive their car. For kids today, breaking early curfew for the first time at the prom has little salience; lots of them drive their own cars, and most girls become competent beauty practitioners well before entering high school. This rendering of youth, perched at the threshold of adulthood (favored not only in popular thought but in scholarly literature), provides limited understanding for how kids experience school life today. Not only does this rhetoric of *becoming* have little relevance to how kids define the experience of being young, it deflects, by glossing over, the contested and contradictory practices through which daily life inside and outside of school is made meaningful. Understanding proms and the different ways that they are organized, experienced, and defined requires that we look at them as more than fleeting moments in the history of kids' lives. The prom is a space in which teens make sense of what it means to be young in culture today, negotiate the process of schooling, solidify their social identities, and struggle against the structural limits in which they find themselves.

*Prom Night* sheds light on how proms, a curiously ignored subject among academics, figure in the lives of high school students.[4] We need to broaden and complicate our cultural understandings of what proms are, how they work and how they are socially organized. A high school prom can be many things: image, experience, and event that comes together through the local activities of students, teachers, parents, communities, and schools, but it is not simply a local event. High school proms everywhere are mediated by a series of external forces, largely invisible within their immediate settings. Understanding how proms work requires that we inquire into the larger cultural terrain in which proms are experienced and defined, not just by kids but by the larger culture in which youth resides. Drawing upon a rich body of cultural studies literature and ethnographic work on proms spanning several years, *Prom Night* traces how proms emerge as moments of tension in the history of kids' school lives.

Such moments of tension often involve far greater stakes than what to wear or what kind of car to drive, as in the following cases. In Wedowee, Alabama, a school was set ablaze after the principal canceled the prom in a last-ditch effort to forestall interracial dating; a gay student sued his Rhode Island high school for the right to attend his prom with his boyfriend; African-American students at an integrated Georgia High School protested because the prom music reflected the tastes of the school's white students. Extreme as these examples may be, they provide some indication that proms, hardly inconsequential, can often be the starting point for the formation of a youth politics. Proms can offer tremendous insight into how kids engage in the cultural politics of their worlds. These examples also demonstrate that proms are not experienced uniformly among youth; historically specific relations of race and socially constituted sexual and gender practices impact in profound ways the meanings kids attach to this event and how they narrate their prom experiences. The prom is hardly just a fun space to dress up in (though it is partly that). Located at the intersection of school, commercial, and youth cultures, proms are contentious spaces wherein kids work through central issues surrounding questions of authority, class, diversity, sexuality, and romance.

Studying proms can tell us much about how students negotiate life in school, how they participate in the ongoing production of cultural life, and the relations of constraint that frame their participation. Understanding the important role proms play in young people's lives has meant listening to kids talk about their proms, taking seriously what they have to say, and then creating a space in which their words can be heard. If we are attentive listeners, we will gain from the lessons they offer us.

### More than Just a Dance: Pleasure and the Commodity Market

Proms are not what they used to be. The prom has gradually moved from the high school gym to the luxury hotel. Many students now rent limousines or expensive luxury cars (e.g., BMWs, Porsches, or Range Rovers) to go to their prom, rather than drive their own or their parents' cars. Just as the process of being schooled can no longer be separated from commodity culture, so too is the prom influenced by a range of practices shaped by market and economy.[5] Buying french fries from McDonalds to eat during study hall, drinking a Diet Coke bought from a soda machine in the school cafeteria, or listening to music on a CD Walkman on the way to class are increasingly part of normal life in school. While consumerism has become part of the dynamics of everyday school life, cutbacks in public resources have given rise to the private sector's involvement in schooling curricula and policy. Multinational corporations like Burger King, Coca-Cola, and Nike are among the many corporations that provide funding to schools. Though few scholars agree on what this actually means for today's schools, most agree it has dramatically altered how schools are organized.

Proms epitomize the expansion of a distinct youth consumer culture and the spending power of youth. How proms are organized and the forms they take express the increasing influence of the cultural industries (e.g., those of fast food, fashion, and music) in schools and, in general, the pervasive force of consumerism in society today. Though scholars seem to know very little about proms, marketers have an astute knowledge of how they work. *Your Prom* and *Teen Prom,* two teen magazines, conduct reader surveys each year to better grasp how and what their readers consume as they prepare for their prom: "How many stores will you visit when shopping for a prom dress?" "Check which of the following you use and which you will buy for prom night." "Would you be interested in looking at gowns like these for other special occasions such as homecoming?" These are just a few of the questions posed in one reader survey.

Much of this market focus on proms is geared toward girls; the emphasis on consumption, beauty, and romance for girls is stunning. Popular girls' beauty magazines, including *Seventeen* and *Young and Modern,* now dedicate entire monthly editions to preparing for the prom, while a small but significant number of romance novels for young adult readers has developed around the prom (including titles such as *Much Ado About Prom Night* and *Girl Gives Birth to Her Own Prom Date).* In these texts the prom is packaged as a feminized space, wrapped up in contemporary conceptions of heterosexual romance.[6] Proms are often marketed as "pre-weddings"—as rehearsals for a young woman's "inevitable" wedding day. This comes as little surprise, given that *Modern Bride,* one of the most widely distributed bridal magazines, publishes *Your Prom,* one of the leading prom magazines.[7] A number of afternoon talk shows, including *Jenny Jones* and *Oprah,* have hosted shows featuring the latest fashions in prom dresses, and both Macy's and Nordstrom's department stores host annual prom fashion shows. (*It's Not Your Mother's Prom* was the title of Macy's 1999 prom fashion show.) Capitalizing on the idea that girls' identities today signify a more modern, hip, and girl-centered form of femininity, the message is clear: This is your prom; you can express yourself in any way you want, just make a statement!

Proms tie kids to cultural industries by harnessing their pleasure in consumption. Limousines, prom magazines, expensive dresses, dinners at upscale restaurants, luxury hotels, and long weekends at the beach (a common occurrence for wealthier kids who live on the East and West Coasts) are central aspects of experiencing the prom for many students who appear in this study. Their investments in the prom are mediated by their consumption of these prom products, so significantly that at times it was difficult for me to distinguish between the girls I talked to and those who appeared in the fashion magazines. Young people spend an exorbitant amount of money on their prom; one prom website estimated an average of $500 per person is spent in going to the prom. A 1996 prom poll featured in *Your Prom* magazine reported that $800 is the average cost of a prom per couple, $188 is the average cost of a prom dress, and 45 percent of students rent limos. Once an evening lasting a few hours, "the prom" now lasts a period of several days. While a number of students finance the event by saving their earnings from after-school employment or from their weekly allowance, others (those who are able) turn to their parents for support.

Proms can hardly be understood today without attention to the overwhelming influence of a commodity-based culture over modern constructions of the self, school, and cultural life. The prom is a historically specific event; its particular organization is shaped by time, place, and space. What, then, is the historical context within which the prom has emerged? What are the prom's historical roots? In what follows, I provide a brief sketch of the particular historical and cultural currents that have shaped the organization of proms in contemporary social life.

### Proms and the Rise of the "Adolescent"

Young people have to learn gracious manners and social good taste just as they have to learn anything else, and well managed school dances and parties provide excellent opportunities for practice.

—*Parent's* magazine, 1935

Proms first emerged in the early twentieth century amid significant economic, social, and institutional changes. First and most significant to their development were changes in who was able to attend school: throughout the nineteenth and the early twentieth centuries, more youth began attending high school. Schools had once been open to the children of the middle and upper classes only, because working-class youth had been forced to work in the fields and the factories. School, in a sense, was a luxury.[8]

With this increase of student enrollment, public schools came to play a greater role in the organization of the social body, the management of social order and the maintenance of class divisions.[9] In the service of state and economy, schools helped to shape which occupational identities youth would occupy in their adult lives. At the same time they were (unofficially) responsible for the transmission of middle-class values to the working (under) classes.[10] School clubs, school dances, and student government increasingly became a significant part of kids' lives. [11]

While the expansion of schooling played a key role in the prom's emergence, also of importance were the social reform movements of the early twentieth century (organized largely by white middle-class women) to secure democracy for a rapidly changing nation.[12] Like changes in school, widespread social reform was largely a consequence of rapid urban and industrial expansion and the social unrest these expansions caused.[13] Scholars have argued that these democratic reform campaigns were organized to gain the participation of the working class in upholding democracy. To foster democratic allegiance among those who theretofore had not experienced the benefits of democracy, democratic reformers worked to open a range of social practices once reserved exclusively for the governing elite.[14]

While the initial efforts of these social reformers were genuine attempts to extend democracy to the economically disadvantaged, the effects were dubious.[15] Such democratizing impulses reflected a broader aim of the governing class to secure their own economic interests, though much of this remained hidden by a rhetoric of democracy.[16] Opening the leisure spaces that had been once closed to the downtrodden, the governing class was able to advance what William Graebner refers to as a program of "democratic assimilation."[17] Accordingly, the prom was a democratized version of the debutante ball, an event historically attended by only the leisure class.[18] As a "popularized" debutante ball, the prom afforded anyone attending high school the opportunity to feel as though they too were "coming out," that they could transcend the boundaries of class. The message was that you did not have to be rich to wear a fancy frock, to be adorned with a corsage, or to waltz the night away.[19]

Gaining the consent of a governed class of laborers and their children for the notion of democracy secured the continued advancement of a rapidly expanding capitalist economy.[20] Work and education became an expression of a democratic commitment; leisure was organized to serve the interests of capitalism. A plethora of organized social activities such as proms, sports events, and parades, and social spaces such as dance halls and parks, emerged.[21] Regulating these spaces, the governing class was able to manage in less visible (and less physically coercive) ways how disenfranchised groups, particularly these groups' younger members, came together not just within the work setting but now also outside it.[22]

Though proms emerged sometime after the turn of the century, they did not gain in popularity until the early 1930s. Their popularity stems largely from the discursive changes in how youth had been culturally identified and constructed as a distinct age group. Though youth had been treated as a cohort having distinctive habits and traits by scholars since the mid-nineteenth century, by the 1930s the idea of the *adolescent* was firmly entrenched in both popular cultural lore and scholarly work (shaped in part by the popularization of the discipline of psychology). At the threshold of adulthood, adolescence signified a tumultuous stage in the life course, a period of uncertainty and angst.[23] Accordingly, middle-class experts urged parents and schools that adolescents (belonging to both the working class and their own class) needed guidance to ensure their development as morally upstanding citizens and responsible adults.[24] The best plan of action was to provide well-structured, adult-supervised social activities.[25] A growing concern for adolescents' moral and psychological development, combined with the fact that their lives were increasingly consumed by activities outside of the home, led to more concerted efforts to socialize youth.[26]

By the 1940s, kids' leisure lives were tied less to family and bound increasingly to commodity culture. *Teens* had emerged as a distinct consumer category.[27] Realizing the economic potential of middle-class adolescent buying power resulting largely from the expansion of a middle class and its growing prosperity following World War II, the market transformed the leisure activities of kids, the spaces they occupied, and the activities in which they engaged. Kids had money to spend, and marketers knew it! As a newly discovered niche, youth activities were harnessed, mobilized, and redirected for accelerated capitalist growth. The leisure of youth was radically reinvented around consumption; the market was dramatically redesigned around leisure.[28] Entire markets developed around the idea of distinct teen commodities: makeup, clothes, and soft drinks promised to ensure a particular kind of teen experience.[29]

Though this "discovery" was presumably good for the economy, it also meant that parents (particularly the middle class) had less direct control over their children, from where they spent their free time to what they consumed. The emergence of a teen leisure market generated questions of concern about youth sexuality, delinquency, and complacency among (largely middle-class) adults. A wealth of organized activities for youth sprung up to guard against youth complacency and delinquency.[30] By the mid-twentieth century, high school proms, along with teen canteens and sock hops, were a mainstay of middle-class cultural life.[31]

In the late 1940s, juvenile delinquency also had gained growing public consideration and was treated as a pressing domestic social problem; "bad" teens were understood as a threat to U.S. democracy within an expanding global context.[32] While schools functioned as sites of ideological control, proms especially performed the role of fending off the supposed propensity toward youth degeneracy. As William Graebner, one of the few scholars to address the social meaning of the prom, explains, "The prom was another class-linked celebration of maturity, a sort of coming out party sanctioned by parents and characterized by youth voluntarily shedding cultural and subcultural apparel for "adult" tuxedos and evening gowns, dancing to a traditional orchestra rather than popular records or rock n' roll and, in theory and outward appearance, sublimating sexuality in romance."[33] Elevating traditional notions of heterosexual courtship and dreamy romance, schools worked to contain what seemed to be an urgent problem not only among our nation's youth but for the future of democracy.

Vestiges of these programs to socialize youth to particular forms of adulthood can still be documented today. For the contemporary prom, formal invitations are sent to each of the class members; corsages and boutonnieres are worn by most prom attendants; dress codes are enforced; and students purchase their "prom bid" under the assumption that the bid is for two (heterosexual) people, not one.

Following World War II, high school proms were once again harnessed in support of a larger political project of "democratic assimilation" shaped by the uneasy Cold War climate felt at home and abroad. Graebner argues that during the 1940s and 1950s, extracurricular activities like the prom were part of a program to advance American democracy and in so doing, asserted and celebrated the political and economic power of the United States. Proms, student government, and after-school sports were organized to create a more cohesive, assimilated, and homogenous student body united against communism. Concerted attempts to impose social controls through the management of the social and sexual practices of youth were particularly heightened during the Cold War. Participation in school activities reflected a willingness to embrace one's patriotic duty and democratic commitment.

The prom's popularity waned in the late 1960s and early 1970s. With countercultural movements, antiwar protests, and an antiestablishment stance, many "irreverent" youth brought proms to a halt. However, the

---

The Class of 1958
Bristol High School

requests your company at the

Junior-Senior Banquet

on Thursday, the second day of May
nineteen hundred and fifty-seven

at six-thirty o'clock
Stacy-Trent Hotel
Trenton, New Jersey

Dress Formal

R. s. v. p.
by April 8th

---

The Class of 1989

of

Westfield High School

requests the pleasure of your company
at the Junior-Senior Prom
"This Is The Time"

on Friday, the twentieth of May
Nineteen hundred and eighty-eight

at eight o'clock in the evening
L'Affaire
Mountainside, New Jersey

reassertion of a conservative political agenda in the late 1970s and early 1980s combined with the concerted and accelerated efforts by marketers to carve out and expand youth markets, proms once again gained in popularity.

### *Proms as Contested Sites: School and Youth Cultures*

Given that proms are central to many students' experiences in high school, an important part of this study is what it can tell us about schooling. Specifically, *Prom Night* directs attention to how relations of power organize social settings connected to school. Like sports fields, locker rooms, the cafeteria, and cheerleading squads, proms are sites wherein students construct and make sense of a complex set of local social relations that order school life.[34] Only recently have educators begun to take seriously how these sites work to secure the pedagogical and social organization of modern schooling systems to forms of domination.[35] By and large, most studies of education have focused exclusively on the practices and politics of the classroom, ignoring the different ways ideologies of schooling shape a set of extended relations and spaces. The danger, of course, is that in overlooking these sites we belie consideration of the extent to which schools not only organize kids' academic lives but their leisure lives as well.[36]

Understanding how schools authorize and legitimate specific ideological practices by regulating spaces like the prom is important to understanding how identity and culture are mapped through day-to-day life in contemporary American institutions, and how power works within these local sites. The culture of schools actively works to secure kids' participation in the dominant organization of society and to imbricate kids in the relations of state and economy, though in vastly unequal ways.[37] Yet the power ordering school life is hardly a one-way process. Schools are contested spaces, organized around contradictory cultural and historical practices. They maintain forms of social domination by producing students' assent to hegemonic relations and ideas, but at the same time the very practices that work to control give rise to students' dissent.[38] Students find a range of ways to resist and evade schools' control over their lives and struggle, whether in the classroom or at a school dance, to exert influence over what forms of schooling are authorized.

Looking at schools as sites of struggle requires taking seriously not only those activities legitimated by schools, but the activities kids participate in, and the spaces they occupy outside the classroom, such as proms. The selection of music for the prom, though long overlooked by white students, administrators, and teachers, was seized by students of color at one integrated school in this study as an occasion not only to debate the place of multiculturalism in their specific school setting, but to create a space for "whiteness" to be interrogated. These sites and practices are repositories for youth to express their sense of culture, articulate their everyday class, race, and gender selves, and struggle against forms of authority. Attention to the meanings students develop about particular cultural practices inside and outside school, the type of investments they make in these practices and the pleasure they derive from participation in them requires a closer examination of popular cultural forms and how they shape the process of being schooled. To study schooling today, then, demands recognition of the impact of popular culture on the social organization of schools and school culture.[39]

Proms were historically tied to a schooling project used to govern the uncontrollable (youth). By enlisting youth to participate in middle-class rituals like the prom, schools were able to advance a program that reigned in students' emerging and increasingly public sexualities. Idealizing dating and romance, proms championed heterosexuality. Though they function to uphold a normative sexual and social order, proms figure more significantly as a space wherein these social forms, hardly secure, are negotiated. This is best highlighted in the recent emergence of the "gay prom." Given the considerable homophobia that permeates most high school life, queer youth organizations have begun hosting their own proms. The prom, an event that not only normalizes but institutionalizes heterosexuality, has been taken up by gay and lesbian youth as a space to solidify their identities and contest heterosexuality as a taken-for-granted cultural practice.

In other ways beyond the gay prom, kids use the prom as a site at which to counter their school's control over their social lives and self-expressions. At every level, proms include the negotiation of social meanings and social space. The meanings kids construct for proms within their local settings can disrupt the dominant organization of sexuality, gender, race, and class.

How do they cause such disruptions? What resources do they use? A range of rhetorical tactics including irony, mimicry, and parody are all employed to reconstruct social meaning, narrate students' shifting cultural identities, and disrupt the prom as a school space. For example, a group of students at a New York City high school decided not to hold a conventional prom. Instead, they organized a graduation dance called the MORP (which was, but was not, the prom). Such discursive plays represent an important part of youth politics this book seeks to capture and explore.

While the prom is resolutely a space of constraint, it is also a space of infinite possibility and self-(re)invention, a rich tapestry of spectacle and pageantry. Proms are spaces of performance and often emerge as meaningful sites in which to express a range of confrontational youth stances. Through what kids wear, how they style their hair, and how they dance, they negotiate and sometimes challenge dominant social forms, and in so doing forge a politics that arises from their places within social life. Using the resources offered within commodity culture (dresses and tuxedos, limousines, music, and corsages), kids struggle to define the prom outside the context of school and middle-class adult culture. How these commodities are assembled on or in relation to the bodies of these promgoers is key to deciphering the meanings they create at the prom.

Through dress, kids playfully mock and, in so doing, disrupt how the prom gets defined as a "sophisticated" social event by an adult world. One group of students at a suburban school outside Los Angeles abandoned the traditional prom regalia (tuxedos and gowns), choosing instead to outfit themselves in full gangster costume (replete with floor-length boas and pin-striped suits), thus enjoying an evening of rich role-playing with the prom as their stage. I myself can remember my placing an ostentatiously large, bright red artificial poinsettia in my hair moments before having my photo taken with my prom date by the hired photographer. (My mother still looks at the photo of me wearing this ridiculous flower behind my ear with a measured degree of motherly disgust.)

The surface of the body is a key site in articulating a youth politics of place, space, and identity at the prom.[40] Race, class, gender, and sexuality shape the expressions kids offer and the meanings they create. My placing that poinsettia in my hair had everything to do with the tension I felt around adolescence and white, middle-class femininity and how I chose to display this tension at the prom.

## On Methodology: Proms as Popular Culture

Culture is created in the dressing rooms of department stores, in the hallways of schools, in the cafeteria, and as teenage girls browse magazine racks looking for the new issue of *Your Prom* magazine. This project bears the unquestionable influence of John Clarke's "bricolage," a strategy that builds by examining pieces of cultural life, not to provide a single and cogent picture of what culture "is," but to make visible the multifarious and contradictory processes through which meanings of cultural life are made and shared.[41] This approach to studying culture is guided by the understanding that the processes of meaning-making occur within a play of forces, patterned by social structures but not fully determined by them.[42] There is agency in the production and reproduction of dominant culture, the ideological controls that secure it, and the social and material conditions upon which it relies. Yet just as cultural actors consent to and actively participate in re-creating the prevailing organization of culture they are also participants, though often in smaller ways, in the disruption of that culture. In this sense, Graebner explains, "the dominant culture is held to be something less than monolithic, beset by differences and divisions that create the opportunity for alternative ideas and practices."[43]

Influenced by the ethnographic work of scholars most often associated with the Birmingham school of cultural studies, *Prom Night* begins with the understanding that (popular) culture is made in the relationship *between* representational systems and lived social relations.[44] Culture is defined as an ongoing process that requires not only a close examination of those practices, symbols, artifacts, and texts that comprise and organize daily life, but also recognizing that these aspects of daily life carry different meanings for the people in these settings as they do for the dominant culture.

To capture what the prom means to kids and to schools, and at the same time to understand how social forces mediate the ways proms are experienced and defined, this study draws upon a range of materials for analysis, including observation, in-depth and informal interviewing, archival, electronic and contemporary print documents, and narrative analysis.[45]

I began studying proms by asking college students to write narratives about their prom memories. Reading through the narratives these students wrote, one of the first things I noticed was that a number of their accounts of the prom never actually mentioned the dance itself. Instead, students constructed their narratives around other related sites and activities, some focusing on their preparations for the prom, some writing about their school's social structure, and others centering their narratives on the postprom events. Many young women wrote about the difficult process of choosing a dress, while others wrote about their romantic expectations for the prom. What I realized from this early research is that the term *prom* (the *in* the *prom* is usually silent) is deployed by students in shorthand to represent a series of events, practices, and relations. The prom dance is just one of a series of sites and events that comprise this event.

*Prom Night* also draws upon fieldwork I conducted at four public schools during a two-year period. In addition to attending these schools' proms, I spent countless hours visiting the schools, talking with students before and after the proms and observing their preprom and postprom activities. In the school cafeterias and hallways and at their preprom events in the weeks before prom night, I had the opportunity to speak with a number of kids about proms and prom dresses, school, dating, popularity, life after high school, being young, and life in their local communities. Interested in how kids narrate cultural identity, I conducted twenty-three interviews with male and female students, mostly seniors, before and after their proms (appendix B). I also spoke with countless administrators, teachers, and parents to gain a sense of the institutional forces influencing kids' prom experiences. I studied "gay proms" primarily through an examination of newspaper articles chronicling their development. In addition, I interviewed four queer youth, two of whom had attended a "gay prom," and several queer youth leaders who had been active in organizing such proms. Analyzing contemporary and historical prom documents, including a wealth of films, prom websites, magazine articles, and advertisements, I was able to understand how proms are encoded in a wider cultural terrain (appendix C). Combining ethnography and cultural studies, I immersed myself in all aspects of the prom—even those that seemed, upon first glance, only peripherally related. I observed other settings connected to the actual prom dance including two prom fashion shows; the junior-miss sections of several department stores; a hair salon; a girl's bedroom, where a group of middle-class girls prepared for their prom; a florist shop; tuxedo rental shops; and a school-sponsored postprom party. Understanding the prom means understanding how these different settings contribute to its social organization.

## *The Schools*

Alhough I draw upon a range of materials for analysis, the core of this study centers on the development of the prom at four public high schools. How proms are arranged, experienced, and defined varies enormously from one school to another. To understand these differences and the varying social, economic, and political realities that give rise to them, consideration of how proms are arranged in each school is critically important. I specify the significance of race and class practices in shaping proms, and the different institutional contexts in which race and class are expressed. In selecting schools, I also chose to avoid making broad comparisons between the opposing extremes of the urban poor of color versus the white suburban rich. So often the complex configurations of class and race are collapsed into this binary. The four public schools are: Woodrow High School, Rudolph High School, Hudson High School, and Stylone High School.[46] Though similar in some ways, these schools differ in racial, ethnic, and class composition, in location, and in curriculum.

Woodrow High School, located in a midsized city in New York, was the first school studied, in 1996. Its student population is racially diverse: 40 percent of the student body at Woodrow are African American, 40 percent are

European American, and the remaining 20 percent identify themselves as either Latino/a or South Asian. Students also represent different class groups. Because of its proximity to a large university, many students have parents who are employed as university faculty or administrators, while a significant portion of students attending Woodrow belong to households that are a part of the growing number of poor and working poor. The city in which this school resides has suffered from rapid downsizing spurred by deindustrialization, which has resulted in significant economic decline and higher rates of unemployment for many households. These changing economic arrangements are reflected in the school's student population: 36 percent of students participate in the subsidized free lunch program. Fifty-four percent of graduates attend four-year colleges.

In 1997, I returned to the field to study three more schools. Rudolph High School's prom was the first. Rudolph is predominately white and is located in an affluent suburb, approximately one hour from a large northeastern city. A large percentage of parents are part of the professional, managerial class. Many are corporate leaders and executives, doctors, lawyers, and other professionals. Eighty-five percent of the students attend four-year colleges, and the students, on average, score in the 98th percentile on standardized scholastic assessment tests. Many of these students, following in their parents' footsteps, will occupy positions reserved for the professional middle class.

The following month I observed the proms at Hudson High School and Stylone High School, both of which are located in a large northeastern city. Like Woodrow, Hudson High School has a student body that is mixed in both race and class. Hudson High School, like the majority of the 126 schools that comprise this city's public school system, occupies the middle stratum of a three-tiered system. Hudson, referred to as an "ed op" (for *educational opportunity*) school, essentially works as a "magnet" school, attracting students from different neighborhoods across school districts. Hudson is in neither the top nor bottom scholastic stratum.[47] Sixty-four percent of the students go on to attend four-year colleges, although less than 12 percent of the student body receives Regents' Diplomas, a requirement for entrance to most competitive colleges. Unlike the top-tier public schools in the city or the neighborhood low-tier schools, midstratum schools like Hudson tend to be racially integrated. Twenty-five percent of the students at Hudson are Asian or Asian American, another 25 percent are Latino/a, another 25 percent are African American, and the remaining 25 percent are European American. Many students are recent immigrants, a number of whom live in poverty or are of the working poor. Thirty-two percent of students are eligible for the free lunch program, and 22 percent are classified as limited in their English proficiency.

Stylone High School was the final high school I studied. Stylone is a highly competitive school with a primarily white and Asian student population (over 80 percent of its enrollment), located in the same northeastern city as Hudson High. Students generally come from households that are socioeconomically above average, though roughly 22 percent qualify for the free lunch program. Stylone is one of the most academically rigorous high schools in this city's public school system. Ninety-eight percent of the students attending receive the Regents' Diploma. Stringent entrance exams ensure that the school draws only the most academically successful students from the city and maintains its placement at the top of the educational strata. From the outset it was easy to recognize this school as an elite public school remarkably similar in some ways to many northeasten boarding and private day schools.

## Organization of the Chapters

This book is centrally concerned with the self-organization of youth in and around school settings. I explore this in connection with three broad themes: (1) how proms are defined within an organization of gender and heterosexuality, and how this organization shapes the process of becoming masculine or feminine for kids as they prepare for and attend their proms; (2) how proms work in connection with school and today's educational process; and (3) how proms figure in the formation of youth cultures, youth politics, and youth identities. This discussion considers how the organization of social relations around the prom is shaped by the institutional and historical contexts of schooling by examining the different ways kids take up, define, narrate, and experience the prom.

Why have proms come to occupy such an important space in the school and social lives of youth, and what role do proms play in the identity projects of youth? How are kids' identities formed within the context of larger structures of constraint, and how can we identify and understand these structures as they take shape within local settings? How are the boundaries of self and self-formation mediated by relations of race, class, gender, age, and sexuality within this cultural scene? How do proms work to gain the consent of youth to the daily operation of dominance? How does pleasure pattern their investments in the prom, while also working to hide the political workings of power? What possibilities for resistance exist in this space? These are the questions that occasioned this study and will be explored in the following chapters.

Chapter 2 examines how proms have appeared in popular culture in order to understand the cultural currency they carry. Examining films, television, and print media, this chapter considers how cultural representations of proms have shaped the discourses and practices that frame this event and help to define youth identities in contemporary American life. Special attention is given to how students themselves use these discourses as they describe their prom experiences.

Chapters 3 and 4 examine how the construction of the prom as a feminine space shapes how students come to occupy this site, and how their participation actively reconstructs the prom as a space belonging to the feminine. In Chapter 3, I examine a central aspect of the prom—the process of preparing for prom night, by looking at how girls get ready for the prom. Locating the production of this feminine "body work" at the prom within the intersecting forces of school, romance, and commodity culture, this chapter explores two social currents: first, how the prom emerges as a space for girls to perform and solidify their feminine identities, and second, how girls' bodies emerge as sites of struggle over what it means to be feminine within culture today.

Chapter 4 explores how ideologies of romance and the designation of the prom as a site of romantic promise shapes dating. While an important aspect of everyday school life, dating at the prom takes on increased significance because of the highly public nature of the event. Examining the meanings students attach to having a date for the prom, this chapter explores how their understandings of the prom are mediated by contradictory meanings formed around gender, class, heterosexuality, and romance, and how the organization of this space as a feminized space patterns boys' and girls' investments in it.

Chapters 5, 6, and 7 explore the connections between the processes of schooling and the formation of youth identities and cultures of resistance. Concerned with how schools operate as spaces of social control, chapter 5 examines the different rules schools deploy to manage students' interactions and actions at the prom, how they are enforced, and the underlying logic that gives rise to specific sets of rules. Exploring the social organization of rules around the prom, with particular consideration of the rules around alcohol and drugs, the aim of this chapter is to make visible the ideological workings that underlie and mediate the adoption of particular rules by schools to manage the prom space and its attendants. I investigate how students understand and define prom rules and the creative strategies they develop to work around them.

Chapter 6 focuses on the development of the prom at Hudson High School. Tracing how the prom is organized and planned at this racially integrated urban school, this chapter examines how proms are patterned by changes in the organization of school life stemming from the rise of commodity culture, multiculturalism, and the decline in resources for school. How these social changes shape the different investments students make for this event is also explored. This chapter gives particular consideration to how larger economic and social processes, specifically those formed around relations of race, pattern the organization of proms in high school.

Chapter 7 provides an examination of how adult structures of control mediate the meanings kids construct through their participation in the prom, and how this process sometimes gives rise to their articulations of resistance. Through a critical reading of style, I look at proms as locally negotiated events that are central to kids' understanding of politics and struggle, culture and context, school and identity. Consideration of the notion of "gay proms" is also explored in this chapter. I draw upon the semiotic practice of "reading" everyday life as "lived text" to examine not only how kids define the prom's significance in their lives, but how they negotiate those cultural struggles that penetrate everyday school life. These negotiations emerge as central ground where kids make sense of their school and extended social lives. In the last chapter, I offer a summary of the findings from this study and recommendations for how proms might be used toward developing a critical pedagogy, whereby youth politicize their own identities, within schools. Appendix A, "Methods," provides a more extensive look at the research strategies I used to study proms.

Several years ago, when I first undertook this study, I did so reluctantly because I was unsure whether or not I would "find" anything substantial enough to warrant my writing this book. Looking back now, I realize the extent to which I had accepted the standpoint (of a scholar and adult) that proms, because they are sites belonging to youth, are frivolous and trivial, or worse yet, unscholarly. Of course, the analysis I provide suggests otherwise; proms are key sites at which a politics of youth is formed, where identities are fashioned and cultural struggles waged. Whenever I remember that time, I am reminded of my being an adult and how that shapes my understanding of youth and ultimately the cultural account of youth identities, realities, and worlds I offer here. I keep this memory with me as a reminder of where I am and its vast distance from where the kids are. I encourage readers to do the same.

# Two

## Coming of Age at the Prom

### Adolescence and Popular Culture

Proms are a big deal. A much anticipated event for juniors and seniors, proms tend to take on a larger-than-life importance for many students, parents, and communities. It is not uncommon for preprom planning to begin early in the year. Teachers and students assemble after school to decide on the most important prom decisions: the theme, the location, the decorations, the menu, the remembrance gifts, the price of tickets, and the music (band or DJ?). By the time spring arrives, proms are the focal point of school life. The flurry of talk about who's taking whom, who's wearing what, and plans for after the prom often fills the halls between classes and spills over into the cafeterias. Most public schools and many private and parochial schools today organize a junior and senior prom each year. By the time students graduate from high school many have attended several proms; one young woman in this study had gone to ten proms by the time she graduated!

The appeal of the prom is understandable. For many high school kids the prom represents a momentary break in the monotony of daily school life; a departure from what are often considered mundane school routines. For others, the prom provides an occasion to shed one's school identity and become someone else, even if for only one night. Yet there is more here: the overwhelming messages from popular culture, parents, and teachers make it clear that the prom is an important cultural rite of passage. These messages shape how students come to think of the prom and its significance to their

lives. Students often feel that they *must* go to the prom, that if they don't go somehow they have missed a once-in-a-lifetime chance. The message conveyed in films, television shows, prom magazines, and advertisements is that the prom is the most momentous night of the year. Don't squander this once-in-a-lifetime chance to make memories by not attending this significant social rite! Make the prom a night to remember!

Constructing the prom as an important cultural rite works to ensure that students will go to the prom. Subtle social controls are at work here in shaping how kids come to think of the prom and, subsequently, of themselves. Examining how proms are constructed through popular cultural texts, such as magazines, films, and television shows, the first portion of this chapter identifies the discourses that have helped to define how proms are understood. The second portion explores the ways kids use the prom narratives presented in popular culture to talk about their proms. Particular consideration is given to how these narratives work to give meaning to youth identities.

## A Night to Remember: Reading Proms in Contemporary Cultural Life

Proms are a part of our everyday cultural imagery, possibly more so now than ever before. A range of media have provided a bevy of images of the prom, testifying to its importance not only to the lives of high school students but to American cultural life as well. The 1980s witnessed an explosion of teen films organized around high school life and, most notably, the prom. Films like *Carrie, Pretty In Pink, Fast Times at Ridgemont High, Valley Girl, Back to the Future, Grease, Just One of the Guys, Teen Wolf,* and *Footloose* provided our culture with a collective imagination of the prom. Just as in the 1980s, movie theaters in the late 1990s have been inundated with box office hits that either develop entirely around the prom (*10 Things I Hate About You, Trippin', Never Been Kissed, American Pie,* and *She's All That*—all released in 1999), or include prom scenes as a major part of their plot development (*Jawbreaker, Something About Mary, Dance till Dawn, The Rage: Carrie 2, Romy and Michele's High School Reunion,* and *Grosse Point Blank*). Many recent television shows, such as *Beverly Hills 90210, Roseanne, That Seventies Show, The Simpsons, Boy Meets World, Saved by the Bell, Friends, Sabrina the Teenage Witch, The Golden Girls,* and *Buffy the Vampire Slayer* have also incorporated the prom into their story lines.

These films and television shows identify the key players of the prom. The prom queen tends to receive an inordinate amount of airtime. She is both adored and reviled, envied and scorned. She is pretty and popular, fashionably dressed, usually rich, and almost always white. She is consumed with her appearance and the appearance of others. She spends most of her time with her exclusive entourage of girlfriends, ruthlessly stepping on the little people. Then, there are the minor players, the teachers and parents. Teachers serve as reminders that proms are institutionally linked to schools. They are the chaperones, there to ensure that students don't dance too close together, to keep a watchful eye out for any tomfoolery, to make sure the punch hasn't been spiked.

Images of the prom and its attendants are everywhere in today's popular media. In the course of researching this book, I was struck repeatedly not only by the pervasiveness of prom images (the prom has been used to market *Tide* laundry detergent), but by how proms are framed around particular discourses of contemporary adolescent life. How proms are portrayed in popular media has everything to do with the current notions of the "adolescent."

It is not surprising that different narratives of adolescent life are employed to give the prom meaning; the prom is, after all, an event *for* adolescents. And just as there is not a single version of what an adolescent is, there is neither a single version of what a prom is. Images of the prom rely upon opposing and contestable readings of youth's worlds and realities, emerging as competing narratives. The narrative of nascent romance, for example, is central to how proms are understood culturally, and will be discussed in subsequent chapters. But equally salient is the narrative of sex on prom night. Is the prom about romance or sex, good clean fun or wild abandon?[1] Based upon the media images of proms, it is difficult to know—though certainly the allure of heterosexual romance, in general, is often linked to the prom. What is always clear, however, as pointed out earlier, is that the prom is a rite of passage; for better or worse, the prom is not to be missed.

Images of proms, as varied as they are, provide a basis through which "adolescence" is culturally defined, interpreted, and made meaningful as a socially organized experience. Through these cultural representations, both the young and old are educated about the social role of adolescence, and what "adolescence" means via its relation to adulthood. In effect, we become readers of a generation of youth through these images.[2] What is significant about these images, however, is that they actually tell us little about how youth see and define themselves. Their importance as cultural artifacts lies in the fact that they speak volumes about how youth continue to be defined by the adult world. Cultural ideology is at work here, providing us as consumers of culture with an all-too-often limited number of meanings of youth's lives and realities.[3]

## Coming of Age: Constructing the Teen

While representations of proms are laced with symbols of youth cultures, most also harbor adult agendas and anxieties about how youth should or should not organize themselves. Within a context in which youths themselves are increasingly seen as social liabilities, most films and TV shows reflect adult concerns for the development of youth into upstanding, morally correct adults. Teen violence, teen pregnancy, and youth crime—most recently the shooting at Columbine High School in Colorado—are regularly broadcast on the nightly news. In the wake of these increased (and inflated) representations of demonized and morally impoverished youth, the prom is often nostalgically and reverently celebrated as a tiny capsule of youthful innocence and hope. In a recent article in *Harper's* magazine titled "Home After Dark: A Funeral for Three Girls in Kentucky," a feature about three girls who were shot by a fourteen-year-old student as they left the regular morning prayer session at their high school, it is worth noting that one of the girls, Kayce, was buried in her prom dress. The girl's mother explained to the mourners at the service that, "She's thankful Kayce went to her first prom last year. At the time it seemed almost overblown, the flowers, the pictures, the dress and preparation, but the memory of those preparations are her only indication of what it might have been like to plan a wedding for Kayce, with Kayce."[4] In this way, we can see that the prom is memorialized as an event that offers the promise to reclaim honor and youthful innocence (and possibly youth redemption).

In other cases, the prom is depicted as an important though somewhat trivial part of the process of coming of age. The following passage, taken from Jean Shepard's short story "Wanda Hickey's Night of Golden Memories," tells the tale of Shepard's high school prom. Shepard threads together the series of awkward, often painful and humiliating adolescent moments he endured not only to gain entrance to the prom but to ensure its success, noting, in retrospect, "I leafed through the pages [of the high school yearbook] . . . suddenly there it was—a sharply etched photographic record of a true puberty rite among a primitive tribe in Northern Indiana. The caption read: 'The Junior Prom was heartily enjoyed by one and all. The annual event was held this year at the Cherrywood Country Club. Mickey Eisley and his Magic Music Makers provided the romantic rhythms. All agreed it was an unforgettable evening, the memory of which we will cherish in the years to come.' True enough. In the gathering gloom of my Manhattan apartment, it all came back."[5] Drawing upon a similar discourse, *People* magazine, in one article featuring photos of Hollywood celebrities at their proms, enabled its reader to look on and "remember when," saying, "Ah, Spring! It's the time of year when a high schooler's thoughts turn from SATs and fake IDs to that other adolescent rite of passage: the prom. Years and even decades later, mere mention of the event, for those who have partaken, can conjure memories of baby-blue tuxes, big hair and really, really bad cover bands faster than you can hum the opening notes of 'Stairway to Heaven.'"[6]

The idea that the prom is a significant social event specific to being an adolescent permeates these cultural images. Whether the kids are fighting for their "right" to experience this rite of passage, as in the popular 1984 movie *Footloose*, or mark their coming of age by the loss of their virginity on prom night, as in the 1999 film *American Pie*, these images of kids at the prom rely upon and recuperate the idea that coming of age is a natural, incremental, and essential progression.[7] In Susan Shadburne's recent documentary *Street Kids and Tuxes*, about the lives of street kids in Oregon and their journey to a prom held for homeless youth, the promotional brochure reads as follows: "Here, for one brief night, they strut, eat, dance, laugh and forget their lives in the only traditional rite of passage they will probably ever know."[8]

In the popular 1999 teen film *She's All That*, about a young woman's struggle to "find" herself, her journey to selfhood culminates at the prom. Laney Boggs (Rachel Leigh Cook), is a slightly offbeat girl, disinterested in the daily banter of "popularity," disaffected from school, and alienated from her peers. By Hollywood standards, she is not your "typical" teen. Rather than shopping endlessly and fixating on romance like other (Hollywood) girls, Laney spends much of her time alone in the basement of her father's house, where she painstakingly pores over her politically inspired artwork, awaiting the arrival of adulthood. The meager social life she maintains exists outside of school.

When not painting, Laney spends her time watching over her younger brother, Simon, and her well-intentioned but inept widower father. Mired in the responsibilities of adult life, Laney hardly has time for such trivial matters as being a teen. In the opening scene of the film, we find Laney outside Simon's bedroom door, beckoning him to get out of bed; they are already late for school, she warns. In her hand she is holding a glass of orange juice for him. She pounds on his door, pleading with him, but he is slow to stir. Just as we are convinced that she is the maternal figure to Simon, and our remorse for her lost adolescence begins to wax, she hocks up a "loogey," threatening her brother that she will deposit the phlegm in his orange juice if he doesn't get out of bed. Alas, she is just a teen after all.

From this opening scene and throughout the movie, it is clear that Laney is responsible for the care of her family. Without the direction of a mother, it is she who must maintain family life and manage even its most mundane features. The tension between normative ideas of "adulthood" (real responsibility) and "adolescence" (carefree fun) underlies this film as a coming of age tale.

Laney's life, however, takes a sudden turn when Zack Syler (Freddie Prinze, Jr.), the most popular boy in school (who recently had been "dumped" by his horribly wicked longtime girlfriend and anticipated prom queen) accepts a bet wagered by his best friend that he can turn even the most pitiful wallflower into the prom queen. Laney, unequivocally recognized as the weirdest girl in school, is chosen for the bet. With a mere six weeks left before the prom, Zack gets to work: he enlists his younger sister to make her over into a teen beauty queen, and takes Laney to parties attended exclusively by the popular clique.

Determined to win the bet, Zack relentlessly pursues her. Inevitably (and predictably), both Zack and Laney begin to realize their emerging affections for one another. But eventually Laney learns the truth, that her newfound popularity has been a ruse and the mysterious but welcomed attentions of Zack Syler are the result of a cruelly inspired bet between two boys. Defeated, she returns to her artist's perch in the basement, and denounces "teen" life. She is determined not to attend her prom, even though she has been nominated for prom queen. On the night of the prom, we find Laney down in the basement, dressed in the disheveled, paint-splattered uniform of a "serious" artist, completing her self-portrait, when she is interrupted by her father. "Don't you have a prom or something to go to?" he asks.

"No, I'm not going," she replies. Disquieted by his daughter's decision not to attend her prom, and what it might mean for him as a "suitable" father, he pauses for a moment before he begins his Father Knows Best speech: "Sometimes I think you take on so much, so you don't have to deal with the business of being a kid. I can't imagine being seventeen is easy, especially with your mother not around. I'm just afraid if you keep putting off your life like this, you're gonna wake up eighty-five years old, sitting on a porch somewhere [he pauses evidently unsure what he should say next] . . . looking for your teeth."

"Thanks Dad," she replies, "That was graphic." Yet, she is sufficiently persuaded by her father's not-so-compelling treatise on coming of age that she trades in her artist's smock for a black-sequined, floor-length gown, attends her prom and is all the wiser for doing so, even though she is not elected prom queen and the promise of romance at the prom never materializes.[9] Stories such as these, depicting proms as modern-day Cinderella tales of transformation from disheveled, drab girlhood to sexy and glamorous femininity are common. *Pretty in Pink*, *Carrie*, and *Never Been Kissed* are all versions of this tale. Such tales work to secure femininity in our culture as well as the importance of heterosexual romance. While Laney is not elected prom queen and seems as if she couldn't care less, she still submits to the trappings of an idealized feminine image. She trades in her nonconformist style for a fashion makeover straight out of the pages of *Seventeen* magazine.

The prom is also constructed here as a quintessentially important part of the business of being a kid. Implicit is the idea that one cannot legitimately speak about the experience of high school—or of growing up, for that matter—if one is unable to reference the prom. In other words, having missed the prom, one might as well have missed all of what's important about high school. The prom is the capstone of teen life.

While relying upon a particular understanding of adolescence as a distinct stage in the life course, these images also naturalize what it means to be an adolescent. Equally significant, the construction of adolescence only becomes meaningful in relation to the construction of adulthood. In this way adolescence, more than being defined by what it is, is defined by what it is *not*.

It is also worth noting that these prom images, because they are based fundamentally on an all-American teen rite, revolve around white, middle-class teens. While narratives on proms vary, the characters in these films rarely do. Representations of youth in prom films are totalizing images; they work to erase class and racial differences among youth. They resecure the idea that the typical teen is white, suburban, and middle-class. By providing a narrow vision of youth, these images of kids at the prom reproduce prevailing cultural notions that adolescence is ahistorical and universal.

### Prom as Horror Story: Teen Angst and Disaster

Proms occupy a precarious place. They are celebrated, packaged in particular ways that serve to designate them as important life events, but they are also easily satirized. The prom is an event adults may remember, but it is attended by teenagers only. Because of this, the prom is frequently depicted as an event that we adults may have taken seriously as teens, but only because we were "silly" teens, preoccupied with such ignoble and frivolous issues as "popularity" and "self-image." In popular films, as well as everyday talk, the prom is mockingly constructed as a moment besieged by teen angst and tumult—so profound disaster and disappointment are inevitable. One news radio talk show I listened to asked callers to call in with their most "horrifying prom episodes."[10] The idea that proms are riddled with disappointment, to be rendered inconsequential once we reach adulthood, was easy to recognize as part of our culture's coming-of-age lore.

The 1998 popular comedy *Something About Mary* is a film about an ill-fated prom whose narrative depends upon the notion that the teen years are a period of abject humiliation and social awkwardness. The story develops around Ted Stroemann (Ben Stiller), a caricature of male adolescence—nerdy, pimply, and with a mouth full of braces—who is beguiled by the pretty, popular, and smart Mary (Cameron Diaz). Like other high school geeks, he admires her from afar. On a whim, he musters up enough courage to ask Mary to the prom. Much to his astonishment, she actually says yes. On the awaited day, Ted arrives at her house outfitted in a brown tuxedo with a brown-trimmed frilly tuxedo shirt to pick her up. Mary descends the stairs, dressed in a sky-blue floor-length frock. She is an image of loveliness, embodying all that is innocent and pure: her long blond hair cascades over her shoulders, her blue eyes sparkle.[11] Just when Ted thinks on this night of nights that nothing could go wrong, it does. Before they leave for the prom, he visits the bathroom; as he is zipping up his pants, he catches his penis in the zipper. Not only painful, it is painfully humiliating. In an effort to salvage what appeared to be a magical evening, he struggles to gain composure; he is determined to resolve this dire situation, but in the end only makes matters worse. Before long, Mary is alerted to Ted's most compromising predicament, as are her mother and father! The scene concludes with him strapped to a stretcher, surrounded by a small crowd, before being carried off in an ambulance to the hospital, his one chance of love lost. We find Ted ten years later, pining away in a bar with a bunch of dimwitted pals and wondering, What if? What if they had made it to the prom, had had that special dance—would Mary have realized that he was her prince?

In many of these representational forms, proms are constructed through a filter of adult memory; in fact, the narrator is often an adult. While understood as an important event for youth, the prom also occupies a privileged place in the individual and collective memories of American adults.[12] Proms tend to be events that adults remember, which may help to explain why the themes of adolescent disappointment, fragility, and embarrassment are recurring themes in these texts. Proms, then, are a part of how adults remember and rewrite their pasts (even so for those who didn't go to their proms). Adults get to define their current self in relation to their past self; who adults were then shapes who they are now.

In the 1999 prom film *Never Been Kissed* this theme presents itself again. The story revolves around Josey Geller (Drew Barrymore), who eight years after her high school prom works as a copy editor for her hometown newspaper. Just as in high school, she is plain, shy, and meek—in short, nothing special. She is given the opportunity to return to high school, this time as an undercover, investigative reporter; she eagerly accepts her assignment. Once there she is reminded of the torture and ridicule she had endured at the hands of her merciless peers (even as a twenty-five-year-old she still can't pass as "cool"). Through a series of flashbacks, we gain a sense of Josey's former high school self. In the first flashback, we see Josey in school—painfully awkward and drearily dull. In the background we hear a cacophony of voices chanting "Josey Grossey" (her nickname in high school). That she was repeatedly taunted and tormented by her classmates is a theme established early in the film. In the second flashback, Josey learns she has been asked to the prom by the most popular boy in school, on whom she has a secret crush. Not realizing she is being set up for disappointment and humiliation, she readies herself for her prom. She twirls before the mirror as she admires the image she sees before her—a lucky girl who is about to be whisked off to her prom by a popular boy. The phone rings; it is her date calling her outside. Filled with the promise of a wondrous night of fairy-tale romance, she rushes out to her front stoop and awaits his arrival. Yet instead of being presented with a corsage, as she had hoped, she is assaulted with raw eggs by her date. Devastated by this unexpected turn of events, she drops to the ground in tears as her date drives off with another girl to the prom.

Harboring this memory, years later she admits she has never fully recovered. "All I wanted was to be accepted and they tortured me . . . I lived a lifetime of regret after my first time at high school," she explains. Unlike her real high school days, her second chance at high school eventually brings her popularity, the man of her dreams (her English teacher), a date for the prom, and the much coveted honor—the throne. While she was prevented from attending her first prom, at her second she is crowned prom queen. Unlike the wallflower she was, she finds herself this time the unexpected recipient of male attention.

On prom night, we find her once again on her front stoop awaiting the arrival of her date. As he nears in the limo, she shudders as the painful memory of her past prom is momentarily relived. Unlike last time, she is presented with that long-awaited corsage, finally getting to attend the prom escorted by a dream date! What is significant is that as she reconstructs her past, she is also able to reconstruct her present. As an adult returning to high school, Josey Geller is given the opportunity to rewrite and renarrate her high school history, and significantly her prom. Only after she returns to high school, eight years after she has graduated, has she finally blossomed. She is hardly able to recognize her former self.

### Not to Be Missed

Despite the inevitable disappointment that accompanies the prom, it is generally assumed that proms are events not to be missed. In the popular 1986 John Hughes movie *Pretty in Pink,* the older and wiser Iona (Annie Potts) tries to cajole the young Andie (played by then teen star Molly Ringwald) into attending her prom:

Andie:   Did you say you went to your prom?
Iona:    Yeah, sure.

Andie:   Was it the worst?
Iona:    Yeah, but it's supposed to be. You have to go. Right?
Andie:   Well, you don't have to. It's not a requirement.
Iona:    I had this girlfriend who didn't go to hers and every once in a
         while she gets this really terrible feeling something is missing.
         She checks her purse, she checks her keys, she counts her kids.
         She goes crazy and then she realizes nothing is missing. She
         decided it was side effects from skipping her prom.

Even if a terrible time is had, the prom is still supposed to be remembered.
While this framing is resolutely patterned by an adult ideology, reflecting
how adults define and remember their own proms and themselves as adolescents, kids also used this discourse to make sense of the prom:

I wanted to show face so I can say twenty years from now, oh like,
when we have our twenty-year reunion, you know like, "I went to my
prom." I wanted to go and get dressed up and just showcase anyway,
you know. (African-American female student)

In my school, going to the prom was a big deal. Everybody couldn't
wait to show off their new clothes, limo, and their date. The prom was
considered to be the event of the year. Some go for the once-in-a-lifetime experience, while others go so they can tell their grandchildren
they went. My reason for going to the prom was of obvious reasons.
All my friends were going. Other reasons included that feeling of
regret. I felt if I didn't attend my prom, that I one way or another
would regret it in the future. (Asian-American female student)

Themes of regret, of the prom being an important social rite, of it being
a night to make memories pervaded kids' accounts as they discussed their
prom experiences:

It was May 27 and I still couldn't believe the long-awaited day was
finally here. When we arrived we took more pictures. We walked into
the dining area where we were given the most grotesque food ever
imaginable. Somehow the food wasn't even important. Too many
things were going on at the time. Friends were socializing, camera
flashes were being shot and excitement saturated the air. We all danced
the night away. The entire night seemed to breeze by like it was only
one hour, if that long. I couldn't believe the night was gone. I knew in
my heart that although it was gone, the memories of my friends,
boyfriends, and fellow classmates would stay with me forever. (Asian-
American female student)

The lingering feeling of regret in having missed the prom is so powerful that many of those who do not attend their proms operate with a similar understanding of what proms are and the significance they have for American culture and the overall life course. The regret that one African-American woman expressed about not going to the prom again testifies to the cultural notion that the prom is an important milestone in the process of becoming adults:

> When I first began high school I was under the impression that my senior year would be one of the best years of my life. I held onto this hope until approximately my junior year, where everything went downhill. I hated school more than ever. I really couldn't wait until my senior year and not for any other reason except the fact that it was to be my final year of school ever. I had no plans of going on to college at this point. Prom preparations began the first day of classes for most of the senior girls. But not for me. I was not interested in anything that had to do with school whatsoever. I was not banning the prom for reason of rejection from a potential prom date. I basically knew I could get a date and that made it worse. As the prom time neared I began to feel slight regret about my decision not to attend, but it was too late to turn back now. All the good dresses would have been taken, and all the good dates would have been taken. So prom night came and went for me just like any other night. I was alone because everyone I knew was attending our senior prom. I look back on my decision and I must admit I regret it. I regret that I missed out on many high school activities simply because of my negative feelings toward everything. I definitely know if I could turn back time I would have attended my prom.

The sense of fatalism expressed here points to how social controls work in this space. The fear of having missed the prom is harnessed as a mechanism to gain students consent to this event and the material and ideological conditions it secures. As in cultural representations, the prom is interpreted here as a critically important part of the coming-of-age process.

### *Making Memories*

Implicit in the occasion of the prom itself is the idea that it is a night in which to make memories that will be recollected alongside those of other important adolescent events: the first kiss, the first date, and the first day of high school. So significant are proms to our memories of high school that taking pictures on prom night is a central part of the event itself. At the four proms I attended, I saw scores of kids walk around with cameras, both taking and posing for pictures. Samuel, an African-American student from Hudson, shared with me the scenes and events he thought were most important to record.

AB:     What did you take pictures of?

SF:     Um, I took pictures of people dancing, also I took a couple of friends with their dates and their girlfriends, some group pictures. I took some pictures of the hotel. What it looks like inside and that's basically it.

AB:     Did you take pictures after the prom, too?

SF:     Yeah, like by the restaurant. It was at the seaport also and when we were coming home. Everybody looked tired. I took pictures when everybody was sleeping. Everybody fell asleep in like a half hour, almost six o'clock.

Students customarily have their photo taken before they arrive at their prom. Parents of promgoers often organize preprom photo sessions as social events at which community and extended family come together. Sandy, a white student at Rudolph explained the process:

AB:     So, your parents took pictures of you guys before you went to the prom and I think you said there were a couple other couples there, and some parents.

SAG:    There were three other couples there and some parents. It wasn't bad, my boyfriend's mom had a little party. She had dinner for us beforehand, like pastas and vegetables and fruit salad and everybody sits around and talks for a while and then goes outside on the porch and takes pictures.

AB:     What was that like?

SAG:    Confusing. There was a lot of us. It was like couple and then, couple and then, we all had to gather and then, we did it [take pictures] with the parents. I had to do it with my parents and then, I'd do it with his parents and then, with his grandmother and me.

At one upper-middle-class school in suburban New Jersey, a young woman's parents threw a very large and extravagantly catered preprom party for both parents and kids. After the kids left for the prom, the parents stayed for the rest of the evening drinking champagne and speculating about what their children might be doing at the prom. At another upper-middle-class school, the entire town came together around the activity of preprom pictures. An entire block was sectioned off and a large number of the town's residents attended.

Once at the prom, students usually have their photos taken by a professional photographer. At each prom I attended, a table was set up near the entrance to the prom for kids to select and purchase a variety of photo packages.[13] Mark, an African-American student at Woodrow, spoke about the importance of these photos, explaining,

They are pictures you are going to always have. You're gonna always want pictures. Everybody took the pictures. Like the day we got our pictures everybody was around school saying, "Ah, see my pictures, see my pictures." Everybody took pictures and everybody wanted the biggest packet ever. I got the biggest packet and I still came to find out I didn't have enough because everybody wanted a prom picture. I didn't have enough. I went somewhere and I was showing somebody— "Oh can I have this?" Everybody just wants a prom picture, like, "You make a cute couple." Everybody I showed was like, "Can I have one?"

The effect of these pictures is to provide a particular kind of memory of the prom. In other words, these pictures inscribe within our cultural consciousness what a prom is: The Girl Pinning a Boutonniere on Her Date's Lapel; The Boy Arriving at the Doorstep of His Date's Parents' Home; Stepping into The Limo; Table Pictures; The Crowning of the Prom King and Queen.[14] Not just to be remembered, proms are to be remembered *in a particular way*.

As in the case of popular representations of high school proms in popular culture, these pictures work as narratives to define reality within a narrow range of possibilities. Kids record the events they have come to understand as significant to the experience of the prom. These pictures tell a story—a story that is in keeping with how proms have been culturally narrated and understood. Like the cultural representations of proms identified earlier in this chapter, these pictures (re)construct the prom as a rite of passage laden with pomp and circumstance.

## A Time to Remember

In popular representations and in kids' talk, the prom is often thought to be especially meaningful because it represents one of the last times kids can appreciate their connection with students who share similar histories of place and space. "It's the last time you get to be with your friends, have fun," one student offered. "I really enjoyed the night. It was a night to remember, a night to remember." This theme pervaded students' narratives:

My prom for me was very special. It was the last night I'd spend with my friends from home. It was a lot of fun because we were on a boat and the DJ started playing many old school songs, the Electric Slide, Doing The Butt among others. It was so much fun doing all our old dances and just reminiscing on the old days. It made us wonder how different things were going to be once we were all apart when we went to school. (African-American female student)

Proms are supposed to capture heartfelt emotions about leaving and loss, the disbanding of a unified class of students who are moving on. It is not surprising, then, that songs with titles like "We've Got Tonight," "Hold On to the Night," "Make it Last Forever," "Sweet Days," and "Only Time Will Tell" will be used as prom night themes year after year.[15] The song chosen for the last dance of the night often incorporates themes of change, continuity, remembrance, and commemoration. Consider these lyrics from Billy Joel's "A Time To Remember," which was a favorite when I attended high school in the 1980s, and continues to be a popular choice as a prom theme today:

This is the time to remember, cause it will not last forever
These are the days to hold onto, cause we won't although we'll want to

These are the days, but times are gonna change
You've given me the best of you and now I want the rest of you.
Some day we will both look back and laugh
We've lived through a lifetime and the aftermath.

Another song by Billy Joel, "Just the Way You Are," is also another of the popular prom songs:

> I would never leave you in times of troubles
> We never could have come this far.
> I took the good times, I'll take the bad times
> I'll take you just the way you are.

The prom is celebrated as a moment of togetherness, as a place of belonging to a group of students who share a collective history of the past.[16] (Of course, what is often overlooked is the fact that proms, like everyday life in school, are beset with divisions and distinctions.) The imminent departure from high school and entrance into an adult world is crystallized in the prom. The prom signifies a bridge between the past—life in high school—and an unknown future.[17] Two students responded:

> Being a very tight-knit class we went through a lot together. The class of '95 always got along well. Our senior prom would be one of the last times our class would be together in its entirety. We were determined to make the most out of this night so we could look back and have very fond memories of everything and everyone. My senior prom was unforgettable. We made the most of one of our last times together and the memories we made will bond the members of my class for life. (White female student)

> It was like, "Ah, remember this and how funny was this?" It was basically the fact that like . . . the senior prom weekend was really like the end of the year. Everybody gets back and after a weekend like that, who wants to think about school, you know? It's usually like school is ending in like a month. And for us that weekend just like ended it. You know, because like before prom weekend it was like, "At least we have prom weekend coming up," you know? And then like, after that the only thing you have coming up is like graduation. So there's nothing, like, to look forward to, you know, because school's pretty much done with. (African-American male student)

Many students talked about the prom as a moment in which to come together. A student from Woodrow High School, drawing a parallel between the prom and a dance ritual celebrating solidarity in a tribal society (which she was unable to name but had remembered reading about), told me the prom highlighted the harmonious coming together of diverse groups in their celebration of difference.

As is the case in popular cultural texts, kids' talk works to reconstruct adolescence as a universally shared experience; even across their differences these kids belong to a "common culture." What is assumed here is that all young people come to this space in similar ways, but of course they don't. Relations formed around race, class, gender, and sexuality shape the types of investments kids make in this space and how they ultimately define it. These kids' narratives privilege age over other social relations and in doing so elide attention to these differences.

## Proms as Popular Cultural Sites: Representation and Everyday Life

What is the consequence of the repeated invocation of the theme of coming of age? Sociologists have long argued that ritual serves to stabilize the current organization of cultural and social life because it forcefully "unites a particular image of the universe with a strong emotional attachment to it."[18] While structuring kids' investments in the prom, these images also shape *how* kids read the prom. Viewing cultural narratives that define proms, the beginning of this chapter makes visible the ways in which the construction of the prom as an important cultural event relies upon prevailing definitions of adolescence as a distinct stage in the life course. Not only do these images *depend* upon our culture's willingness to accept adolescence as a "natural" given, but these images *confirm* and *reify* this reality. In other words, these images resecure the notion that to be a teenager is to be something entirely different from being an adult. Proms have been made meaningful in the wider culture through this lens, a lens that belongs fundamentally to adults, not to kids. However, kids do use these narratives to narrate their proms, as is clearly demonstrated here.

How, then, should the relationship between everyday life and these representational systems be understood and theorized? Since most of these prom representations are narrated by adults, the prom is interpreted through a discourse that defines adolescence by its relation to adult life and in so doing belies consideration of the series of ongoing relations that make the prom a complex and multilayered space of meaning. These images, while providing us with a clear sense of the cultural currency proms have, tell us little about the way kids invest in or define the prom. What an examination of these images does offer is a framework through which to understand what youth respond to as they fashion their identities at the prom. As kids make sense of who they are, they are profoundly aware that history and reality already has been defined for them. The challenge youth face as they solidify and articulate their identities (as working-class youth, white youth, middle-class youth, gendered youth, youth of color) is the struggle against these discursive and material forces that limit the possibility for meaningful self-representation. For this reason, understanding how youths' lives are shaped by adult agendas and ideologies, and how youth negotiate and struggle against them in local settings, is critically important at this historical moment. Popular culture may be made through these representational systems, but popular culture is also made through everyday local life.[19]

While these images work to provide youth with a limited range of options in understanding themselves *as* youth, there are always possible alternate readings. As will be demonstrated, many students reject the conventional narrative of the prom as a coming-of-age rite. Many struggle to define the prom outside these conventional frames; theirs is a struggle over meanings. Unlike the neatly packaged meanings conveyed through the popular cultural texts identified in this chapter, the process of meaning-making as it occurs within the context of kids' everyday culture is complicated, messy, and contradictory. An examination of how kids come to define the prom, and the investments they make offers an understanding of how youth experience control, how they participate in the ongoing production of cultural life, and how they use and create cultural meanings to understand themselves as youth. It is to these issues I will turn next.

# Three

# *Fashioning the Feminine*

## Dresses, Jewelry, Hair, and More

Before the twentieth century, girls simply did not organize their thinking about themselves around their bodies. Today, many young girls worry about the contours of their bodies—especially shape, size, and muscle tone—because they believe the body is the ultimate expression of the self. The body is a consuming project for contemporary girls because it provides an important means of self-definition, a way to visibly announce who you are to the world. From a historical perspective, this particular form of adolescent expression is a relatively recent phenomenon.

— Joan Jacobs Brumberg, *The Body Project*

The popular 1999 teen prom films *She's All That* and *Never Been Kissed* are Cinderella-inspired tales of transformation. As the narratives unfold, the central female characters, both wallflowers, submit to a series of changes culminating in their emergence as beauty queens at the prom. Each wins the adulation of her peers, and best of all, each gets the man of her dreams. In these Hollywood productions, the process of getting ready for the prom is a privileged space in which bodies are magically reworked and identities completely refashioned.

Predictably, the popular construction of the prom as a moment in which to reinvent the self is a gendered one; this narrative is almost always told through the voice of a girl and the transformation that occurs is mapped fundamentally through her body. This is because the prom belongs to "the feminine." The prom is a feminine space, conventionally thought to be the domain of girls. Constructed as such, it is a site where girls are expected to be heavily invested because they can use this space to solidify and display their feminine identities. Such expectations are inscribed in both popular culture forms and everyday talk. Girls are repeatedly told that going to the prom is a fundamentally important part to their being and becoming feminine. In prom magazines, "making a statement" is the very promise of the prom: "the prom is your night to shine." "Dare To Stand Out" and "Be The

Babe of the Ball" these magazines tell their readers. One magazine article asks, "On your special night will you steal the social scene?" The message is that a carefully fashioned feminine self is the key to an unforgettable prom. The packaging of the prom in this way virtually ensures girls' participation in the consumption of goods and in feminine body work. And why wouldn't girls want to make a dramatic statement about themselves at the prom? There is tremendous pleasure in the project of self-change.

Yet while girls are expected to take up the work of becoming feminine at the prom, they are also confronted with the inherent contradiction in doing this kind of work. The very practices that girls are expected to invest in and to find pleasurable are also dismissed as trivial. "When I was a freshman I couldn't wait to go. I worked at the postprom party at my school but by the time senior year came around it all seemed so irrelevant and unimportant to the future," one young woman wrote. The basic paradox lies in the following: the project of becoming feminine is defined as frivolous, and that which is frivolous is also feminine.[1]

So profound is this contradiction for girls that many young women I talked to expressed an initial ambivalence about going to the prom.[2] One white young woman wrote,

> I wasn't originally going to attend my prom simply because I was broke and didn't want to get dressed up for one night. But somehow my best friend convinced me to go. So then I went home and told my mom that I was going and she didn't believe me until two weeks later when I shelled out $50 for two tickets.

Elise, a biracial, bisexual student at Woodrow, originally rejected the prom because she felt it reflects a space ordered by a set of gendered practices that privilege consumption and heterosexuality. "At first I was like, screw the prom, you know. It's kind of cheesy. Everyone's going parading around, this is my dress, and who's he bringing?" But she also said later in the interview, "You know, I'm kinda getting into it." Elise did end up going, as did many young women who originally thought they might not. Most girls found themselves—for some reason or another—mysteriously "caught up" in the preparations for the prom despite their initial resistance. Only a few girls in this study decided they were not going to attend their proms. One young white woman discussed her decision to not go:

> I choose not to attend my junior or senior prom because it was not important to me. I had opportunities my sophomore, junior, and senior years to attend and I worked on the prom committee to organize the event. I think that the prom is blown completely out of proportion. I came from a small town and there were some people who became obsessed with the prom. This was the case with one of my

friends. She got mad at me because I didn't want to go. I think my mom was a little hurt by this too because we didn't go dress shopping, etc.

Even the marketers of the prom magazines realize the weight of this contradiction. Consider one article from a 1997 special prom edition of *YM*, which began, "In your opinion, the prom is so, well, not hip. So though you're majorly excited for the big night, you're saying 'See ya!' to flowing ball gowns and stretch limos—you've got to make a statement girl!"[2]

The contradictions among delighting in the work of getting ready for the prom, of wanting to be seen, and of feeling that the prom is an event having little true social value point to an ongoing tension (significantly beyond that of the prom) that many girls experience when taking up a position of femininity in a culture organized around consumption in which men and the practices authorized by masculine ideologies are privileged. Leslie Roman and Linda Christian-Smith, in their book *Becoming Feminine*, elaborate the connections between the contradictory nature of popular cultural forms and the struggles girls face in becoming feminine. As they explain, "At stake in the struggles and contestations over these meanings are not only textual representations of femininity and gender relations in particular cultural commodities, but also their place and significance in the lives of actual women and men who consume, use and make sense of them in the context of their daily practices and social relations. The struggle for girls and women, then (whether they are feminist or not), over gendered meanings, representations and ideologies in popular cultural forms is nothing less than a struggle to understand and hopefully transform the historical contradictions of becoming feminine within the context of conflicting sets of power relations."[3] This chapter explores how this struggle, a struggle fundamentally formed in relation to the self, was narrated by girls as they prepared for and then attended their proms. While the prom highlights more general dilemmas about the continuing influence of dominant gender meanings on girls' lives and their bodies, it also emerges as a distinct site where context-specific forms of femininity—that surprisingly cut across race and class lines—arise. From hairstyles to dresses, these girls' narratives tell the story of the work and the lessons offered by the prom.

## *Seeing and Being Seen: The Making of Feminine Bodies*

I want something that makes my dad a little nervous . . . something pretty . . . maybe make him lose a little sleep. I want something that will make me the center of attention . . . I want something the other girls wish they could wear . . . something that makes everyone stop and stare.

—Advertisement for Flirtations, *Your Prom*, 1996

Despite the tensions some girls initially felt about investing in an event that had been framed as silly and superficial, many young women looked forward to the prom as a place to be seen. As John Berger explains in his important book, *Ways of Seeing*, "A woman must continually watch herself. She is almost continually accompanied by her own image of herself. Whilst she is walking across a room or whilst she is weeping at the death of her father, she can scarcely avoid envisaging herself walking or weeping. From earliest childhood she has been taught and persuaded to survey herself continually."[4]

Proms are moments in which girls in particular are on display. The structuring of physical space at the four proms I attended ensured that the prom would be designated in this way: the entrances to the prom sites were situated so that girls could be looked at by others. "Even at the prom, people said it was the best looking dress, I remember," one young white woman offered. Many purposely delay their arrival to the prom so that they can make a grand entrance. As one African-American young woman wrote,

> When I stepped out of the limo I remember thinking that I was just the princess of the night. All lights were on me and this was my night. No one and nothing was going to spoil it for me. So we walked in about an hour late. When I made my entrance everyone's eyes were on me. I even remember one of my enemies sitting on the table that was right next to the door. And when she turned around and took a look at me her whole face fell. By the way she looked, it seems like she had just decided at the last minute she was going to the prom.

Though especially pronounced at the prom, being looked at is a normalized and naturalized dimension of life as a girl; as a result, its embeddedness within a gender and heterosexual order usually goes unnoticed.[5] One girl related,

> I'm looking forward to seeing everyone in a different dress. Everybody keeps telling everybody else what their dress looks like and

you can get an idea but you can't *really* get an idea until you actually see it. You can get rolls and rolls of film and take lots of pictures.

As this young woman suggests, seeing carries as much significance as being seen in this cultural scene. While suggestive of the agency girls can claim in the space of the prom (being able to look rather than just being looked upon), this agency continues to be lodged in an organization of gender; the practice of seeing chiefly centers on girls' bodies, and in this way offers little room for girls to reject fully their participation in the project of becoming feminine.

### Getting Ready

Your 30-Day Beauty countdown. Don't let prom put you in a panic! With one month to go, you've still got tons of time to get perfect skin, beautiful hair and a hot bod. Just follow our head-to-toe guide to getting gorgeous.

—"Your 30-Day Beauty Countdown," article in *YM*, 1997

Because of the importance of being seen in this context, preparations of the body are extensive. Many girls spent considerable time during interviews and in their written narratives providing detailed descriptions of their dresses and hair, how they came to select their dresses, and their efforts to coordinate what they wore with what their date wore. Sally, a white student from Woodrow, had originally bought two dresses, the first of which she returned once her friend found her a new dress.

AB:   So what made you choose this dress over the first dress?

SB:   The first dress was like, I would have to buy jewelry too. Like, dress it up and get, like, different shoes. It was very plain. It was, like, something you would wear out to a nice restaurant.

AB:   How did you find your first dress?

SB:   I was so lazy. I was like, I went to the prom last year. I don't feel like shopping again so I was like, I'll just look through catalogues. And I looked through a *Victoria's Secret* catalogue and I just picked out the first dress that I saw.

SB:   That was the short dress?

AB:   Yeah, so that's my big mistake. I didn't go looking around at stores or anything.

Sally, while initially ambivalent about the work required to experience the prom in a feminine way, ultimately acquiesces. Her self-critique for not initially engaging in the work that is in many ways for girls the very foundation of the prom points to the ongoing pressure many girls experience in fashioning themselves to be seen.

For a number of girls, how they worked and "disciplined" their bodies directly related to their having a successful prom. "When the day started off I thought it would be the best day. I had the perfect dress (no one had anything else like it) and my hair was done beautifully," one African-American young woman wrote. Success for her not only centers on but is bound to the body.

The process of preparing for the prom for many of these girls was as important as the end product, if not more so. Many girls declared that getting ready for the prom was an entire day's commitment (though preparations began months in advance). Hair, nails, and face were thoroughly worked over; many girls attended tanning salons, while others reported that they dieted to lose weight before the prom:

> All I can remember was that the prom wore me out. From half a day at school, to a morning appointment to get my hair done to an afternoon appointment for my friend to do her hair I was literally exhausted. I also remember fasting so that I could fit into my prom dress.

Another girl wrote,

> We all went shopping for dresses. This didn't take just one trip to the mall. We looked at dresses at every mall in the area and even traveled to malls where there is more selection. Some of my friends even had their dresses made by professional seamstresses. We all had our "dream dress" in mind and it was all a matter of finding it. Then, of course, we had to look perfect in those dresses, so a bunch of my friends and I joined the gym. We exercised three months before.

Social class emerges to organize these feminine practices in a range of ways. One girl, discovering on the day of the prom that her dress was too small, went out and bought another. Sally was able to buy two dresses, though she planned to return one. Clearly the availability of disposable income made this possible. For these girls, class status often means whether or not their parents are able to "support" their prom by covering the significant expense.

The availability of unlimited money enabled some girls to organize the activities in ways that directly hooked them into the spheres of consumption. Several young women enlisted the help of beauty professionals. One girl reported that she and her friends had rented a limousine to take them from the hair salon to lunch at a local café, while another girl and her friends hired a cosmetics representative to come to her home and do their makeup. One white middle-class girl wrote,

> I remember the preparation for my senior prom being really formal. I remember going to NYC to pick the dress, which took two days, starting to get ready at 10:30 in the morning. That day a group of six friends including myself made a day out of it: hair, nails, pedicures, facials, lunch—the works. Even though we all rode in the limo during the day while getting ready and going from place to place, we all took separate limos to the prom.

Most girls, constrained by limited money but also wanting to participate in this beauty work, compromised by getting just their hair, nails, or face done. Tracey, a young African-American woman, explains,

> I know it's like I have to get my hair done and then I have to get my nails done and that costs a lot of money. My dress was expensive, you know, my dress was $275. So it's like I'm broke. I have no money, you know, so if like somebody loans you jewelry or something, you know, that's a lot cheaper than going out and buying it.

Several girls, deciding that this beauty work should be done by professionals, sought jobs to pay for these added expenses; some even started separate bank accounts to save for the cost of the prom.

As many of these young women suggest, these preparations for the prom, while fundamentally being about setting oneself apart, were often a collective process. For many of these girls, talk started about how they intended to prepare for the prom months before the actual event. Some girls reported that these conversations transformed their initial ambivalence about the prom into excitement about the prospects of working on their bodies for the upcoming event.

The process of getting ready came to represent for many a space of shared experience. It was not uncommon for female family members, friends, and more experienced promgoers to assemble at one girl's house to get ready together. Consider my fieldnotes from observing as one young white woman, helped by two others, got ready for the prom:

Susie came in from having taken a shower in a panic, wrapped in robe and towel. Her day, she said, had been a succession of preparations: getting the campsite ready for after the prom, having her nails done. She had had a French manicure. Susie left to put some clothes on after calling a friend to remind her to bring the boutonnieres. We, the three helpers, sat on the floor in the middle of the room, talking casually about last year's prom, which one of the girls, Lori, had attended. Lori told us a story about sticking her head out the sunroof of the limo they had rented and messing up the big curls she had so carefully put in her hair. Lori was supposed to put those same big curls in Susie's hair. Before they began working on Susie's hair, Lori and her friend Donna decided to go have a smoke, on the roof, while Susie began drying her short bobbed hair. After a few minutes Lori came through the window "refreshed" and began working on Susie's hair. As Lori styled Susie's hair around the curling iron, the three girls chatted about the prom, how Susie had found her dress, their skipping school to lay out in the sun that day and the boys outside playing basketball in the driveway across the street. The conversation jumped from one topic to another quickly. From the pace of their talk it was easy to tell these three girls were good friends and that their lives were bound up with one another. What I realized after being there for just an hour was that while these girls came together ostensibly to help Susie prepare for her prom, the social significance of this space was more meaningful. More than just getting ready, this was a space to "rehash" aspects of their daily lives with other girls who shared in it. (May 1996)

The pleasure many of these girls expressed as they spoke about this collective process was difficult to miss. Consider the following three narratives written by young African-American women:

The house is going to be filled with people coming to help me. My mom and her friends they're gonna come help me get ready and stuff and do my make-up. I'll already have my hair and nails done and then my friends are gonna come help me get dressed. They're gonna be taking pictures and videotaping. One of my friends, she's a year younger and then her sister's a year older. She graduated last year and I went last year and helped her get ready and get her stuff together. Her and her mom are gonna come help me. My grandmother will probably come over. My brother, his girlfriend and my niece, they're gonna come over and take pictures and watch when I leave.

I woke up out of bed about 9:00 a.m. that morning because I had a million things to do. I called my cousin and we went shopping. We picked up my dress, accessories and shoes. After doing that I spent another 10 hours getting my hair and nails done. I didn't get home until about 6:15 and the limo was scheduled to pick me up at 6:30. So thanks to my mother and cousin I was able to get ready in about 25–30 minutes.

I have to go get my nails done. I don't want my hair to fall. How do I do this? How do I do that? I have to make sure I do the make-up, this that. Well, I don't wear make-up, but this is just what we were all talking about, just the girl-type of stuff. Like, "Oh make sure you bring an extra pair of pantyhose, make sure your shoes are this, that everything matches, you don't put on too much make-up because the light looks this way on your face." All that type of stuff.

Pictures were often taken to record the elaborate work that goes into getting ready.

### The Burdens of Beauty

Beauty Make Me Over: From Toned-down to Terrific, From Low-key to Luminous; From Sweet to Sophisticated.
—Beauty article in *Your Prom,* 1996

Some girls, while enjoying the process of getting ready for the prom, were also aware of the extent to which these preparations are distinctly feminine. One white middle-class girl wrote:

This elaborate process of preparation was done by most of the people attending the prom (well, girls). It was ridiculous when you think of all the time and money that went into one night. But it was fun.

Another young white woman wrote,

This whole procedure for preparing for the prom was pretty hectic. That's because, I mean, I don't mean to create more stereotypes for my gender but, girls who do go to the prom have the tendency to over-exaggerate things. Speaking for most of my friends, we worried too much. There were many questions that ran through my mind as the prom night got closer and closer: what type of dress should I wear? Should I wear long or short? What color dress should I wear? How should I get my hair done? Who should do my hair? Should I do my nails? What type of jewelry should I wear with my dress? What type of shoes? While on the other hand guys have one major question: Should I rent or buy?

Like these two girls above, most took it for granted that boys and girls engaged in a different set of practices as they prepared for the prom. These young women are drawing from a set of social assumptions about what it means to be a "man" or a "woman." Treating gender as simply a matter of social difference and not social power not only works to naturalize a gendered division of labor, it also obscures how this very talk produces and maintains a social organization of gender. Mary and Sarah, two white students from Woodrow, related,

MD: I don't think they [boys] really care quite as much as the girls do. I mean, like, what they care about is what they're doing before and what they're doing after and with who.

SJ: They don't really have a lot to get ready.

MD: "My tux is a double-breasted gray." [she laughs]

SJ: The girls are—the girls have to do a lot more planning with their dress and their . . .

MD: Yeah, go through their hair and their nails, their dress.

While many girls were willing to acknowledge that the work required of them was entirely different from the work required of boys to get ready for the prom, few referred to these preparations as burdensome. Exceptions to the rule, two white young women described their experiences as follows:

I'm all through with dress shopping. I'm done. It's tiring. You go from store to store trying on dresses, taking off clothes and putting it on, oh no. It's very tiring shopping for a dress. I'm glad that part is over with.

Shopping for all the prom stuff was a hassle. I went through four dresses and two pair of shoes until I was set on the perfect outfit. The night before the prom I ended up puking my brains out all night and was running a high fever. My mother dragged me to the beauty parlor drugged up, while I had my nails, hair, and makeup done. They had to put extra makeup on me because I was so pale from being sick.

As this last young woman suggests, mothers are central players in the prom, often as invested as these girls in the project of becoming feminine. One young woman laughingly reported to her friends in the bathroom at the prom that her mother had "attacked" her with mascara. In these last two scenes, it is mothers who enlist their daughters to do the work of looking feminine for the prom. One girl is "dragged" by her mother, while the second had been "attacked." Though clearly expressed in jest, both provide compelling imagery of the ways the practices of femininity are passed from mother to daughter.

While at the prom, a lot of girls talked openly among themselves about the labor-intensive work they do on their bodies to achieve an idealized feminine image. Most common were girls' tales of struggles to find the right dress and their efforts toward having the "perfect" hairstyle. Stories of this kind were exchanged and compared at the prom in the girl's bathroom, a space at the prom reserved exclusively for girls. After observing four proms, I realized that these bathroom discussions about their bodies, dresses, and preparations were not only a source of pleasure, but were also an integral part of the actual prom. In my fieldnotes from Hudson's prom this is most evident:

> I watched girls come and go and check themselves out in the mirror as they passed. Three girls came in the bathroom and I started to talk with them as they primped. One girl was wearing a green dress, with a green sheer shawl and full tulle skirt and I told her how pretty it was. She twirled around for me. I asked her if she'd had it made and she said she had. She told me she wanted it to be fuller on the bottom so that she would get more attention. She also told me that her jewelry came from the makeup artist who did her makeup. She was heavily made up in green eye shadow with her hair pulled up into large ringlets. Her friend, who had also had her dress made to look like a traditional ball gown, with a purse to match, said her sister had done her makeup. The girl in the green dress told me she had only had hers done by a professional because she didn't know how to do it herself. I asked her if she normally wore makeup and she said no. The three of them talked among themselves about their lipstick, comparing prices, mostly. One girl had bought hers for $2.00, while the other had gone and gotten her lipstick from Lancome for close to $15.00. Another girl walked by showing off her gold shoes and said, "These are toe crackers." Soon after another girl came by whose dress was bursting at the sides. She and her friends were in search of a pin of some sort. They had done a botched job to repair the dress by the bathroom stalls. This led to the three girls' discussion of the mistakes about their own dresses. The girl in the green dress pointed to some gapping around the neckline, while the other pointed to her uneven hemline. (June 1997)

While in many ways this kind of "body talk" represents an articulation of feminine identity and mastery, it also undermines the idealization of feminine display because it exposes it as work that requires money, time, and body alteration. Contrary to the idea that femininity is something girls simply possess, their talk helps to define femininity as something one actively undertakes.[6] I overheard one girl as she rushed up to greet her friend in the beginning of Rudolph's prom, pointing to the top of her head, exclaiming, "Three hours, it took three hours to get my hair to look like this!"

More than just a set of frivolous practices of primping, these are fertile sites of identity negotiation and construction, where girls are making sense of what it means to be women in a culture that treats the surface of the body as the consummate canvas on which to express the feminine self. There is also a clear sense that many of these girls enjoyed the attention they received after such significant transformations—their labors were not in vain. Indeed, this is the very promise of the prom, highlighted in girls' talk, and telegraphed in prom films and magazines. The pleasure in being seen in "a new light" helps to gain girls' consent to consume, to ensure their participation in beauty culture and the ongoing creation of gender.

### The Politics of Pleasure

The achievement of femininity for the prom depends on an endless consumption of products; makeup, clothing, hair accessories, shoes, lingerie, handbags, and jewelry are all products readily available in a commodity market and heavily marketed as tools for feminine display and self-reinvention at the prom. These are tools that require time, patience, and skill to master. Susan Bordo elaborates on the more lasting effects this kind of exacting and intensive work has on women and how they experience life in their bodies, explaining, "Through the pursuit of an ever-changing, homogenizing, elusive ideal of femininity—a pursuit without a terminus, requiring that women constantly attend to minute and often whimsical changes in fashion—female bodies become docile bodies—bodies whose forces and energies are habituated to external regulation, subjection, transformation, 'improvement'."[7] But this kind of body work is not just about producing disciplined bodies for consumption; there is more here. The meanings girls themselves attach to this work is significant for understanding why they engage in such practices in the first place.[8]

Engaging in the work of becoming "beautiful" for the prom represents a struggle to stake a claim to one's identity. For many of these girls, participating in beauty work enables them to occupy a position within a public space, a significant fact when considering women's historical relegation to the private sphere. As consumers of beauty culture, these young women are able to possess a sense of power and visibility by claiming public space that often is not experienced in their everyday lives in school, with family, or in their relationships with young men. They occupy hair salons, nail salons, and dress shops in a way similar to that of middle-class women in the 1920s who, just after winning the right to vote, proudly (and paradoxically) announced their new freedom by wearing shorter skirts, bobbing their hair, and smoking cigarettes in public.

Not only are these girls able to demonstrate a public commitment to feminine practices, they are also able to express their competence as beauty practitioners. The desire to do so is so significant that girls who were either unable (or sometimes unwilling) to indulge in the extravagances of the beauty/hair salon performed this work in private spaces, most often their homes. These girls created a situation resembling, in remarkable ways, the experience of going to a salon. Friends and female family members were enlisted to perform the beauty work provided to other girls by service workers. Though done in the private setting of home, getting ready signified a public act.

While young women arguably do beauty work for the prom to express their heterosexual desirability, they also do this work to experience a self-pleasure by making themselves feel special.[9] For many of these girls, the prom presents itself as an opportunity to indulge themselves in ways that many of them are simply unable to in their day-to-day school lives. Part of what makes this body work around the prom worth undertaking stems directly from how they experience everyday life as young women.

Teenage girls are often denied control over their bodies, their desire, and their self-definition. Engaging in this elaborate consumption-oriented body work enables them to craft a space of self-control, self-definition, and self-pleasure that is experienced immediately. Many girls perceive adult women as possessing greater control over their lives than they as girls can. Transforming themselves to look more like adult women through these beauty practices allows many of them to feel more like adult women, to possibly experience adult freedoms and liberties, even if momentarily, and to negotiate those everyday constraints they experience because of their age and consequent position in society. Of course, the result is that the pleasure of excess conceals the ideological workings of the prom; proms structure girls' investments in both gender and heterosexuality, exacerbate their anxieties about the body, and focus their attention toward the all-consuming project of the body.

## Fashioning the Feminine Self

### The Dress

I had been looking for prom dresses for months and I hadn't found anything I really liked and I just happened to walk back to where they keep the more expensive dresses in my store and I saw this dress and went, "This is the dress." Before I even put it on I was like, "This is my dress." I tried it on and all the ladies in the store were like, "Oh my god, that's so beautiful." I did my hair up a little bit, you know and it looked really nice. So I decided to get the dress.

Like this African-American woman, most of the young women in this study made some mention of the prom dress, detailing their efforts in finding it, as well as how it felt to wear it on the night of the prom. There was anxiety for some girls as they figured out what to wear; others enjoyed looking for a dress as a part of the process of doing beauty/body work. One white girl wrote,

> I don't remember anything eventful about the prom itself. I remember the major preparation that went into it, namely—FINDING THE DRESS. Everyone discussed first what style they wanted: long, short, strapless, black, sequined, etc. When we walked into the prom everyone (girls) greeted the other girls immediately with compliments on dress and hair.

Consider an African-American girl's comments:

> You can have the same hair style as anyone else. It doesn't matter, but that dress. I know me, the dress I picked out two years from now I don't want to look back on my prom pictures and be like, "What am I wearing?" So, I won't be like other girls. I won't regret having this dress.

Her statement is suggestive of the complex thinking girls engage in when selecting a prom dress. A range of factors must be considered: not only must she set herself apart through what she wears at the prom, the dress must also be remembered in a particular way. It must be able to endure changing styles and outlast current trends. She is conscious not to make the same mistakes as other girls. Her good taste, keen sense of style, and feminine judgment will be admired not only at the prom, but in years to come. How she remembers the prom is contingent on how she remembers the dress. One girl reported feeling like "a million dollars in my beautiful red dress" and that she had the time of her life, while another girl commented that she felt like "a princess for a day" because of what she wore—an unforgettable dress secured an unforgettable night. Significantly, one young woman ended up not going to her prom because her dress was not ready:

> Oh gosh, it's so sad. She's, um, my best friend and she basically didn't make it to the prom because her dress wasn't ready. She started, her sister goes to the Rhode Island School of Design, so she was designing her dress and everything. Doing it by hand, no pattern and they

basically waited till the last minute to go to New York and get the fabric and they started her dress on Tuesday. The prom is Friday so she was all prepared except for the dress. She had her nails done, her hair done. She had the shoes, the pocketbook, everything, but her dress wasn't ready until 12:30 that night. Like, we were calling because she was supposed to sit at our table and she's just like, "It's not done. I can't come. It's not done," and I'm like, "You can't just slip on any dress? You spent all of this money on preparations. Just because your dress isn't made, just come anyway. You bought the bid." Like, she spent all of this money getting ready. She probably spent more money than I did because she didn't go last year, either, so I'm like, "Just come." But she wound up not coming.

Many girls spoke about their dresses not only with an uncanny attention to detail, but with a striking familiarity and understanding of the meanings that underlie the style codes defined by the fashion industry:

My dress, I believe, it's called watercress satin. It's the satin that has the sort of wood grain texture. It's not a shiny satin, it's a duller satin and its got a scoop neck and it has puffy sleeves. Mary and I used to call it a princess dress and this is the actual thing. My dress is more flared than hers is going to be. It's not way out. It stands a bit above the floor. So it's gonna be cream satin and then it's going to have some flowers on the collar.

Another white girl said,

> It's long, but unlike most long dresses it's not tight. It's not really squared off. It's just kind of like not fitted. It's like A-line and backless but, it's not like high cut in the neck and its got crisscrossing straps in the back and it's shimmery black . . . when it ripples, it ripples sparkles. Not just silver sparkles but multicolored sparkles. It's really, really faint glitter and you wouldn't see it normally. It has a silver image but, it's really blotted. Everybody else is going black.

Elise referred to her dress as "a great dress" because it showed off the new tattoo on her arm, a significant departure from how other girls spoke. Displaying her tattoo counters the cultural expectation that girls will relate to their bodies as spaces to demonstrate their commitment to feminine practices. Yet this can also be read as a dramatic statement she makes about herself through her body. As Joan Jacobs Brumberg has argued in her book *The Body Project*, tattooing and body piercing, though often considered outside the realm of the feminine, is still work on the body. Whether dramatic or subtle, work on the body is a feminine form of work.[10]

### Hair

Just as the dress signifies an expression of the feminine self, enabling girls to make a statement about who they are, so does hair. For the prom, many girls treat their hair with the utmost care. Great attention is paid to how it looks, and whether or not its style compliments the style of dress worn. In many girls' narratives, hair was critically important to the overall construction of a "prom look." As mentioned earlier, many girls had their hair professionally styled. Several girls reported that hair salons were so overbooked on the day of the prom that they were forced to take hair appointments early

in the morning and pray their hair would hold its shape until the fateful moment arrived. Hairstyles varied: one white girl discussing her hair offered, "I have a feeling I'm going to have braids and pearls. I have long red hair and I'm wearing a princess dress, so the hairdresser immediately said pearls and braids." Another girl, who wanted to create what she considered a more sophisticated look through her hairstyle, explained, "Since, I'm going to be wearing rhinestone jewelry, I'm gonna slick it back or something. I could do curls, but I look silly in curls. I'm going to be Miss Elegant for the night." For many girls the "up do," a symbol of sophistication and elegance, was most popular.

Hair seemed to be a particularly important site for some African-American girls in the articulation of a sense of self, perhaps even more so than the dress. Many African-American girls at the prom creatively displayed their hair through hair extensions, braids, and wraps. Glitter and rhinestones were artfully placed to draw attention to hair, often overshadowing the prom dress.

While few white girls would have been able to connect how they styled their hair to their being white, to see their hairstyles as an expression of their race identities, predictably, for African-American girls, hair seemed to have everything to do with race. Historically, hair has been an important symbol through which both style and identity politics have been expressed within the African-American community. Lisa Jones writes on the meaningfulness of these hairstyles, "These are elaborate constructions, with hair piled high, woven with ornaments and shaped like fans, wedding cakes, hourglasses and halos. Maybe they're crowns, maybe they're altars. What links African American/Africa-diaspora cultural practice with African traditional cultures is not the naturalness of the braids, it's the idea of construction. Hair in both traditions suggests spectacle and pageantry. It's always handled and adorned; hair is never left 'as is.' Hair exists to be worked."[11]

Challenging the idea that black women work on their hair to conform to white ideals of femininity, Cobena Mercer has argued that hair stylization within the black community signifies a creative play of identity rooted specifically in African-American beauty culture.[12] Similarly, I would argue that these creative expressions represent an attempt to resist hegemonic images of femininity and beauty rooted in white middle-class culture by articulating pride in racial self. This act may be especially meaningful at the prom because it is a highly visible and public spectacle formally tied to white institutions of schooling.

### What He Wears Matters, Too

Night of Nights. The best looks for this year's ball. "Suitable style" for him is just a page away, too.

—"Night of Nights," article in *Your Prom*, 1996

Some girls express their feminine skills through the outfits they selected for their dates. Several of the girls I interviewed stated that what their date wore was more an expression of their own ability, not his, to assemble and organize appearance and style. I, too, can remember negotiating with my date what he was going to wear when I went to my own prom. I had insisted he wear a red plaid cummerbund and bow tie with his tails and went with him to the tuxedo rental shop to make sure he picked the right suit. "The guy matches to the best he can," one girl offered. Mark, an African-American student, discusses how he came to select his prom outfit and the role his girlfriend played in the decision:

AB:     So how did you pick out your tuxedo?
ML:     Well, I really didn't pick it out. Me and her went to get it and she was like, she got her dress way before the prom. But I had to match what she had so I didn't want to get a regular black tuxedo.
AB:     How come?
ML:     Because I figure everybody would have a regular tuxedo. I wanted to be different. I wanted to stand out. So I went there and she was like, This is what I want you to get. Like, not a regular one. She picked out everything. This is what I want you to get. Like, so, I got the white jacket. Like I said, she picked it out.

While his desire to be different may have been independent of her, Mark's girlfriend exerted considerable influence over how he was able to express his individuality. How a boyfriend dresses is often perceived as an expression of the girlfriend's good taste and style. Consider one white girl's comments about what her boyfriend wore to the prom:

He had a little baby-blue handkerchief so it would match my dress. We didn't want to be tacky with a baby-blue vest or anything. I remember he got the cummerbund and I was like, "You need to get the vest." Everybody was getting vests and I was just like, "Why didn't you get a vest?"

This suggests an extension of the spaces where femininity can be demonstrated. Boys' bodies, in addition to girls' bodies, signify meaningful sites for the display and management of femininity at the prom. What matters is how it all comes together: how the dress looks beside the tux, and how well the corsage compliments the dress. Of course, this very coordinated presentation relies on an organized, even rigidly regulated, heterosexuality.

### Class Talk: Distinction and Taste

There is some indication that girls' talk about their dress, their hair, and their date's tux is also embedded within a particular set of class relations and class meanings. Although rarely explicitly stated, class emerges within these girls' talk about their dresses as an ideological mechanism used to define and distinguish among a range of practices within an economy of "taste."[13] Consider Erin's discussion of what constitutes an "ugly" prom dress, what she likes and what she doesn't like; her narrative hints at how the management of style and femininity is organized through a discourse of class:

> Ugh. I don't like sequin dresses. I don't like stuff that's real, real shiny. I like, like my dress has diamonds on it but it's not that many. I don't like, like, real lively stuff, stuff has a whole bunch of diamonds or lacy stuff. I don't like different color dresses, like a red top with a black skirt. Something else like that is ugly is the big ruffles on the shoulders or something, the ruffles on the bottom, I don't like that.

Through her talk about different dress styles, she seems to be imposing a distinction between what has been designated culturally as "overdone" and what she implicitly defines as a reserved elegance, similar to the old adage "less is more." Erin's narrative suggests that class is significant in organizing her relationship to a discourse of style. She implicitly invokes the concept of "taste" to delineate between class groups and forge a connection between social class and style. Another young white woman addressed this issue in relation to her hair:

> My day started off from the hairdresser from hell. She totally did my hair wrong. I wanted a simple french twist because I had a simple dress. Well, what I got was a BIG poof that cost $40. When I got home I called my cousin and she came over and did my hair.[14]

Many girls deployed the discourse of "taste" to set themselves apart from other girls, though often the distinctions were subtle, as in this girl's description of her dress:

> I have to say a lot of the dresses are going to be tacky looking. I mean hopefully mine won't look like that. I tried really hard. I didn't want it to be shiny. It's not going to be shiny, it's going to shimmer. It's not the same thing. The kind that can't be worn more than once because it's a prom dress. It's like the bridesmaid dress that's obviously a bridesmaid dress. There are prom dresses that are obviously prom dresses.

This idea of "distinction," defined chiefly by what is *not* distinct, is central to both the production of femininity and the reproduction of class relations. Many girls spoke with clarity about the importance of looking distinctive at the prom. One white middle-class girl wrote,

> My dress was long and fitted with gold sequins that shimmered different shades of pink, yellow and green in the light. I liked it because it was unique. I knew that no one else would have it. Everyone wants to have their own dress.

Another girl's narrative suggests that those girls who did not look distinctive were chastised. For her, distinctive meant wearing a brand-new dress, which is suggestive of the extent to which ideas about distinction are ordered by a class logic that relies upon the availability of disposable income:

> The women who didn't go out and buy a new dress for that particular event were made fun of. Although most us, if not all of us, wanted to get a new dress, some couldn't afford it. Many of my friends made fun of such girls, when it wasn't their fault.

Although most girls talked about how they chose their dresses, these girls spoke in vastly different ways. For some, the price of the dress was central to how they thought about the dress and determined its value. Many girls spoke proudly about finding their dress for a reasonable price, which suggests that they considered this a fundamentally important skill in negotiating femininity. Their concerns with the cost of their dresses also may have particular salience because most of these girls do not have their own disposable income and are reliant either on part-time, low-wage work or on their parents' disposable income. A young African-American woman wrote,

> Well I knew I was going to the prom long before it came up in school and one random day I found my prom dress. I paid like $45 for it. I wasn't about to go out and spend like $200. Later I bought a pair of nice shoes and they were like $25, I think.

Money is a huge issue for girls. While some girls are willing to splurge for a $300 dress, most can't. Finding an inexpensive dress while still being able to make a statement carries tremendous importance. Lots of girls mentioned the price of their dress and whether or not they would be able to wear the dress again, "I know me, the dress I picked out I want to be able to wear this dress other places." Magazines and local newspapers, acknowledging the significance of limited money to purchase a prom dress, often offer suggestions to cut costs. "Don't Break the Bank" was the title of one article featured in *HJ*, a teen magazine read by Woodrow students, that offered, "One way to cut down on prom costs is to share dresses. . . . Why let the dress you wore last year sit in your closet this year? Do you have a friend who looks good in blue? Ask her if she wants to borrow your dress in exchange for that great one she wore to the winter formal. Form a dress network among you and your friends with everyone's old dresses."[15] Recognizing that the dress is often the most expensive purchase for girls for the prom, prom magazines usually picture less expensive dresses alongside dresses costing well over $200; "tons of great looks for under 100 bucks!" these magazines promise. The caption from one photo layout featured in the 1997 *YM* special prom issue read, "Sexy Steals: Dope dresses for around $100. Floor him with a little black dress, the whole posse looks totally hot." The lesson here is that even girls with limited budgets can afford to have a new dress for the prom—they can still consume!

Yet many of those girls who bought their dresses for what they had defined as an inexpensive price stated that they actually desired the more expensive dresses. As one girl put it, "The dress I found that I liked was $250. So we shopped and found the only other prom dress in the world that I liked for $80." The idea of "having expensive taste" is often given as testimony of an "authentic" social class position. The ability to distinguish between "high quality" and "low quality" or to appreciate "the finer things," much like in the story of the princess and the pea, is assumed to be, within a cultural logic of class, a characteristic specific to the middle or upper middle classes. [16] I interpret this as a form of "class talk" that enables these girls to assert a higher class identity than their material conditions might allow.

### It Has To Be an Original

The importance of setting oneself apart is such a significant aspect of feminine consumption that one small dress shop from which many girls from Woodrow High School bought their dresses kept a record of who bought which dress and which school the girl attended to prevent girls at the same

school from wearing identical dresses to their prom. Mary, a white student at Woodrow, elaborates on the importance of having an original look:

> The two other girls I'm going with, one girl is going to be wearing a silver dress with stockings, heels. She's dying her hair, well it's black now and she's gonna put silver hairspray in it and she's gonna, everything is gonna be silver. She got the idea from me, which is why I'm not doing it. I was going to go silver until two of my friends said, "Oh, we're going to go silver," and bought the dresses before mine was made. Okay, forget that.

Some girls went to great lengths to ensure that their dresses were originals. One young woman traveled out of state to find her dress, while another bought her dress from a small dress shop where she knew few girls from her school would shop. Terry, an African-American student at Woodrow, discussed how she would feel if someone had the same dress as she:

> I would die if someone had my dress. I would die! Because I just love that dress and I really don't, I would be really surprised if someone had that dress. I really would. And my friend saw it and she's like, "Oh, my god! That dress is so pretty." And she's like, "I want to get that dress, after I saw it." I was like, "Too bad, you ain't gonna get it. That's my dress." I would die. This is like my prom and I own it. No, I don't want anyone to have the same dress as me. I would say, "Well I look better than anyone," to try to make myself feel better, but I would still be upset. I would still be mad. I know they [the store] have three of my dress.

Girls' talk about prom dresses in the weeks before the prom can also be a deliberate way of ensuring that other girls do not wear the same dress, as is suggested by Erin:

> The worst thing that could happen is to run into somebody with your dress. That's why you have to be kind of sneaky about it. Like, lots of girls will go around and ask, "What color are you wearing?" to make sure that we have a different color and always ask what does your dress look like. And you make sure someone doesn't have it and it's nothing close to yours. You know some people will draw their own dresses on papers and like, my friend she drew a dress, designed her own thing and she was going to have somebody make it for her because she wanted to make sure she had something like nobody else. She showed it to me, not to other people, because she didn't want other people stealing her idea.

*Rethinking the Dress*

While the discourses on beauty, pleasure and consumption regulate girls' investment in femininity, girls also use these discourses in ways that enable them to push the boundaries that contain them, though in limited ways.[17] Resistance to these discourses often arises because of budgetary constraints. Many girls simply do not have the money to buy expensive dresses and are forced to develop alternative plans. Other girls think it too indulgent to spend considerable money on one night unless they are able to find that "perfect" prom dress. And some girls buy their dresses at secondhand consignment shops. Sandy, a student from Rudolph, discusses why she didn't buy a new dress for the prom:

> My prom dress was something in the back of my closet. Like, I looked forever for a prom dress. I could not find one that I liked. [Last year's] was really expensive and I didn't want to do it again because it was three hundred and some dollars. I would never ever pay that much again. I started looking for a dress for this year and in the beginning of May, I guess. I kept looking and I couldn't find anything I liked.

Although most girls struggled to make sense of their investment in the feminine project of getting ready for the prom, a few, like Elise, a young bisexual woman, more actively rejected the ideals of femininity and its anchoring within a heterosexual order. For Elise, the dress symbolized her rejection:

EV:    I don't know, I figure I ought to go all out, put on some makeup, the shoes.

AB:    Can you tell me a little bit about your dress?

EV:    It's white, it's long and it's kind of lacy. I've had it for like a couple of years and I only wore it once. I said, Okay, I'll wear it to the prom. It's nice.

AB:    Any other preparations?

EV:    Like jewelry and stuff like that. Yeah, jewelry, a necklace and that's probably it. I don't know what she's wearing [her date]. She wants to wear some vinyl pants and probably a shirt.

AB:    Is she going to wear like a tuxedo suit jacket?

EV:    No, I don't think so, that'd be cheesy. I think that's cheesy. It's like to try to conform in a way, you know, the male-female relationship like, you know? That's not what it is. It's just a different relationship, we're two women.

Instead of buying their dresses in a store, several of the girls interviewed had them made by their mothers or by friends. Many girls who had handmade dresses spoke about how they decided on the design. As one girl explained, "I basically knew what I wanted and I knew I wasn't going to be able to find it because I looked." Several of them began by exploring department stores and smaller dress shops, inspecting the different styles of formal dresses provided in the market before deciding what their dresses would look like. Borrowing dress styles from department stores but not actually buying the dress there, these girls creatively used the market toward their own end.[18] As one girl related,

> My mom's making my dress. Mainly because we couldn't find any in the mall that was not too expensive, not immodest and what I wanted. The first trip my mom dropped me off [at the mall]. And she said, basically, "Go store by store because you'll never know where you're going to find something." So I went store by store and everything was way out of my range. But it was basically just to look around and see if there is anything out there that I liked. So I got a lot of pieces of dresses that I liked but, no real full dress. Plus, the fact that what's in style now is either short and flared, or long and tight, or short and tight. But you can't really get flared and long in the stores. And both of those were like $250, which nobody in their right mind buys for a prom. They were very pretty, but. . . . So after that we went to bridal boutiques and a couple other malls.

Making their own dresses also sets girls apart from others and guarantees the dresses' originality. One girl who designed and sewed her own dress commented, "For the next couple weeks after the prom—I'm not lying—people were still talking about how beautiful my dress turned out." Most of these girls did not reject the project of inscribing images of femininity on their bodies; they welcomed the idea of working on their bodies, but challenged the direct connection to a commodity market.

### School, Dresses, and the Body

Getting ready for the prom enables many girls to cultivate and demonstrate their skills at coordinating and assembling a range of signs and symbols upon their bodies in a way that transforms who they are in school. As one African-American girl wrote,

> I wanted to wear something that would totally surprise people. In school I was known to constantly wear all black, if not mostly black outfits. So as my huge surprise to everyone, I ended up wearing a long white dress. It was white stain and chiffon with black lace on the side with white pearls on the lace.

The prom is a space in which young women can play with a range of identities, many of which are closed off to them within what Nancy Lesko refers to as the "body curriculum" of schools, a curriculum that operates to regulate and discipline girls' sexuality and desire.[19]

Most girls construct their appearances in ways that suggest their willingness to be seen; as one girl noted, "I remember everyone being surprised I had on makeup and all that." Without romanticizing the practices of dressing up, I do want to suggest that the prom represents a safe and playful space in which many girls may negotiate, in some ways challenging how adolescent girls are culturally represented. For many girls the style of dress worn is tied to sexuality and to sexual identities. Consider a Latina middle-class girl's comments,

> I'm such a tomboy. I never let my hair down and I rarely wear dresses. The prom was an experience. Everyone kept commenting on how beautiful I looked, "Why don't you let your hair down more often?" "You have a great figure; you shouldn't hide behind jeans and a T-shirt." My friends barely recognized me. People who've known me all my life stared at me.

The prom dress is critically important to this invention of a sexual self; as such, many girls buy dresses that are significantly beyond what they can normally afford to spend on everyday school clothes. Many girls at the proms I attended wore long, fitted dresses, many of them black, often with exposed backs and deep slits running up one leg. As one white girl described her dress,

> It's got rhinestones and spaghetti straps. It's got a scoop neck with rhinestones going all the way around. It's long, it's got a slit up the mid-thigh and then rhinestones going in the back criss-cross and then the back is completely open and then it kind of comes in at the sides so your sides are showing.

These young women are able to display their bodies in ways that they usually can't at school: arms and legs are bared, necklines revealed. "It was cut in here and here [gesturing to her sides] and came up around my neck and all this was beaded and it was like an open back with just the crosses and it was real tight and it just went out to like here. I loved it." As another described hers, "It's blue chiffon and it comes down to like the heel of my shoe, and it doesn't have a split in it which surprises me cause I wanted a split." I also overheard many girls proudly exchanging stories of their fathers' utter discomfort in seeing their daughters in such sexy dresses, testimonies that the girls had succeeded in transforming themselves.

When understood within an organization of schooling that emphasizes modesty and reserve in dress for girls, a sexy prom dress signifies a way to negotiate the sexual terrain of school.[20] Girls have so few spaces in which they can claim sexual agency.[21] Those who attempt to articulate their own sexual desire must negotiate their sexuality within a discursive organization of adolescent female sexuality most often ordered around images of sexual victimization, teen pregnancy, and sexual promiscuity.[22]

Through what they wear many girls seem to claim a visible (hetero)sexual identity that counters a (racially coded) bourgeois image of the adolescent girl as the bearer of sexual innocence.[23] While the activity of dressing up binds girls to an unequal order of gender, their actions and the meanings they attach to them reflect attempts to generate alternate meanings that enable them to exert some control over those sexual and social struggles that shape and pattern their everyday lives.

## *Can Girls Contest the Prom?*

At stake here are familiar concerns. What leads girls to invest in feminine practices, particularly those that require the dramatic altering of their bodies? The transformation of self many of these girls desire reflects the ideologies organizing not only beauty culture within consumer capitalism but its entrenchment in an organization of class, gender, and (hetero)sexuality. For most girls choosing to attend the prom involves a series of negotiations that express a struggle to understand these social forms in relation to their lives. Their narratives illustrate the tensions girls experience as they make sense of the cultural codes of femininity.

There is a clear sense that many girls in this study are not normally as invested in femininity as they seem to be for the occasion of the prom. Many indicated to me that they usually do not wear makeup and only visit the hair salon to have their hair cut. In this way proms are much like weddings: women who might normally reject the conventions of femininity suddenly find themselves strangely seduced by their appeal. Just as many women do for their weddings, girls pulled out all the stops for the prom: nails were manicured, eyebrows plucked, and hair professionally styled. In fact, for some young women, the prom is seen as a dress rehearsal for weddings. If young women invest in the body work for the prom or for their weddings, but not necessarily elsewhere, what, then, are the connections between gender and these settings?

Proms, as cultural sites, work to secure girls' consent to prevailing feminine forms. The gender and heterosexual controls within this cultural scene are so rigidly organized and so profoundly connected to bodily pleasure and self-pleasure that acts of resistance seem to be possible for only a few. The limits of resistance to these gender precepts seem to be determined by the very social organization of this space—proms are the domain of the feminine, where girls' pleasure in doing feminine appearance work and their desire to make a statement about themselves are especially pronounced.

On the day of my junior prom a close girlfriend, who had decided to wear pajamas and no makeup to school, approached me to ask why I had worn makeup and chosen to wear a skirt and nice sweater on the day of the prom, of all days. I didn't understand what she meant; since I wore skirts almost everyday to school, why would this day be different from any other? She told me pointedly that girls are supposed to look awful on the day of the prom so that when we arrive at the event the statement we make is more dramatic. In short, her plan ensured that on the night of the prom she would really wow them! This memory of my prom was recalled as I struggled to make sense of why girls, many of whom reject these aspects of femininity more generally, used these feminine codes as they defined, experienced, and talked about their proms.

What girls wear to their prom and the activities they participate in tie them in many ways to gender structures that concentrate their energies on body work. Yet at the same time, their actions provide an opportunity for them to respond to how their schools defined adolescent femininity, and defined the girls themselves. Understanding what girls respond to—specifically, how schools restrict their sexual identities and expressions—is essential to understanding why girls invest in these activities, the pleasure they derive from them, and the meanings they attach to them.[24] Likewise, understanding how girls engage in negotiations over definitions of these activities is central to understanding how gender continues to operate as a pervasive force in our society.

*Four*

# Romancing The Prom

## Boyfriends, Girlfriends,
## and "Just Friends"

"Oh God, it's the prom! This is no time for that feminist crap."
— *That Seventies Show*

Kiss me out of the bearded barley. Nightly, beside the green,
  green grass.
Swing, swing, swing the spinning step. You wear those shoes
  and I'll wear that dress.
Oh, kiss me beneath the milky twilight. Lead me out on the
  moonlit floor.
Lift your open hand. Strike up the band and make the fireflies
  dance, silver moon's sparkling. So kiss me.

— *Sixpence None the Richer,* "Kiss Me"

The second of these two epigraphs is taken from the theme song to the pop-ular 1999 prom film *She's All That.* The idea of dreamy romance invoked in the song "Kiss Me" is one of the central organizing concepts upon which meanings of the prom hinge. Girls' magazines and a host of Hollywood films have constructed the site of the prom as a site of romantic possibility, where the promise of sweet love and tender affections are infused to create a magical night.

Though often obscured from view, gender and heterosexuality provide the foundation upon which this romance rests. To assert this claim is to rec-ognize that gender and heterosexuality are critically important to how romance is culturally understood, classified, and "experienced" within the context of the prom and beyond.[1] The social importance of romance is defined by a repertoire of images and cultural symbols. Romance carries tremendous ideological force; it naturalizes and normalizes heterosexual and gender controls, and shapes and organizes modern constructions of the self.[2]

### *Prom Romance*

> As a little girl, I always fantasized about this famous night where I would resemble Cinderella in my gown, with my best friends at my side as we all prepared for a night out in New York City. My Romeo-type boyfriend that showers me with flowers and compliments me the whole night through. Nothing would go wrong on prom night and *perfect* would be the only word to describe it.

Like this young Asian-American woman, many students spoke and wrote about the prom romantically. Most stories had a sort of dreamy tone to them, as though they had been rehearsed. Most were vague if not evasive, and there was a distinct sense that the meanings about romance and the prom were pieced together not from the students' experiences, but from a preexisting discourse of romance. Consider the following account by a young African-American man:

> The atmosphere was very casual for it to be a formal affair. All of the popular music from the time was playing, drinks flowed from peoples' cups like water and everyone was dressed to kill. There were few tuxedos but most of the boys had five- or six-hundred-dollar suits. They were very impressive. Every female had a gown that was even better than the last I had seen. I wouldn't trade the experience for anything.

His narrative is comprised of a collection of "props" already coded in a discourse of romance: "Everyone was dressed to kill"; "It was a formal affair"; "drinks flowed"; and "every . . . gown . . . was even better than the last. . . ." He does not actually tell us anything about his own prom experience—instead, in invoking images of heterosexual romance, he creates an impression of what the scene felt like.

Girls, in particular, seem to find pleasure in thinking about the prom within a discourse of romance.[3] Consider one white girl's narrative:

> I remember commenting that night that I felt like a princess and that I wished I got this type of treatment all the time. It is only one of the nights where the guys actually seemed to care if you are having fun or not. Everyone should feel that special. Those nights are some of the only nights where girls are treated like ladies.

Conjuring the familiar image of the princess at the ball, she narrates her prom within a fantasy of respect and romance. The prom signifies a momentary escape from her ongoing relations with boyfriends and other male peers; it is distinctly different from other school dances, the average Saturday

night out, or classroom life.[4] Here but not elsewhere, girls are treated as they "should be."

Many girls read for romance; some find romantic meaning in the gestures their dates make toward them:

My prom experience was very typical. When he came to the door he gave me a kiss on the cheek and a single long-stemmed rose.

As another girl wrote, "Since it had gotten chilly, my date let me wear his jacket."

Obviously consumers of popular romance, the two girls above are able to recognize these gestures as acts of chivalry through which romance can be experienced. Recognizing these gestures as "important" enables these girls to locate their prom experiences within a specific discourse of romance organized primarily around chivalry and sexual innocence. Drawing upon such symbols provides girls with neatly packaged meanings of what the prom is, and offers them codes that define particular relations, utterances, or actions as romantic. Compare these two narratives with two offered in one prom magazine article titled "Romance: Your Mushiest Prom Night Moments": "He suddenly put his arms around my waist and pulled me in tight—it sent shivers up my spine!" "He took my hand in his and looked deep into my eyes and said that he loved me! I was so incredibly happy I started to cry."[5] The similarities are indeed striking.

Girls' discussions of romance tend to center on their being the recipients of boys' "kind" treatment. Rarely do girls raise the issue of sex or discuss their own sexual desire or sexual agency. In many ways, ideal romantic moments (admittedly shaped by middle-class notions of love and courtship) are patterned by tenderness and attention to girls' emotional desires instead of their sexual desire.[6] Girls offer stories of their success in this type of romance as testimonies of their femininity.[7] Only one young Latina woman ventured to explicitly name sex, though she makes little mention of romance:

> It was a crazy night because many of us did things we never expected. Some of us got drunk for the first time and others lost their virginity, like me. I look back on it and remember how special it was. I also laugh because I always promised myself I would not be like everyone else and lose it on prom night. Even though I let myself down, I don't regret it.

Boys who spoke of romance also seemed to define it in terms of their treatment of women. As one related, "I spent the rest of the night with my girl. I cannot get too specific about what happened because some things were meant to be private." Consider the following narrative written by a young white man who was elated by the simple fact that he was able to enjoy a few moments of companionship with his date. What is especially compelling is that he sees this as a departure from the standard prom night:

> The thing that stands out the most was that my senior prom was just me and my date. We just hung out afterwards on the rocks of a beach. I didn't feel the need to go out drinking or to some motel. I was amazed at how wonderful a night I had had with my girlfriend just sitting and talking to each other the whole night. Sometimes the little things in life mean the most and stay with you for a lifetime.

In the following conversation I shared with a young African-American man, prom night is constructed as a night of closeness with his girlfriend:

> MC:  It's a night to remember, a night to remember.
>
> AB:  Why is it a night to remember?
>
> MC:  Well, like, how should I put it like this. Me and my girlfriend [he pauses], we just felt close, a lot, a whole lot closer, you know what I'm saying? It was like she was in my arms. To me the prom is like a wedding to me so, it was just, I just met this girl and we'd been together like six months but I just met her and this was like the first time she spent the whole night with me. It brought us together like real close.

He alludes to sex, though it goes unnamed.

These young men draw upon cultural ideals of romance and intimacy in ways that are pointedly different from those of most boys. Predictably, most boys avoided a discourse of romance (though perhaps not romance itself). Masculinity places enormous constraints upon men's emotional expressions, providing limited avenues with which boys may affirm their heterosexual

and masculine identities. Yet, investing in romance is also a way boys can demonstrate their identities as men at the prom, given that they are still able to claim heterosexual agency, a central component of masculine identity.[8]

## Tales of Power: Unsettling Accounts of Girls Who Settle

Power is a central point in the narratives about love, romance, dating, and the prom. I have heard countless stories about unequal power relations between dates, and an equal number of stories of failed romance. Power is naturalized through a discourse of romance. Ideologies of heterosexual romance and girls' investment in it work to uphold traditional conceptions of femininity and, thus, diminished power for them. Discussing romance in relation to weddings in her book *White Weddings*, Chrys Ingraham points out, "Viewing the various sites in popular culture where images and messages concerning white weddings dominate, it becomes clear that the intended audience is women, particularly white women, and that weddings are the domain of the feminine. More importantly, examining all of these sites together reveals the extent to which the dominant social order seeks to produce feminine subjects whose very existence and identity is organized by the ideology of romantic love. In addition to gaining the consent to the heterogendered division of labor where women are responsible for unpaid domestic and affective labor, the less obvious outcome is the privileging of romance discourse in women's everyday lives."[9]

The discourse of romantic love restricts girls' claims for equality in dating relationships, whether at the prom or not. As a result, girls rarely enter their relationships with their dates on the same level of power. The struggle to claim equality in their dating relations often requires that they forfeit the promise of romance. If girls are to challenge the power boys exercise over them at the prom they will be forced to construct alternative understandings of themselves as nonfeminine. For many girls deeply invested in femininity this creates a paradox many are unwilling to confront at the prom.

### The Race For A Date

Don't gamble on your prom date. Scour your school for Mr. Perfect . . . the guy with the winning smile, feet that won't crush yours on the dance floor, and a stellar personality that will keep you entertained all night. Clueless on which guy to choose? Just study our crash course in Prom Date 101 to pick the right guy for you.

—"The Dating Game: Who's Right for You?" article in *Your Prom*, 1997

Securing a date for the prom carries tremendous importance for many girls. This was a theme that pervaded the written narratives I collected and emerged over and over in the interviews. For girls, having a prom date was internalized as a means to both measuring their feminine self-worth and to solidifying their heterosexual identities. It's not surprising, then, that the pressures to have a date for the prom are considerable. "Early on in the year everybody had their prom dates and I was one . . . who didn't," one girl wrote. "It took about two weeks before the prom to get a date." Mary, a white student from Woodrow, expressed the tension girls often feel about being dateless:

MJ:    There's like people like me and half the other girls who are like, "No, we don't have a date." And they are calling on everyone asking for dates. I personally think it's way overblown. I want a date just because it's gonna be a threesome and I don't want to be part of a threesome with my friends. It has to be a foursome. It tends to be paired off. It happens in every group. That's why they make sidewalks so only two people can walk side by side.

AB:    Are you willing to go to the prom without a date?

MJ:    Yeah, I'm pretty much willing to. I wouldn't have a problem with it. The only person I might be going with is from my church but I called him yesterday and he doesn't know. I wouldn't want a real date, because I'm not going out with anyone important. I mean, I want a date, but it's not necessary. It's nice because you have someone to dance with and you don't have to worry about having someone to ask.

One white young woman in search of why having a date was so meaningful offered,

I thought about going stag. A lot of my friends are going stag and then I thought I'd rather spend the night with someone just for the fact that sharing the memory and stuff. My problem is I really don't know boys in school very well.

Unable to find a date, she went with her brother. She relayed to me later that she had wanted to go with her older brother because he was taller than she; she thought it would look better. She ended up going to the prom with her younger brother who, though shorter, allowed her to maintain a particular construction of the prom as a heterosexual event, and herself as legitimately feminine.

The social pressure many girls feel as they struggle to find dates for the prom leaves them with little room to assert agency in this process. As one girl explained,

All high school dances with my group of friends were the most disastrous occurrences because all of my friends and I would try to manipulate who would go with who and it never worked out the way we planned. There was always a crisis date situation about a week before the dance, making all of us so upset and stressed. Our senior prom was different, though. . . . All of the guys asked early, which was good because you know that the girls want their dates about two months before the prom and the guys never even think about it until three weeks before it. But this time they were considerate to our frenzied state and asked early so we could be sure that we're going to our senior prom and have time to get a dress and all.

This young woman forfeits control, but voluntarily. While she holds boys accountable for girls' anxiety, this largely goes unrecognized as an expression of boys' social power. The field of dating is defined as a masculine ter-

rain where boys are seen as having a monopoly, but it is girls who often must do the work of getting a date.

The close association between having a date and expressing girls' feminine identities works to conceal both the ongoing operation of power and the heterosexual imperatives that pervade these dating schemes, while also obscuring the double bind many girls face: finding a date is ostensibly "girls' work," but girls are also prevented from being the subjects in these dating arrangements. As one prom magazine suggested to its readers, "The best plan of action is to make him feel safe about asking you. Keep in mind that guys like the game, so you are going to have to make him think that he thought of the idea first."[10]

It is not surprising, then, that finding someone to go the prom with is a source of enormous anguish for many girls, significantly more so than for boys (a theme I will discuss later in this chapter). Many young women I interviewed reported that they began strategizing early in the year to make sure they had a date for the prom. Fiona and Mitch, two white students from Rudolph, elaborated on the nature of this work in their school:

FJ:    I guess, pretty much you try to look for someone almost when you think prom dates are starting. Everybody just kind of like looks for someone, like, they are trying to hang out with them more. Where I'll try to like be with this person more, kind of like I don't want to get stuck without a prom date.

ML:    This year a lot of people have boyfriends.

FJ:    A lot because they got together just for almost [the prom].

ML:    You think so?

FJ:    Yeah, I think after the prom a lot will separate.

ML:    Oh really?

FJ:    Yeah, a lot of people will not be together.

In the following narrative, another young white woman guides us through the steps she took to secure a date for the prom:

In high school it seems as if guys just didn't find me attractive. So finding a date to the prom wasn't easy. I'll always remember the tension and panic that filled my high school junior class in the months that preceded that day in May. It seemed as if each one of my dateless friends was dropping off one after another. It appeared as if one of my good male friends was going to ask me. But alas, at the last moment he asked one of my best friends. So as Spring Break approached I was getting desperate. My family and I were going on a cruise and as I boarded the plane I was dateless but not hopeless. I started a letter campaign to my friend Doug in hopes that he would help me out. Well

I really threatened that if he didn't find me a date there would be dire consequences. And it worked. I went with this kid Mike whom I had never met before. We actually had a great time because we were in a group of 16 other people. This certainly wasn't the guy of my dreams but I had a date and that was all that really mattered.

For this young woman, as for other girls, "all that mattered" was having a date. "I barely talked to my date, I didn't have much interest in him but he asked me so I went with him anyways," another girl wrote.

Desperate to have a date but unable to find one from their class, many girls resort to taking dates from other schools, while others search the lower grades. As one African-American girl explained,

I can remember having trouble finding a prom date. I didn't have a boyfriend and there was no one in the vicinity who I really wanted to go with. My prom date flew in from Atlanta, Georgia to attend my prom in Cleveland, Ohio. He was the first guy I ever had a crush on. We met in the fourth grade.

One white girl asked a neighborhood boy who was a first-year college student to attend with her, though she would have preferred to be accompanied by someone of her senior class:

Many of my friends didn't go to the prom because the guys they wanted to go with were already going with someone else. They didn't go because either they couldn't find a date and didn't want to go alone, which is seen as negative in my school, or because they only wanted to go with that guy and wouldn't lower themselves to go with anyone else.

The anxiety many girls articulate about the possibility of being dateless for the prom seems to be especially pronounced for girls who do not consider themselves to be "popular." For girls not seen as popular, having membership in the popular group translates into a series of resources—resources, many grudgingly reported, they were without.[11] As one girl related,

My prom was very influenced by the social structure of my senior class. It seemed that the most popular of students were guaranteed a date just because of who they were and who was in the group, especially the most popular group because it seemed to have an equal number of boys and girls. Even those who were at the bottom of the social structure, those who were at the lowest ends had dates just because of the organization within the group. But once you got to the rest of the class—the people who weren't the most popular nor the least—there was no one to go with. My female friends and I had a very difficult time finding someone to go with, just because of the group. So basically most of us looked outside our own school for dates. It was probably the worst time in my senior year because I felt so inadequate among my peers.

The system through which popularity gains currency is bound to normative constructions of masculinity and femininity; typically the most popular girls are also viewed as the most feminine girls, and social power is concentrated in the hands of boys who abide by a code of hegemonic masculinity.[12] In contrast to that of boys, however, girls' popularity is based principally upon standards of attractiveness. It is men's assessment of women's attractiveness that chiefly determines women's location within this status system.[13]

Whom one takes to the prom indicates social status and social capital. Fiona, a student from Rudolph, had this to offer:

Last year it was a big thing to, to like, oh, you have to go with a senior. Everybody was like. "I don't care as long as I go with a senior." I think it's a big deal, a lot of people think it's a big deal with who you go to the prom. I'm sure it's the first thing people think, okay who am I going to ask out. I know that's the first thing I think of . . . and then people settle like, okay, I'll settle for him because they can't get that first person.

Unable to find a "suitable" date, unwilling to go alone, some girls ended up not going to their prom:

Wasn't asked to my junior prom. I was devastated. I spent the whole night crying and my mom took me to the movies. I was very shy in high school—went through an ugly phase in junior high and I don't think anyone wanted to be the first person to ask me out. I never had a boyfriend throughout my high school years. I went to my senior prom with a "nerd." He was the only guy who asked me and I felt compelled to go. I was stupid. I really didn't have a good time. I think mainly because I really didn't like my date; he was annoying. I was glad it was over with. Too much stress and only the cool people seemed to really be enjoying it.

I didn't go to my prom because only one guy asked me and he was a nerd. I guess I was too shy to ask anyone else for fear of rejection.

I think the prom is a special event that you share with the right person (or I thought that two years ago) and I didn't have a boyfriend. I wasn't going to go with anyone just to go. So many people go with people they never talk to or were friends with because they were date-less. All my guy friends were younger (that stereotypical thing that a female shouldn't be with a younger man, especially at the prom) or had girlfriends. I pretended like it didn't matter but watching my friends prepare was kind of weird. I went with one of my best friends when she got her dress.

## The Politics of Dating: Failed Romance

Many girls I interviewed reported a profound sense of disappointment because their expectations of romance never materialized. These girls' stories clearly demonstrate the unequal power relations that continue to persist in their relationships with boys. Though power is rarely named, it is always present. Consider one young African-American man's statement about how he and his friends selected their dates for the prom:

> From my experience and most of my friends' experiences, they had girlfriends but other people asked them for dates. With me, it got into conflict. I'll just tell you from the beginning. We [he and his girlfriend] hadn't really been going together. I just asked her to the prom. We wasn't boyfriend-girlfriend. I asked her . . . but there were other girls that asked [me]. I felt bad. I asked her and [then] I [took] another girl. First I was up to doing it but it made me felt bad. So, I had to take her. [She said] "You say you would take me to the prom," and dis, dat, dat and the other. She wanted to go and like, fight [this] other girl. So I was like, "Naw, I'll take you to the prom." It happened to my friends too. One of them, a guy who had been dating this girl for a while, going on two years. She found out that he was talking to another girl and asking her to go [to the prom]. They, like, separated.

There is a clear sense of male entitlement expressed here; boys are the decision makers. In this young man's story, he and his male friends take the liberty to hold out or even withdraw prom invitations to their girlfriends in the event that other, presumably more desirable, girls come along. Though on some level he seems aware that his and his friend's actions toward the girls they are dating are insensitive, he is also unfazed by such callousness. He speaks with a surprising frankness about the politics of dating in his school and the power that boys claim in their relationships with young women.

So taken for granted are these dynamics of power that many girls accept poor treatment from boys in order to have a date for the prom. Consider the following account by one white girl who went to the prom with her former boyfriend:

I remember I almost didn't have a date. I ended up asking and going with my ex-boyfriend. The actual event was really fun. He was being really nice to me, and a perfect gentlemen. We ended up being picked as one of the best looking couples at the event. Afterwards we went to a friend's house where everyone was getting together. I'll never forget that part. My date ended up with another girl at the party. They were in the dark room together all night. I was so devastated. Ironically, quite a few girls also got dumped by their date that night! We all tried to make the best of the situation and ended up having fun overall.

This girl's reaction is striking. Though upset with the outcome of the evening, she accepts her date's action, which admittedly may be easier for her to do because other young women found themselves in similar situations. Perhaps she accepts his dismissive treatment of her because she is grateful that she at least had a prom date. Through girls' resignation, power is concentrated in the hands of these young men and normalized as a fundamental feature of heterosexual dating.

Though many girls carefully try to manage these dating relations, often their efforts are fruitless. Consider these two narratives written by African-American girls.

The memories of my prom begin with the fact that my boyfriend waited until a week before to tell me that he did not want to go. He was older and didn't feel like going through the motions of getting a tuxedo and all that. That was very hard for me. I was then forced to find a date last minute, which my boyfriend did not approve of, he thought I should not go to the prom. I told him that I was [going] and there was no way I was not.

My date [boyfriend] went to college an hour away. He said he had classes on the day of the prom so he wouldn't . . . come home till a few hours before the prom. The prom started at 6:00. At 5:00 I hadn't heard from him. At 6:00 he still hadn't called, so after crying, I decided to call one of my girl friends to ride with her. I arrived at the prom in tears. I called my date's grandmother and she said he just walked in the door, so I told him I was already at the prom and for him to hurry up and get there. When he arrived it was about 8:00. His tuxedo didn't match my dress and he didn't even have a corsage for me, luckily I had bought one in case he forgot. When it came time to take pictures he gave me like $10!!! He didn't end up spending any money except to rent his tux and $10 for the pictures. Afterward I told him I wanted to go home early. What a disaster.

One white girl wrote:

Everyone makes the prom out to be this great fantastic experience, well I was disappointed. Sure I had fun but it wasn't incredible. After the prom my friends and I stayed in a hotel and drank a little. My boyfriend was there, and he got drunk, got sick and passed out.

Another young white woman's narrative reflected upon how her expectations for a night of romance were foiled at the prom:

I went to my junior prom with my boyfriend at the time and another couple that we were really good friends with. We had it planned out and thought it was going to be great but it ended up a disaster. The couple we went to the prom with were Harry and Michelle and my boyfriend's name was Bill. Harry had a yacht so before the prom we went to the yacht (all dressed for the prom) and took the yacht to a restaurant across the lake. This sounded like it was going to be so much fun but it turned out it was very windy that day. As we were going on the lake in the yacht that wind was messing up my hair and water was coming up onto the yacht because Harry's father was going too fast. So right off the bat I was in a bad mood because I had spent so much time doing my hair for the prom and it was a mess. We docked the boat and went into a beautiful restaurant on the water. Sounds nice but Harry didn't really want to be at the prom a long time so he tried to take his time eating and ordering more food to drag it out as long as possible. This made me nervous because I wanted to go to the prom. We got to the prom late. My boyfriend would hardly dance, took a limo back to the yacht to stay the night and got into a big fight with my boyfriend.

Not only does her story help clarify the extensive work girls do to create the "perfect" romantic night and its importance to the project of femininity, it also sheds light on the ongoing operation of masculine power, how it works and is sustained through a series of minor events: Harry prolongs dinner, causing them to arrive late at the prom and, once there, her boyfriend would hardly dance. Another young white woman's narrative tells of a similar series of power struggles:

My clearest memory of my prom was when I was in my junior year. I had been with a guy for most of that school year and had planned on going to the prom. I had my dress, tickets and everything was all set. Not more than a week before, he told me he had been with someone else and planned on taking her. I was shocked, hurt and didn't know what to do. He really didn't seem to care. I wondered how I could have liked him so much. I ended up calling a friend and begging him to come with me. I paid for everything for him. I didn't mind but we only stayed 45 minutes before he wanted to leave. I remembered seeing my "ex" at the prom and realizing what a jerk he was. In my mind I wanted to show him up.

In this story, the first struggle emerges with her boyfriend because he has cheated on her before the prom. The fact that his cheating has left her without a date seems most significant. The second struggle involves her new date. Desperate to have a date, she "begs" her friend to escort her. She is willing to cover the sizable expense of attending the prom just to have a date. Despite the fact that she has paid for the evening, her date's actions still determine the outcome of the night. No longer about romance, this young woman struggles to find other meanings in the prom; the prom becomes a site at which to "show him up" (her "ex"). The fact that she is able to find a date on such short notice enables her to assert agency, though limited, in this cultural scene. Significantly, both boys end up controlling her night. Another white girl wrote,

> I went to the prom with my boyfriend of three and a half years. It was a *nightmare*. I was class president and had many responsibilities to take care of during the night. However, my boyfriend became angry because he wanted me by his side all night. So after the prom a group of us rented a hotel room and after we got there, he and a few friends got back into the limo and left. He came back two hours later drunk. What a lovely night. Needless to say the $350 dress was a waste and all the hype of a romantic night was quickly diminished.

In this girl's narrative, contradictory readings of prom romance produce an irresolvable conflict with her boyfriend. For her, there is room for both romance and friendship, sociability and school duties. His expectation of romance, however, is that she will be by his side throughout the night and refuse all other commitments. Interference by others encroaches upon his vision of a romantic night, while her expectation of romance can be reconciled with her other responsibilities. For him, it seems that it's either his way or the highway; because she is unwilling to meet his demands, his seemingly retaliatory act (leaving to get drunk) spoils the possibility for romance after the prom.

Many girls I interviewed found themselves in dating situations at the prom that were laden with power. These are unsettling accounts. A mixture of anger, devastation, resignation, and acceptance can be found in their stories. The key issue in each narrative is that the agency the girls demonstrated was not immediately expressed, but eventually materialized. "My best friend and I double-dated with our boyfriends. I think we would have had more fun if just us two girls went by ourselves," one young woman wrote about her prom. While many girls expressed anger with their dates for being controlling or for ruining their night, there is little suggestion that these girls confronted their dates at the prom.

At the proms I observed, I did see a few girls challenge the power their dates expressed, though in small and contained ways. I saw girls walking off the dance floor, leaving their dates behind. I also witnessed girls struggling with boys to get them to dance. I remember with clarity arguing with my boyfriend at my own prom because the way he danced with me felt overtly sexual. Admittedly embarrassed, I walked off the dance floor. Aside from these minor transgressions, however, I saw few public conflicts between dates. Expressions of masculine power often go unchallenged by girls when they occur in public settings. Because so many girls have expectations of romance at the prom, many are unwilling to sacrifice these expectations for greater equality.

### Rejecting Romance

> I think the nice thing about the prom is it's generally treated as something special but also sort of more casual. They don't play it up to be a big romantic night, maybe like they do at some dances. If it were built up as a very romantic thing I don't think I'd be very comfortable because I don't have romance [laughs]. But I like that fact. (white female student)

> I went to the prom solo. Everyone was talking about me behind my back and felt sorry for me. BLAH, BLAH, BLAH. I was excited. I had no worries of what corsage to get, how to act fake, and that social concept of what to wear. (White female student)

Considering the disappointment that pervaded a number of girls' accounts of romance discussed earlier, it does not seem surprising that some girls, like the two writers above, would pursue dates—or reject them altogether—for reasons other than romance. Many girls rejected the promise of romance in favor of a date who would maximize their ability to socialize.[14] In speaking with a mother of a young woman who attended Woodrow's prom, she told me that even though her daughter and her daughter's best friend had boyfriends in college, they opted to go with "guy friends" from school instead. Some girls thought it more important to go to the prom with a boy who would be willing to dance. One white girl wrote,

> During the prom a song from the movie *Grease* came on. My friends and I are fans of this movie. Therefore my best friend and I grabbed

one of our guy friends and started dancing. We were all singing and dancing and laughing. He was kind of laughing at us but it was fun just to enjoy this last social event together.

Another white girl, who initially had hopes of romance, found herself pleasantly surprised that she had so much fun with "just a friend."

> I went with a good friend, John. We had an incredible time together dancing, drinking and just hanging out. After the prom was even better. We went on a booze cruise.

Consideration of how their dates might navigate local school relations was important for Serena and Katy, two young women of color, in selecting dates:

S:     You've been with these people so long that you know them as friends, then it's hard asking somebody in that way, seeing someone because if you ask somebody or they ask you, you get, "Oh, they like you."

K:     Yeah.

S:     And then bringing somebody that doesn't go to the school, it's also difficult because you're pretty much in a womb, where they don't know anybody, especially if you were supposed to take, okay, if they knew, like, a couple people at the table. But let's say I'm the type of person where I have school friends and I have outside friends and when I'm in school I hang out with school friends.

S:     Yeah, neighborhood friends. It's hard bringing somebody from that atmosphere into this one because then they don't know anybody so, now you want to get up and you want to dance and . . .

K:     Socialize.

S:     And you can't because he's there and he's like, "Wait a minute, you're leaving me by myself."

S:     I know some girl, she brought her boyfriend to the prom, he didn't dance with her one time.

K:     He sat down the whole time.

S:     He didn't dance with her the whole time and that, wait a minute, you're going to her prom and you're not going to dance and she had to sit there with him.

AB:    So why didn't he dance with her?

S:     He was tired, supposedly. They probably got into an argument before. And then you're stuck and he rains on your parade, too. It's the same thing whether it be a guy or a girl. If they don't want to dance then, you can't say, "Oh, all right, you sit down

and I'm gonna dance." You're kind of sitting there, so then it's a
waste of money.

Both Serena and Katy approach the prom pragmatically, offering the story
of another girl whose prom was ruined by her date's unwillingness to dance
as confirmation that girls who privilege romance are usually disappointed.
They are more concerned with having fun than with negotiating the bur-
dens of dating. By separating romantic success from prom success they con-
tradict the dominant construction of the prom as a romantic space. Katy and
Serena discuss this issue in relation to the song chosen for the last song
played at the prom:

> S:    It was Celine Dion. I mean, I love the song but as a last song for
>       our senior year? It could have been better than "Because You
>       Love Me." Our year was not necessarily about like, couples. It
>       was about friends.
>
> S:    The yearbook staff, because they have boyfriends and they knew
>       they were going to the prom with their boyfriends, they pro-
>       grammed that song.
>
> K:    "Because You Love Me." That doesn't make any sense.

For Katy and Serena, the last song is a defining moment in the prom, one
that is supposed to evoke and capture heartfelt emotions about leaving and
loss among friends as they graduate from high school. They make clear that
the prom is not about romance.

Other girls also rejected the romantic meanings attached to the prom. As
one white girl wrote,

I didn't go with my boyfriend of two years because he had already graduated and didn't want to go again. So I went with one of my best guy friends I had known since about second grade. I also went with my best friend and one of our close guy friends. Both the guys are hilarious. I swear they could be comedians. Anyway I remember having so much fun hanging out with those guys before we even got to the prom. They are so nice. No one was trying to impress anybody. Out of the two proms I went with my boyfriend trying to be romantic, I definitely had more fun with my friends who didn't care.

This young woman's narrative, which privileges friendship and sociability over romance, hints at how the expectations of romance and efforts to create romance at the prom is work that can be labor intensive. Completely unwilling to do the work of romance, another white girl wrote,

The dance part was fun but mostly I wanted to be with my friends and not with my date. The sentence I said to my date all night was, "I'll be right back," as I went to visit my friends.

An Asian-American girl expressed a similar unwillingness to do the work of dating at the prom:

I ended [up] going to the prom with a friend. I got asked out by a couple of guys I knew but I wasn't really interested. I thought that if I went with a date "date," it would mean that I would be "stuck" with that person the whole night.

One young woman chose not to pursue romance at her senior prom because her junior prom, which she attended with her boyfriend, had been a romantic "letdown":

When we finally got to the [junior] prom he was so controlling. He wouldn't let me talk to my friends, only his. Also, he wouldn't let me dance to the "electric slide" because he didn't know how. . . . My senior prom was not much better. I was asked [by] a really good friend of mine. I thought this was a good idea because there would be no romantic problems, we were just good friends.

Romance, for this young woman, is accompanied by a struggle with her date that ultimately limits her autonomy and freedom.

For Serena, negotiating a romantic relationship also meant negotiating an entire field of sexual relations and monitoring her sexual reputation:

Sometimes it's just better to go with a friend because you know he dances, or meet there or something because you dance. Nobody's to say, "Who's that? Why are you dancing that close to him?"

Some girls, like Serena, forsake romance at the prom because of the difficult ground they must cover in managing their public sexual identities, their feminine identities, and their "adolescent" identities. Barbara Hudson sheds light on the nature of this conflict, saying, "In matters of sexuality the discourse of adolescence is clearly at variance with the discourse of femininity: according to the terms of the adolescence discourse, adolescence is a time of shifting allegiances, rapidly changing friendships; whereas femininity involves the skill to make lasting relationships, with the ability to care very deeply for very few people. Thus, the teenage girl has to tread a narrow line between 'getting too serious too soon,' and being regarded as promiscuous by her elders and as a 'slag' by her peers."[15]

Erin, though personally invested in romance, also spoke about some of the sexual dangers for girls on prom night that might curb girls' pursuit of romance.

My Spanish teacher, um, she just, like she told me, like, don't drink, don't get in the wrong car or something like that. You know, don't be wild, you know, don't get overly excited you know, start doing wrong things and getting crazy and stuff. [After the prom] you don't want to be with one person, you know don't go to the hotels, no, no, no don't go to the hotels with your date especially if you're planning on drinking or something 'cause then it will turn out all wrong. I didn't. I mean, girls mess up their lives by going to the hotel and they end up pregnant. Just don't go alone with somebody, especially if it's a date that you just, you know, you hadn't really known for that long. A lot of bad girls all go and some . . . well, some of them aren't bad, but they just don't know about stuff. I've seen a lot of stuff happen and I know what to look out for.

Implicit is the idea that boys are dangerous, not to be trusted because they are out for a good time, regardless of the cost. Yet also suggested here is that girls are ultimately the ones responsible for protecting themselves—these girls must censor their own sexual desire to do so.[16] Those who fail are the "bad" ones—or at least naive. As Erin suggests, much is at stake for these girls; one slip and their lives can change drastically. Later in the interview, Erin further elaborated these sexual dangers in relation to her relationship with her prom date:

Like my date now, like we've known each other for almost a year now, but still you don't know how people are when they are in a certain situation, so, you just don't take chances with people. You gotta be really careful, really careful.

These girls refuse to read the prom as a romantic moment largely because romantic dating seems too complicated and messy for them. Proms are moments when ideologies of gender, romance, and adolescence often come together in contradictory ways. Some girls reject romance at the prom to avoid these conflicts. Much is on the line for these girls; as Serena, Erin, and Katy suggest, girls must manage their sexual reputations in this highly public scene; sometimes it is easier to simply abandon romance to secure their respectability and to avoid potentially dangerous situations. But there is also a sense that these girls are silencing their own desires in doing so. As one young woman explained, "My date was trying to get me to sleep with him but I was not in the mood for his 'bull.' I had no intention of sleeping with him at all, because I did not trust him." This young woman didn't have sex— not because she didn't want to, but because she didn't trust her prom date. While girls are figuring out new ways to define their feminine identities as they become women, often they must endure hardship, disappointment, or worse, as many of these narratives suggest, to arrive at this space and to forge identities independent of their relations with young men.

## Boyfriends, Girlfriends, and "Just Friends": Proms as Moments of Negotiation

Treat him like a real date (even if he's only a pal). That means holding back your urge to challenge him to an arm wrestle on the buffet table or keeping quiet when you want to gush about how hot other guys look in their tuxes. You may not be into locking lips with your date, but you can make him feel special by acting psyched to be there with him.
—"Five Ways to Make Your Prom More Romantic," article in *YM* special prom issue, 1996

Even if there is little promise of romance and/or sex on prom night, negotiations between dates continue to be mediated by normative ideas about gender and heterosexuality. In the case of going to the prom with a friend, many kids felt befuddled because their dating situation did not neatly parallel the dominant constructions of dating. Consider one African-American young man's narrative:

The girl I went to my prom with was just one of my friends. So I knew nothing sexual was going to happen and didn't expect it to, either. Having already established that, I was able to concentrate on just having a good time instead of trying how to figure out how to get her to do other things. We danced together and had a really good time. When I got to her house she was ready and looked pretty. During the prom and in the limo we took pictures together. We laughed and danced. It felt awkward spending so much time with a girl that wasn't my girl-friend but treating her like she was. I had to keep reminding myself that it was her night too and it didn't make it better if I was constantly running off to dance with other girls.

A clear sense of conflict emerges in this young man's narrative because the "rules" of heterosexual dating do not apply to his situation. What is striking about his account is that despite his feeling awkward because of the expectation that he treat his date like a girlfriend, he expresses relief to be free of certain demands. Because there is no expectation of a sexual encounter, he is excused from the masculine script of sexual conquest. His struggle is less a struggle to demonstrate his masculinity and more one over the meaning of their relationship as it exists in a new, murky terrain. Students who attend the prom as friends and not dates are forced to negotiate this new terrain and in so doing often depart from more conventional dating paths at the prom.

Some students found themselves negotiating dating relationships with people they barely knew. Chip, a white student from Rudolph, faced a particular dilemma because he went to the prom with a blind date, but was dating another woman who was also at the prom.

CP:    I had a date and then, like, I didn't and then, I didn't want to go and then, I did. So, it was kind of like, a last minute thing so, um, one of my friend's girlfriends who lives in another town. She invited one of her friends to go with me. It was a little awkward I guess. It worked out good, you know, because she was nice and she was pretty and she was really cool. She was someone to go with, hang out and have a good time.

AB:    So the woman you were seeing, was she at the prom?

CP:    Yeah, I pretty much hung out with her more than the girl I went with, but I did both, you know what I mean? I wish it had worked out better with the fact of my dates. I wish it had worked out to the point where I asked the girl I was seeing back when I had the chance.

Samuel, an African-American student from Hudson, also went to the prom with a young woman who was an acquaintance. For him, negotiating dating was about meeting her at some loosely defined middle ground. When I spoke with him at the prom, he was waiting for his date to arrive and seemed excited. Because he did not know her very well, there were few established boundaries in their relationship. As we spoke, I sensed from the hesitance in his voice that this produced for him a tension between his expectations of how their relationship might develop and his not wanting to confer too much importance on this potential relationship in the event that she was uninterested. His was a negotiation over a set of conflicting feelings, shaped by the prevailing notion that proms are romantic moments. He did not want to be disappointed, but was willing to hold out for the possibility of a more meaningful relationship igniting because it was prom night.

Dates often must compromise because their expectations of prom night, arguably patterned by gender and class, differ. Consider the following conversation I had with Sandy, a white student from Rudolph, who attended her prom with her boyfriend of two years:

AB:   So what made you decide to go to the prom?

SAG:  I wanted to. I like getting dressed up, it's fun. I mean, my boyfriend didn't want to go, but he knew I really wanted to and we went last year. He didn't want to last year but he had a good time. This year he didn't have a good time 'cause I think he wanted to be down the shore so bad. I mean like, he didn't have a bad time. We left at, like, eleven and I was mad for a while, yeah I was ticked. I wanted to stay for like a half hour more, like, so we ended up having dinner and getting our pictures taken and leaving.

AB:   Did you say anything to him?

SAG:  Oh yeah, he heard about it.

AB:   What did you say?

SAG:  Like, I don't want to leave, he was like, I know . . .

Later in the interview she talked about negotiating with her boyfriend over whether or not they would go to the prom and how long they would stay. In the context of school and youth culture, these private negotiations often became part of a public terrain.

All his friends kept telling me "oh, you're not going to the prom" and I was like, " Yes, we were going to the prom." "No, Randy doesn't want to go," and I was like, "Randy's gonna go!" and then I asked him in the car and I was like, "You really don't want to go to the prom," and he's like, "No, but I guess if you want to go to the prom, I'll take you to the prom." I was like, "Thank you." You know he really didn't have a choice so it was just nice of him to kind of ask me and not be. . . . That's why leaving so early, like, I was mad but I let it go right away because you know, he came for me and I was going to leave for him.

At stake is Sandy's effort to arrive at a decision that satisfies them both. While her negotiation is fundamentally shaped by gender relations, her boyfriend's strained relationship with their school (which was ultimately tied to his class position) also plays a role; he has little interest in school, academically or socially, because teachers and school administrators have treated him badly.

For one girl, negotiating the field of dating was further complicated by relations of race and cultural mandates against interracial dating:

> I could never really have the information to support the argument that proms are not all they are cracked up to be. I regret going through all the hassle. I decided to see if Anthony would go. He was two years younger, so that caused controversy with my family, particularly my father. The largest thing was Anthony was a different race. He is African American and Spanish. I am Irish and Lebanese. I am the "white" girl and he is the "black" boy. I tried to overcome the barriers but didn't succeed altogether. My father banned the prom for me until I lied and convinced him I was going solo. I really had my friend pick up Anthony later.

Not only must this girl negotiate relations formed around gender, but also her sexual identity as a "white girl." Her father's ban, formed by prevailing racial constructions of the black male body as a dangerous one and the fact that the prom is a highly public event, obligates her to manage this racial bind. Though she is unable to outwardly challenge her father's racial politics, presumably because the patriarchal control he wields is so resolute, she is also unwilling to sacrifice her loyalty to Anthony.

Gender and heterosexuality are key principles mediating these negotiations. Another young white woman articulated a conflict she encountered because there was no preexisting formula for her to follow. For her, the negotiation revolved around money and who should pay, negotiations that may have been particularly pronounced because she is working-class:

> I went to the senior prom with a friend named Scott. I remember discussing the costs of particular aspects of the prom, such as dinner and tickets. He offered to pay for both which I thought was unfair. Just because he was the guy he felt that he should pay. I told him that I wanted to give my fair share. We ended up splitting the price of the ticket and he paid for dinner. I gave into dinner because he insisted and I didn't have much money anyway. I had already spent enough on a dress, shoes, hair, etc.

Some girls, wedded to a "traditional" reading of the prom, maintained the expectation that boys should pay for prom expenses and simply were unwilling to negotiate. One young woman, Fiona, offered,

> I guess I'm old fashioned but, I think the boy should pay for it. I mean, yeah, because the boy's picking you out. I mean, the nineties is fine where the guy pays for some and the girl pays for some, but the prom, I think guys should pay for it.

Profoundly aware of what it means to be women in the context of the prom, many girls negotiate carefully, at times monitoring how they are perceived by others. As I listened to more girls speak about their proms, these negotiations began to resemble a running exchange among them as young women and the dominant discourse through which daily practices are coded as feminine or not feminine. Consider Mary's reflection on her having to drive to her own prom:

MF:   I'll probably drive, which is kind of defeating the purpose of being female.

AB:   What does that mean?

MF:   No I'm just always driving, like, whenever I go out with my friends I am always the driver and I was thinking on this one formal thing if I could have the date then they could at least be the one who's driving . . . but assuming I go. I don't know who I'm going with.

Another girl elaborated on a parallel theme:

My stud date got a ticket for DWI two weeks before the prom and his license was suspended for the prom. Meaning his parents made me drive to the prom. They did not actually make me. But it appeared as the only alternative, because in our school taking a limo was trashy. Anyway my mother was a little upset that I had to drive to dinner but I didn't mind. There was a picture taken of us leaving in the car (you would have thought it was my wedding day). And whenever anyone saw that picture they always commented on the fact that I was driving or that my date was an asshole. But people had that impression of him anyways. My whole point here is that nobody could believe that I had to drive, but once we pulled a couple miles away we switched. I didn't feel comfortable driving his parents' brand new expensive car that they wouldn't even let him drive and he felt like a little kid. I can't decide if it was his friends calling me "Mom" or what.

The fact that these girls had to drive disrupted their conception of the prom as a series of gendered practices that ultimately affirm what type of girls they are, though more generally, neither girl seemed to mind driving. Driving is coded as a gendered activity here; taken for granted, the expectation is that when a heterosexual couple drives together, the man sits behind the wheel (though Mary ends up subverting this role by driving to her prom). So powerful are these cultural ideas that the second young woman's date risks driving with a suspended license. This last narrative also highlights the seemingly arbitrary and relational nature of gender. *He* felt like a little kid, "emasculated" because *she* had to drive. So entrenched is the idea that a man must drive to be in control that she is teasingly called "Mom"—the only position women can claim where their power, theoretically, is absolute.

### Going but Not Investing: Masculinity and Proms

It's a girl conspiracy.

I remember being at my prom and thinking, "This is the most boring night of my life." I did not want to be there.

These two statements, both offered by boys about their school proms, have particular salience for understanding the gender organization of the prom and its impact on how boys come to relate to the scene. Boys' disengagement from the prom, expressed in both of these statements was a central issue that emerged in students' narratives and interviews. How boys talk about the prom reflects fundamentally their ongoing relationship with masculinity.

In contrast to girls' narratives, few boys' narratives expressed interest in or concern with preparing for the prom, having a prom date, or the prom itself. When detailed accounts were provided, the prom was often only marginally mentioned. Instead, some young men used the prom to talk about other meaningful events in their lives. A white young man wrote,

I didn't hang out with a very fast crowd [junior year] so my prom was very sober and very boring. However, the next year a few friends and I decided to boycott the senior prom entirely. It probably had something to do with the fact that we were all too lazy to ask anyone to go with us. And just go to the post-prom parties, where we all drank ourselves sick. So much for the prom being the most exciting time of your life. I never really bought into that picture-perfect storybook prom myth anyway.

Another white boy wrote,

I had much more fun at my junior prom and I didn't even go to the prom that year. Instead we all skipped school and went to an amusement park and that night there was a huge party at some [senior] girl's beach house. Me and my best friend were the only juniors invited. We were similarly the only juniors on the varsity baseball team. Most of our teammates were there and so was the entire crowd that they hung out with, including the girl whose house we were at.

When writing about the prom scene, boys' narratives frequently cohered around the achievement of masculinity through excessive drinking and partying, male camaraderie, and/or mental distancing from their dates and the prom setting. Consider this young white man's narrative:

> Senior year in high school, I went to the prom with a friend of mine, yet we weren't close. I had a fairly good time with my male friends but since most of them didn't have girl friends, the males hung out together at the prom while the girls hung out with themselves.

Another white young man wrote,

> My friends and I were drunk after the prom at the hotel. All of the girls were in their bathing suits and we all went swimming and drank more. We had a great time. Some of us woke up in girls' rooms. Others woke up by the pool and some were in the halls of the hotel.[17]

Partying takes on special significance in this last narrative. The night is constructed as having looser sexual rules: girls are in their bathing suits, everyone is drinking, and sleeping arrangements are haphazard. Clearly, sexual, moral, and social boundaries are broken.

In popular cultural texts, the narrative of sex on prom night is an important one. So fundamentally part of our cultural prom lore, this theme has appeared in countless TV shows such as *Roseanne, Beverly Hills 90210, That Seventies Show,* and *Boy Meets World* and in a number of Hollywood films including *She's All That, She's Out of Control,* and *Peggy Sue Got Married.* In the 1999 teen film *American Pie,* the entire film is based on the four male characters losing their virginity before prom night. In most of these TV shows and films, sex is set up in opposition to romance. Drawing from these cultural narratives, boys' talk about sex on prom night seems to be a way for them to invest in the prom in a masculine way. Scott, a white student from Woodrow, elaborates,

> That kind of stuff gets talked about because it draws a lot of attention. It's like, "How much are you going to drink," or, "You're going with her? You'll get some play." Some people are going out with the idea of, "I'm gonna get my date drunk and hook up with her." And I don't want to say have sex with her, cause that doesn't necessarily happen, but at least get with them . . . In some respects it's still a status thing. If you're sexually active you move up on a kind of status kind of thing . . . I guess that's why it's important. A lot of it is based around our perceptions of what we're supposed to do or what we want.

A few boys—decidedly exceptions to the norm—were critical of masculine "sex" talk and its centrality to this process of becoming masculine. An Asian-American young man wrote,

I particularly remember how pressured I was by my friends to ask a friend who I liked. We made several sexual jokes about what we would do after the prom. At the prom I can recall my friends and I rated the appearances of girls. We would make comments like, "Wow, she's hot." It was pretty much me and my male friends and my date and her friends. The girls would make several trips to the bathroom while the guys talked. We would also make fun of other guys in our class who we hated or were the "losers."

While studies in the areas of manhood and masculinity have found that young men primarily demonstrate their commitment to an organization of heterosexuality through talk of their sexual exploits, for some boys the emphasis on sexual bravado produces a feeling of alienation from the prom, though admittedly more pronounced for those whose masculinity is already marginalized.[18] Consider a young African-American gay student's reflection on the nature of this talk in relation to prom night:

I just could never relate. I just never wanted to roll with the boys, go out and get drunk, talk about, "Ooh I'm gonna do this with this girl" and like, bang this girl. I never thought it was nasty or gross. I just wasn't interested. It didn't excite me, like, okay this is what you need to do. I didn't think about sex. I didn't think it was wrong; it just wasn't me.

Still, few boys speak candidly about their anxiety or even uncertainty about dating, because doing so implicates them in a complex field of sexual relations in which mastery is expected. Shedding light on this, Mairtin Mac an Ghaill writes, "In talking with young men about sex and sexuality, what emerges is a picture of complex inner dramas of individual insecurity and low self esteem. In relation to young women, many of them feel shy, inadequate and unable to cope with the demands of initiating and maintaining 'a relationship with a girl.' There is a feeling of immense pressure from peers with whom the collectively fantasized heterosexual ideal is constructed."[19]

Even the marketers of girls' prom magazines seem to have an understanding of the difficulty boys face in dating, though they never connect these feelings to the social pressures masculinity creates. Consider an article in *YM* magazine titled "His Secret Thoughts About Prom: Find Out What He Really Thinks About The Big Night":

*Secret Thought #1:* Who would ever go to the prom with me?

*Secret Thought #4:* Do I look slick in this tux—or like some kind of dorky penguin?

*Secret Thought #5:* Omigod—I'm actually gonna have to dance.

*Secret Thought #7:* All my buds are probably getting some, so I'd better go for it too.[20]

Many boys are simply ill-equipped to speak about these relations openly in ways that still secure their masculinity and heterosexuality. Expressing anxiety about finding a date might be perceived as an inability to manage "feeling" and the complex world of dating.[21] Largely regulated through homosocial relations among men, the pressure to "buck up" becomes a means to measure boys in relation to each other and for boys to figure out where they fit within an organization of masculinity that allows few to reside at the top.[22]

Some boys are actually invested in the prom, and some do develop expectations for prom night, but, just as for the girls, many of their expectations often do not materialize. A significant point of difference between boys' and girls' "prom talk" is how they speak about these expectations. While girls in this study spoke with ease and often without struggle when defining their expectations, boys seemed to experience difficulty when trying to identify exactly what their prom expectations were.

Although few openly expressed their concern about dating, one boy from Hudson spoke in a startling and unabashed way about his discomfort of attending the prom without a date. Consider these comments from my fieldnotes:

A stocky white boy wearing a standard black tux walked up to me and the principal as we were talking. With a short crew, an inflated chest and a sheepish smile, I knew at once he was uncomfortable. His gait was hesitant and his eyes moved disjointedly as he scanned the room, profoundly aware of his own discomfort. His hands clasped in front of his chest, he greeted Mr. Stand. Mr. Stand introduced me to the boy and instantly I forgot his name. He asked me if I knew anyone who went alone to the prom. Mr. Stand and I, both anxious to set him at ease, told him that lots of kids go alone. Mr. Stand added that half the kids here tonight would be without dates. However, our comments didn't seem to placate his anxiety. He still seemed nervous. (June 1997)

The comments he shared with me over the course of the evening provided one of the few opportunities to talk openly to a boy about his anxieties about being dateless. He approached me several times throughout the evening, a number of times asking me to dance (which I refused). When I suggested he ask someone else to dance he told me he was uncomfortable talking with girls because he could never think of anything to say. He had asked one girl to dance and she had refused. Sadly, I don't think he danced with anyone that night. It was clear to me he did not know fully the rules organizing masculine talk about dating, romance, and friendship; he spoke frankly about his anxiety—a huge breech in the rules of masculinity. His comments forced me to realize that to his mind being dateless was in some way a transgression of an informal masculine code (though I was also profoundly aware that male students measure themselves by this code to varying degrees). For boys whose masculine identities are subordinated, like his, not having a date may be more meaningful than for those whose masculinity is secured and legitimated by other boys; many other boys seemed unfazed by their not having a date. Consider one white young man's comments about his not having a date for the prom:

> In my case people are going to look at it like, "He could get a date but he's not going to," because that's the truth. I'm not trying to brag or whatever, but I don't think I would have much difficulty getting a date.

A few, like the following young man, did venture to express their disappointment with the outcome of the evening, although in less vulnerable ways than the young man I met at the Hudson prom:

> My prom was absolutely terrible. I fought with my girlfriend the whole night and after we broke up, never to speak to each other again. It was such a waste of money. I spent so much and had such a crummy time. If I had to go back and do it again I wouldn't. I never wanted to go but it was the thing to do, so I went.

While expressing his regret, this young man's discussion centers on the money he spent, not on any personal feelings he had. At the same time, talk about the wasted money spent was a vehicle to express his profound disappointment.

In interviews, boys tended to elaborate more on their expectations of the prom and what dating meant to them, while still expressing a cool ambivalence. One middle-class biracial boy from Woodrow said,

> Well, like, some people go crazy and they make their own dresses and they start planning months ahead about what they are going to do for one night. I don't know, I usually don't get excited over things so it's . . . I guess it's just me because I do feel it's a special time and it's an important event in my life and the senior prom is pretty big and everything, but usually I try to keep under control in most situations and one way I do that is, just don't get excited.

Though here he tried to actively present himself as in control, later in his interview he offered that, while not hoping for romance he indeed had an expectation of the prom that relied upon the presentation of himself and his date within a particular organization of gender. This became clear to me during a discussion of his date's dress:

> JG:   It's pretty scary. When she showed it to me before she got into it I was like, "Oh my god! You're going to wear that to the prom?"
> AB:   What's it look like?
> JG:   It's purple and it's like short and sort of glossy with a zipper down the middle front. I don't know, it just wasn't what I had in mind as a prom dress.
> AB:   What did you have in mind?
> JG:   Something white or black, maybe velvet or silk or something, usually long. Something like you'd wear to a wedding. I mean I went out and got a tux.
> AB:   When you saw this dress, did you tell her how you felt?
> JG:   I didn't tell her I was sort of like, "Hi." Well, I didn't say I hated it, I didn't say I liked it. I was just sort of, gave her a look and she was like, "Oh my god, he's gonna kill me" kind of thing.

His expectations of the prom had developed around his date presenting herself in a way that corresponds to cultural images of femininity. The dress his date had selected contradicted his expectation of the prom as a space in which he'd be able to demonstrate his masculinity through his date's appearance. He had put time into selecting his outfit ("I mean, I went out and got a tux"); shouldn't her outfit look as though it had been carefully selected as well? Though he never told her she couldn't wear the dress, who was on his arm as he walked into the prom—what she looked like and what she was wearing—clearly matters.

The prom's very organization is contingent on the operation of heterosexuality, regulating not only the actions of "straight" boys, but also making it difficult for young gay men to be "out" at the prom and still claim a space for themselves. Brent, a young gay man who attended his prom with a girl, reflects upon his experience:

> When I went to the prom I just went with someone because I felt I had to go with a girl. That I just had to do it. I went with someone who was very pretty, but she was a bitch. It was the worst mistake. It was not a good experience. In the sense that I said I had to go with her, everybody else was going with somebody from the opposite sex. I didn't ever think about bringing a guy to the prom. If I had the choice I don't think I even would, only because my school, they didn't seem open to it. There was nothing different in my school. Everybody was going with somebody of the opposite sex, everybody was getting tuxes. So I didn't think about it. I never discussed my sexuality and I never confronted it in school. I didn't know anyone else who was gay.

Within this school setting, masculine identities emerge within a complex arrangement of power, influencing how boys relate to girls and to each other, how they talk about themselves, and how they discuss their prom experience. Proms are spaces in which the anxiety that boys experience but rarely articulate about becoming men is especially pronounced. While it is clear that these young men are active participants in the recreation of gender and heterosexuality, it is also clear that some of these young men felt limited by the organization of masculinity at the prom. What emerges is a constant attempt by boys to conceal their feelings and express an outward reserve toward social activities in which girls participate. Like girls, boys must walk a thin line.

### *The Prom Is for Girls*

Rule # 3: Psych Him Up
You want everything to be perfect, but if you're a control freak and insist on making all the decisions, he's sure to feel left out. So get his suggestions on post-prom party hang outs and let him pick the restaurant. That way he'll feel like it's his night too. Help him out with the details. Getting pissed when he shows up with a corsage of lamo-pink carnations is not romantic. Telling him beforehand (in a nice way) which flowers will match your dress and helping him pin them on—is.
—"Five Ways to Make Your Prom More Romantic," article in *YM*, 1996

As discussed earlier, the prom is a feminine space. Girls are central players in the production and organization of both the actual prom and the systems of meaning through which the prom comes into being. This is a terrain in which girls have some measure of power and control (though limited) to define the meaning of this space as a romantic one. As during the planning of weddings, young men are often peripheral players (their involvement, of course, regulated by each other), and most attention centers on fulfilling the bride's needs. Consider this young man's comments:

> Well, the first thing I did was ask someone out on a date to the prom and I had a couple of people in mind. I was sort of procrastinating a little bit and my parents were getting concerned. They were like, "Girls need a lot of time to pick out dresses and everything."

Although this logic sustains an order of feminine and masculine within a hierarchical binary that rests on heterosexuality, it does not necessarily mean that boys or men experience this power in an immediate or concrete sense. A number of boys I interviewed expressed that they only went to their prom because there was an expectation that they should go. Others reported they only went to make their girlfriends happy:

Well, last year I went out and I got a tuxedo, I got a nice corsage . . . I wanted to do this. It was out of respect to my girlfriend because she wanted to take it seriously.

Some boys commented that they had little control over what they wore. Others reported that they only went to the prom because they felt they might regret not going later in life. Many expressed that they had experienced considerable pressure from parents, teachers, and peers to go to the prom, even though they did not want to. A number told me that their mothers selected the flowers for their date's corsage, often without any encouragement from them. While it is difficult to ignore that some boys did exert power over girls at the prom or that some destroyed girls' hopes for romance through their actions, there is also a sense that boys are coerced into actions that they do not fully choose.

The designation of the prom as a feminine space is a designation that is maintained not only through peer talk but through institutional practices. Rudolph High School made arrangements with a local tuxedo shop for boys to rent their tuxedos in the school cafeteria during lunch, when representatives from the tuxedo shop placed orders and took measurements. As one boy explained,

How'd I pick it out? Well, Snappy Tuxedo comes to the high school which is a really, really good idea. That's the way you got to do it. You got to come to the high schools and you got to measure everybody and then they bring it that day, but I wasn't sure I was definitely gonna go the day they came to our school.

The assumption organizing this practice is that the prom is not really for boys. To get them to go, not only does it have be made easy, but the preparations boys engage in can't look like the preparations girls engage in; that is, it can't look like work. Imagine a local dress shop bringing their gowns to the cafeteria; would there even be enough room for all the dresses?

For these boys, masculinity exerts a tremendous influence over their sense of self, regulating their actions and ultimately how they come to define the prom. Yet this does not render inconsequential the entitlement boys are able to assert in this cultural space. Boys actively reconstruct the prom as a feminine space. Many boys refuse to dance, an act that carries tremendous significance given that dancing is such an important dimension of the prom. While their dates and female friends gathered on the dance floor in large all-female groups, many boys stood to the side of the dance floor together. I read this as primarily an expression of masculine disengagement. Consenting to dance with their dates, especially during slow songs, could be interpreted by some boys as a expression of deference to femininity. In fact, some girls reported they felt "lucky" because they had dates who, unlike some of their friends' dates, were willing to dance. Their rejection was especially powerful when collectively demonstrated, and exemplifies how men regulate masculinity for other men and manage each other's investments in a masculine order.[23]

There is some indication of a racial organization in the way boys interacted with one another. How boys came together as men was visible at all the proms I observed, but seemed to be organized differently at each school. The refusal to dance was more common at Rudolph, a predominately white school, than at any other school. At the other schools, Woodrow and Hudson in particular, I frequently noticed black men dancing with women and in all-male groups. The fact that white boys at Rudolph refused to dance, while the young African-American men at the other schools seemed willing to, I would argue stems largely from the racial organization of dancing; dancing is an important expression within African-American communities, one that demonstrates collective membership.[24] However, in white middle-class communities, dance is coded primarily as a gender activity—it's something *girls* do.

I did occasionally witness other boys coming together on the dance floor. At Rudolph, I watched one group of athletically built young white men form a circle with their arms around each others' shoulders, hollering and cheering. This act carries different meaning than just refusing to dance. Their dancing expresses their collective identification with manhood. Masculine camaraderie is celebrated through this kind of dancing, and the power to exclude others—girls, or other boys—from their circle is clearly conveyed. While admittedly about friendship, this kind of dancing also signifies a direct challenge to a culture of femininity through which the prom is defined, in that there is no room for girls here.

## *Walking the Thin Line*

In this chapter, I have explored how ideologies of romance and the construction of the prom as a space of romantic promise shape and organize the meanings boys and girls create as they work through the contradictory and often difficult project of becoming men and women. Students constructed and drew upon a range of meanings to make sense of their dating relationships at the prom—and subsequently themselves, as heterosexual and gendered.

Some students relied on extremely traditional scripts of courtship and romance, and in this way upheld a conception of the prom as a fundamentally heterosexual space. For those girls who invested in romance, many were forced to settle for unequal relationships. Yet many young women rejected romance; for these girls, a discourse of romance worked to silence their expressions of self-pleasure; romance required them to compromise themselves too significantly. Unwilling to implicate themselves in an organization of unequal power or navigate the messy field through which girls' sexuality gets defined, some girls abandoned a project of romance. Boys typically defined the prom with little reference to romance. Many actively worked to present themselves as disengaged from the prom, particularly in connection with its romantic underpinnings. How kids talk about dating, romance, and their prom dates, while varied, reflects the tensions and politics that order and arrange youths' understandings of themselves as masculine and feminine within a culture in which heterosexuality, though conventionally understood as an expression of the "natural," is profoundly social in its origins and upkeep.

While the project of becoming men and women is an all-consuming one, shaped by ideologies of romantic love and conventional notions of heterosexual courtship, it is also a project that is subject to revision. It can be rewritten; for some it is, though for a much larger number it is not. Struggles to redefine romance continue to take shape within a larger set of institutional and ideological forces that may allow for some room, but also continue to secure, naturalize, and institutionalize romance as a mechanism of gender and heterosexual controls.

*Five*

~

# Prom Promises

## Rules and Ruling: Proms as Sites of Social Control

Youth as a self and social construction has become indeterminate, alien and sometimes hazardous in the public eye. A source of repeated moral panics and the object of social regulation, youth cannot be contained and controlled within a limited number of social spheres. Youth cultures are often viewed in the popular press as aberrant, unpredictable and dangerous in terms of the investments they produce, social relations they affirm, and the anti-politics they sometimes legitimate.

—Henry Giroux, *Fugitive Cultures*

### The "Prom Promise"

There is tremendous adult concern to prohibit underage drinking and illegal drug use at proms. Each year at assemblies and in school newspapers officials urge students to abstain from drinking at proms, citing a bevy of frightening statistics on alcohol-related injuries and fatalities that occur during prom season. Parent's associations host all-night postprom parties to keep kids off the road on the night of the prom. Prom magazines warn of the sexual dangers of drinking on prom night for girls. The theme of youth drinking frequently presents itself in television sitcoms and dramas, and in films. The message about youth drinking, similar to the message adults promote about youth sex, is to abstain; to "just say no."

In the final episode of the 1999 season of the successful TV drama *E.R.*, a group of four kids are injured in a serious car accident. It is worth noting that they were on the way to their prom. Dressed in prom dresses and tuxedos they are rushed into the emergency room on hospital gurneys, as a din of grisly screams and cries unfolds around them. What we learn is that the driver had been drinking; significantly though, it is never made clear how much. We also learn that of the driver's three friends also in the car, one sustains such severe burns that he eventually dies on the operating table, and another is left paralyzed. Admittedly, it is a gripping and horrifying scene. The burn victim, as he lies on the operating table in agonizing pain, must say goodbye to his parents. "This was supposed to be the most memorable night of my life," he utters as he dies before our eyes. Faced with an equally harsh reality, the driver slowly realizes the egregious act he has committed; he must live the rest of his life knowing he has killed his best friend. We are left with a strikingly grim, albeit predictable message: because there was drinking and driving on prom night, three lives have ended before they ever began.

Antidrinking and antidrug campaigns targeting youth have become a national concern meriting nationally organized action. The most widespread crusade in the past decade has been the Prom Promise. Introduced in 1990 by Nationwide Insurance, one of the leading insurance providers in the United States, the Prom Promise is a program created to raise greater awareness among youth about alcohol-related automobile accidents. Modeling standard insurance protocol, the Prom Promise works as a contract between the student and the school whereby the student signing the contract pledges to remain alcohol and drug free during the prom. Though none of the four schools I studied participated in the Prom Promise, a number of schools do yearly. An estimated 3.4 million teens in 4,200 schools were expected to participate in the Prom Promise in 1997, according to one teen publication.[1] To encourage greater participation, Nationwide Insurance moderates a regional competition between participating schools; the school with the most pledges from the student body wins a number of prizes.

Though a nationwide campaign, the relative local success of the Prom Promise often depends on the support of individual communities and schools, and of course, the students. As such, local newspapers typically include a list of those schools participating in the Prom Promise. Florists' shops and tuxedo rental stores often promise discounts on prom sundries if students bring in their signed copy of the Prom Promise. One school principal promised his students that if enough signatures were garnered that he would move his office to the roof of the school on the day of the prom.

The Prom Promise is an attempt to regulate primarily from "below"; to ensure its success, students must consent to their own regulation. Students pledge, "Whether or not I go to the prom, I promise Insurance Prom Promise not to use alcohol or other drugs. This is a promise I take seriously. It's one I intend to keep for my sake and the sake of my friends."[2] In theory, students become the direct instruments of surveillance and discipline.[3] One school in New Jersey, featured on the local evening news, deputized students as "prom cops"; stationed at the entrance to the prom, they helped administer breathalyzer tests and encouraged other students to sign the Promise before the event.

What actually occurs at many schools, however, is that students sign this contract with every intention of violating it. Consider a conversation I had with Scott, a white student from Woodrow, about the Promise, which his school had once tried to implement, unsuccessfully:

SD:     The Prom Promise is a thing that is put on by I don't know who. I think it's bullshit. They're [the school administration] not pushing it this year, some years they really push it. You know kids promise and it's a joke. You're signing it in jest. I saw a kid who changed the Prom Promise into the Prom Compromise.

AB      What was his compromise, to not drink?

SD:     To drink, to say, "Fuck this. I'm not going to do what they're asking me to do, I'm gonna go and get, you know, hammered."

AB:     Who's *they*?

SD:     *They* being your safety-minded adult, your adult that feels that you should obey and be boring, basically, and have fun in a very traditional fifties kind of way.

For Scott, the Prom Promise signifies yet another futile exercise in adult control, reflecting nothing more than an attempt by adults to prescribe how students can have "fun."

Other schools adopt different strategies to manage students' alcohol and drug consumption. Most schools invoke a host of rules around the prom, ranging from the simply undemocratic to the truly absurd. One school principal in Pennsylvania prohibited students from renting limousines for the prom, a standard practice at other schools, arguing that this would prevent students from drinking. Unlikely to curtail student drinking, this strategy is additionally ineffective in actually preventing drinking and driving since more students would be forced to drive themselves to and from the prom, whether intoxicated or not. At another school outside Boston, a principal, stationed at the entrance to the prom, required students to breathe in his face so that he might better be able to check for alcohol on their breath. These are extreme examples of the abject control educational "lone rangers" can wield over youth. In most school settings, however, the control teachers exercise is not despotic, reflecting instead the larger institutional constraints and the prevailing organization of schooling that make controlling students virtually obligatory.[4] These controls are generally considered essential to the smooth operation of school.[5]

### Suburban Life and the Middle Class at the Rudolph Prom

They made a big deal about the drugs and alcohol but that's obvious. You know you can't do that so, that wasn't a big deal. And they couldn't do anything about all the kids that wanted to smoke because, they just go outside and smoke. The prom was more relaxed. Nobody was like . . . it wasn't like school at all with the rules and everything. The only rules we had were like the drinking and drugs. If you were caught the same rules applied that were at school. That wasn't a big problem for anyone. (White female student, Rudolph High School)

All high schools have rules. High schools function as regulated spaces ordered by codes of discipline and norms of conduct.[6] Rules reflect the authorization of schools as legitimate sites of control; they express the practices and values that we expect kids to embrace as their own.[7] The specific context of schooling largely determines the different patterns of rules schools develop around the prom. Most often these rules are expressions of the particular pedagogical and ideological commitments of the school and community, organized not only to manage relations between the school and its students, but to connect students to a series of extended social relations beyond the immediate school setting.[8]

Rudolph, a predominately middle-class, white, suburban high school, subjected its students to a most rigid set of rules. Time was used to control the space of the prom. As this is a normalized dimension of the school experience, students are accustomed to having their actions governed by time; the ringing of the school bell is a regular feature of school life, and students have come to expect that their time will be organized in such a manner. At nine o'clock, one hour after the prom began, all kids attending were required to be present at the Rudolph prom. After students arrived, they could not leave the prom. Two plainclothes policemen waited at the entrance, ensuring no one reentered once they left. Guiding this particular rule was an effort to prevent students from venturing to their cars to drink, to return to the prom later. As Ondre, an African-American student, suggests, rules around drinking and drug consumption were particularly stringent and were managed through the use of time restraints:

> I know at Rudolph we were supposed to be there by nine o'clock. The doors would be locked at nine so you couldn't come in and especially like the drinking thing was enforced or whatever. Oh, if they smell alcohol, or even suspect you, your parents will be called and you won't be allowed in.

Direct communication with parents was another strategy the administration at Rudolph deployed. One month before the prom, the principal sent home an open letter to students' parents addressing the issue of drinking and declaring his commitment to making the prom an alcohol-free space. Contained in the letter was a direct plea for parents to join his crusade against youth drinking by urging them not to host any preprom parties. Many students, even their parents, thought this an unreasonable request. Fiona, a white student from Rudolph, explained,

They sent home a letter that they advised us not to have a pre-prom party because it's a new principal. My mom, like, laughed. And they said, "They shouldn't have even the temptation of alcohol or something. 'Cause they think parents might serve us or something. I don't know, but we are [having a party]. My friend right around the block is having it. The parents go and the kids go and take pictures and stuff like that. There's tons of parties.

The assumption here is that when youth drink, they drink excessively and are unable to monitor or restrict their own consumption. The other assumption made by the principal is that students' parents would ally themselves with him and his antidrinking agenda. To the contrary, parents, having their own agenda, allied themselves with their own kids against the school. Indeed, it is not uncommon for parents to loosen strict curfews, or to allow their children to enjoy a celebratory glass of champagne on what many consider the "eve" of their children's adulthood.

Students were required to submit a permission slip with parental approval to attend the prom. The name of their date was noted on the form and any changes in dates had to be approved by the administration before kids could attend. School announcements warned in advance that students would be removed from the premises if approval by the administration had not been granted. Fiona described how this worked at the prom:

At about nine o'clock I guess it was, everybody goes upstairs and you have to find your table and sit at it and the teachers go around and check at the tables to make sure, like they have a card, each teacher gets a set of note cards and you go look for them and make sure they are sitting there. 'Cause if you aren't sitting, if Mike is with some girl, somebody else, then she has to leave. Because you have to have a signed permission slip saying that you can go.

Knowing who is going to the prom with whom enabled the administration to anticipate and ultimately forestall any unexpected surprises. In fact, all students were required to go to the prom with a date, though one exception was made in the case of a developmentally disabled student who was eventually permitted to go to the prom by himself only after his parents contacted the school. Students were also prohibited from going to the prom in same-sex groups or as same-sex couples. (Other schools placed no restrictions on persons with whom kids came to their prom; kids were "officially" free to either go by themselves, with a group, or accompanied by a same-sex partner.) As inferred by several Rudolph students, exceptions to this rule would be honored only if the same-sex couple could demonstrate to the school that they were "truly" lesbian or gay. Consider the following discussion I had with two students from Rudolph about two young women who wanted to attend the prom together last year, but were prevented from doing so by the school administration:

ML:    I think they [the school administration] thought it was just so they could go. They didn't really think they wanted to go together.

AB:    Oh, so did they try?

FJ:    They tried to go together but they didn't want two girls going together, I guess.

ML:    They allowed it this year, but they [the students] have to prove that they are really [lesbians].

AB:    So is there anyone at your school like that's, that's out?

FJ:    What about Jane?

ML:    Is she going with a girl?

FJ:    I think.

ML:    Is she really?

FJ:    I don't know, maybe. I don't think she's going actually, maybe she's not going.

AB:    So how did this come about, was there a discussion around this?

FJ:    With the school? No! Tanya came up to me in school one day and was just like, "They won't let me go," because she just wanted to go with a girl. Because she's not really into [being gay], she doesn't go out with lots of boys or anything like that. She doesn't have many boyfriends or anything like that. It's really hard for her. I think it's hard for those people who don't have like a boyfriend. I feel bad, she's just like one example. Like she's not going this year because she doesn't have a boyfriend or anything. All their guys friends are really already going with someone. There is just people who have to go with someone just because.

AB:    Is anyone allowed to go by themselves? Do you have to bring a date?

ML:    You have to bring a date.

Whether intentional or not, this rule imposed by the Rudolph administration made it virtually impossible for a lesbian or gay student to bring a same-sex partner to the prom.[9] When I asked another student why Rudolph enforced this rule, she said that the school had adopted this rule to prevent any conflicts between student cliques.

Though not explicitly coded in a discourse of compulsory heterosexuality, this practice secured the prom as a heterosexual space. Even gender-specific dress codes were enforced. One student told me that the school required boys to wear tuxedos, and among students, it generally was understood that girls were not allowed to wear tuxedos. However, it is not simply that the school administration sought to uphold heterosexuality as the norm, though that was the effect. This decision has as much to do with regulating youth more generally as it does with specifically regulating their sexuality. This unofficial policy reflects at its core an unwillingness by adults to take seriously the idea that kids *could* be gay, lesbian, bisexual, or transgendered; kids could not decide to take up a position that consciously locates themselves this way "at such a young age."

Aside from a few dissenting voices, by a large measure, students consented to the normative order of heterosexuality. Asking Ondre, a young African-American student, if anyone had challenged the hegemony of these school rules, she responded,

OF:   No.

AB:   They wouldn't do that?

OF:   No, that's not politically correct at Rudolph. You can't say you're gay.

AB:   Because they wouldn't allow it?

OF:   No, like the administration *might* allow it, it's just like the . . . I don't think the students. They would get so ripped on and talked about. They wouldn't do that, just for reputation, for all the big popularity contest and everything. No one would admit to being gay. Not at this age, especially . . . at Rudolph.

AB:   Why?

OF:   Money, wealth, it's one big popularity contest.

AB:   Does money play into that?

OF:   Well, first of all they assume you're rich because you go to Rudolph or [are] living in the area. The township and everything is just like politically correct. I really don't know how to explain it but, it's like, we call it the Rudolph bubble and nothing goes wrong. Everybody lives in their little perfect world. Nobody has, like, family problems. I mean everybody has family problems but they're not heard of at Rudolph. Everybody perfectly has the mother, father, sister, brother. Everybody goes to college, has college funds. It's just the Rudolph bubble. It's just perfect— a perfect world.

Her use of a "bubble" as a metaphor for white suburban life provides a cogent image of how middle-class suburban communities work to insulate and protect themselves and their kids from forces that are designated as disruptive or corrupting.[10] In this instance, students are safeguarded from the threat of transgressive sexualities. To a young African-American woman originally from an "inner-city" community, the school's attempt to contain and segregate the students (whether enforced by the administration or the students themselves) is especially meaningful. In many ways, her blackness and her black boyfriend from the "inner city" whom she brought to the prom signify the very sort of "difference" that communities like Rudolph seek to exclude.[11]

Ondre, one of the few African-American students attending Rudolph, was able to offer this salient critique of the practices deployed by the school to maintain "suburban security," particularly as it took shape within her own community, in a way that the white students could not.[12] These practices were a part of a normative and naturalized order of school at Rudolph, and were largely accepted by the students and teachers. Talking about life at Rudolph, Chip, a white middle-class student, provided the following:

> You don't have to worry about anything, like, bad happening. It's a small school. The kids are really nice. It's really like, cliquey. There is definitely distinctive groups between kids, but, I mean I enjoy it, you know? It's a small school which makes it a little tough. Like everybody knows each other. I mean, everybody has their own reputation in the school. That's about it. It gets kind of old after four years, seeing the same exact people everyday. I pretty much enjoy it, you know, what I mean? It wasn't anything bad. It wasn't like torture. Some of the rules were a little too strict. Like, um, you're not allowed to go outside the building like at all or else you'll get a two-day suspension or something like that. If you have a book in your car you can't even go out to the parking lot without asking permission. I personally think that's a little bit too strict; other than that it's not that bad.

Embedded within Chip's discussion of school life is a tone of resignation. Chip accepts the school rules; they are strict, but such is the trade-off to secure safety in a small town.

I came to view the prom at Rudolph as a "metaphor to separate and sanitize," a phrase developed by Michelle Fine for understanding the ongoing operation of whiteness within institutional settings.[13] The question, of course, is to separate and sanitize from what? Being queer? Listening to rap, wearing hip-hop clothes? Being pregnant? Being a high school flunky? Being in a gang? Not being white, not being middle-class? Hadn't the students suggested earlier that the school administration had wanted to prevent student cliques from forming at the prom? Are students' cliques just a suburban precursor to gang affiliations? Perhaps these rules were an attempt to guard youth from themselves. The school implicitly assumed that these kids, left to their own devices, would veer off track and be headed for trouble.[14]

What are the material forces behind the development of such unyielding rules, and what is at stake? In addition to securing heterosexual and gender uniformity, these rules, ostensibly, are linked to class security, upward mobility, and white privilege. Rudolph High School is an academically driven school, expressed not only in its curriculum but in its culture.[15] Similar to other upper-middle-class suburban public schools, life at Rudolph is structured to secure and ensure the future success of these students. Like other suburban schools, parental and community involvement in kids' school lives is considerable; parents and teachers are enlisted to make sure these kids, most of whom are white and middle class, excel.[16] The rules at the prom, though imposed directly by school officials, are an expression of the larger community's vision of school as an essential stepping stone to secure and sustain a middle class, and their children's location within it.[17] The fact that this is a community comprised of mostly professionals contributes to this being a setting in which the future academic success of its students supplants the immediate need for greater freedom. Students' agency is bartered, bargained, and exchanged for their easy entry into the ranks of the professional middle class. Given the imperative to maintain the school's smooth (re)production of a middle class, it is not surprising that the Rudolph High School prom would be tightly organized.

### Educating "The Best and The Brightest": Reading Privilege at the Stylone Prom

In contrast to the students at Rudolph, where countless rules infringed upon the experience of the prom, students at Stylone, an elite public school for "the talented and gifted," enjoyed considerable freedom at their high school prom. Relative to Rudolph's, their prom appeared to be an unregulated school space. In fact, when I asked the senior faculty advisor at Stylone, Mrs. Stark, a middle-aged white woman, about some of the rules that were enforced at the other schools, she expressed surprise at their policies. As I learned more about Stylone, I realized the aims and objectives of the school were entirely different from those at Rudolph. First, Stylone High School is one of the four most academically rigorous public high schools in its city's public school system, resembling more a private school than a public one. Second, its students possess tremendous cultural and intellectual capital relative to the students at the other three schools I studied. These two factors played a significant role in how Stylone's prom was organized and managed.

When I first met Mrs. Stark at the prom, she invited me to sit down beside her and we started talking about the kids. She began pointing out different kids and telling me about them. "That tall boy over there," she said, "is going to Princeton this fall; he is ranked number one in the state for tennis." Pointing to a young Asian woman she said, "There is a Westinghouse winner" (taking for granted that I was familiar with the Westinghouse Science Awards). Pointing to a young white woman, she said, "And over there is a Westinghouse finalist; she is going to MIT this fall." Nodding her head in the direction of another young Asian woman, she said, "And she played the cello at my son's wedding ceremony last year." This sort of boasting struck me as strangely interesting; I had not experienced anything like it when I spoke with the faculty advisors or teachers from other schools.

Mrs. Stark was actively working to construct my interpretation of the school as an exclusive one and in so doing was trying to distinguish between Stylone and the other public schools in the city. This was expressed in countless ways, as my fieldnotes suggest:

> I asked Mrs. Stark if all the kids were college bound and with a dismissive nod she said, "Oh yes," as though it should be obvious. She told me that some prom magazine had contacted her to ask if they could come to the prom, proudly declaring to me she had said "No." With a distinctive tone of arrogance, she added that their school was the first to decline the magazine and that she didn't care. It was "too disruptive and the kids didn't need that." She told me that *Seventeen* magazine had also contacted them to see if they could come. As I chatted with Mrs. Stark, I watched the kids move about, greeting each other and commenting on the dresses. I noticed it was about 8:15 and a significant group of kids had already arrived, which was different from the other schools. Boys came in their tuxedos and the girls came in evening gowns and cocktail dresses. It was clear to me that most of these kids had spent a lot of money on their clothes. Leaning her head toward me, Mrs. Stark told me there was a 500-person wedding downstairs and she bet none of the guests were as well dressed as these kids! Many of the dresses *were* elegant. She added that these kids all looked so "beautiful, individual and soooo tasteful." She had yet to see two dresses alike, nor had I seen two of the same. I could tell that many of the dresses had been bought in boutiques and women's sections of upscale department stores, like Bloomingdale's and Saks Fifth Avenue. Few of the girls' dresses looked as though they had been found in the teen section of Macy's or JC Penney's. (May 1997)

It became even more apparent to me that coded in her bragging was an attempt to distinguish these kids from not only other city public high school kids, but from public school kids in general. Maybe she was trying to prove to me that this was not another inner-city high school, though I needed little convincing. Her attempts were deeply coded in class discourse, operating not only through a rhetoric of academic achievement but through a rhetoric of cultural style. Her comments about the tastefulness of students' dress styles signified her attempt to place these kids above other public high school students. Amira Proweller, in discussing the social organization of a private girls' school, provides insight into how the operation of schooling works at elite institutions, saying, "As students receive valuable instruction in academic skills, they are also the focus of a larger educational project to socialize a gendered elite. The emphasis here is on the production of a class elite, where students receive daily lessons in class appropriate norms, values and dispositions. Acquired resources then translate into upper-middle class cultural capital that benefit them now in school and hold out promises for educational and occupational attainments in the future."[18]

This understanding of Stylone as an elite school is so pervasive that it was embedded in most teachers' talk about the school, its students, and other schools. Quoting again from my fieldnotes:

> One of the white chaperones, a teacher named Jack, approached me. After chit-chatting for a minute he asked if I would be studying a high school in the Bronx, where he had worked before coming to Stylone. I said no and he said that I would see some interesting differences. He said that the clothes are very "different" and that the kids' expressions in the Bronx were much more "provincial," in short, less informed by current fashion. The exclusion and insularity of Bronx high schools came as little surprise to me. The Bronx is an isolated community, forcibly segregated from the rest of the city, though his comment seemed conspicuously condescending. (May 1997)

Students also helped to construct their school as an exclusive one. Consider the following conversation I had with one young white male student. His story is one of educational privilege serving "the best and the brightest":

RT:    It's unlike any other school. This school is like no other in the United States. I'll tell you a story. We went on a ski trip once and almost everybody [Stylone students] on the ski trip was white. We went to a McDonald's or like, a Denny's and this student, he went to the counter and ordered, and the guy [behind the counter] was like, "Wow, you speak English *good*," and the guy just stares at him [he pauses] and he's like [sarcastically], "So do you." It's a school unlike any other school.

AB:    What do you mean?

RT:    It's a totally free environment. Anything goes. It's also very politically aware. One time we had a substitute teacher and we were doing the *New York Times* crossword puzzle. And she was like, "Students at Stylone are doing the New York Times crossword puzzle?" People think of Stylone as sort of a nerdy school. That you have to be oriented toward math and science. It really wasn't. Although we had a handful of Westinghouse finalists, science competitions, math competitions, and chess competitions, but yet, it was a cool school. It facilitated whatever work you wanted to do. You were encouraged to do everything. We had science trophies but we also had speech trophies and drama trophies. The theater was amazing, so high tech. There are always four or five plays going on throughout the school year.

The first portion of this student's story alludes to how language operates as cultural capital; students at Stylone are well-spoken. His narrative also makes visible that the copious resources available to these students, combined with a progressive pedagogy that encourages students' critical engagement, are what make this school unlike other public schools.[19]

Among their teachers and parents, as well as the larger society, these kids are identified as "the best and the brightest," and therefore it is assumed they are more deserving of the resources that are often absent at other public schools. As Mara Sapon-Shevin has argued, gifted education programs like those at Stylone produce and maintain enormous social and economic inequalities in education that correspond to histories and relations of race and class by providing students with a vastly different and an almost always superior education.[20]

This explains why the kids at Stylone, as one chaperone had commented, were kids who with few exceptions "have a stake in society."[21] These kids largely consent to the organization of their academic, social, and school life, primarily, of course, because they benefit directly from its organization. Accordingly, these kids willingly manage themselves. Their consent, though apparent in the student's talk above, was most clearly displayed through the way they related to their teachers. While the prom, a nonacademic space, may have required less rigid forms of surveillance of students by teachers, I witnessed a camaraderie between the teachers and their students at the prom that was noticeably absent at other schools. Stylone was the only school in my research where the kids selected and invited their chaperones. One white student talked about this within a larger context of how the school was organized:

RT: Sometimes teachers get offended when they are not chosen. You have the teachers who are teaching the most talented kids in the country . . . we choose everything. Our speaker at graduation we chose.

AB: So, how come the kids decide?

RT: Well, I think it is because you are dealing with gifted children. I mean, I don't necessarily agree that they are dealing with gifted children so that you have to treat them with a certain dignity or a certain respect that the other schools or the other students don't get. I think it's important that the administration allow students to make more decisions. Even important decisions, like with school policy. We have a parent-teacher-student administration. Like, once a month we have a big meeting, five students, five parents, five teachers. There is some stubbornness with the old-school teachers, you tell the student what to do and he follows. But the principal is different. She is fair and she loves the students ... they really do push the students to behave how they expect them too. And it's one thing to expect them to behave and then you don't give them the freedom to express themselves. So, if you expect them to behave in an adult way, but you don't really give them the choice. They have to give us the opportunity to go both paths.

Although consenting to supervision, these kids (because they were identified as "gifted") were able to define the terms of their supervision by selecting certain teachers as supervisors. One of the chaperones boasted to me that it is quite an honor to be invited as a chaperone to the prom. Viewing this as an honor instead of as a faculty responsibility radically reframes teacher-student relations as less antagonistic or hierarchical because teachers are unable to categorize this as burdensome work.[22]

The differences between the way Rudolph kids and Stylone kids related to their teachers at the prom were striking. At Rudolph's prom, in the beginning of the evening I watched the kids walk to the very back of the cocktail room, the farthest possible distance from where the chaperones stood at the entrance, while kids at Stylone lingered by the chaperones' table; they hugged and kissed each other "hello" and extended these courtesies to the teachers until Mrs. Stark had to ask them to move inside because lines were beginning to form behind them. I came to see this spatial ordering as a reinscription of symbolic divisions between the teachers and the students, divisions that operate as fundamental features of the everyday ruling in schools. The tension between how teachers relate to school as a work space and how students relate to school as a supervised space often generates antagonism between teachers and students.

These tensions, typically easy to see in most schools, were virtually absent at Stylone. While many students at Stylone cheered and hollered when two chaperones came onto the dance floor to dance, the chaperones at Rudolph (or at Hudson) did not venture to the dance floor. Instead, I watched two female chaperones at Rudolph dance together on the rug lining the perimeter of the dance floor. The dance floor at Rudolph's prom was a space designated for students alone—suggestive, I would argue, of the way kids understand school and school-related sites as spaces of control.

The absence of direct control of the students by the school and its teachers at Stylone, although reflective of a progressive pedagogy of "openness" for these kids, is ultimately about securing their class privilege by allowing these kids to exercise decision-making control (though this is only meaningful as a form of privilege insofar as other students at other public schools are denied it).[23] The prom space was structured for kids to practice privilege, a privilege heavily coded in and ordered around relations of class and race.[24]

At Stylone, one student told me that the prom is completely organized by the students. A small committee appoints a larger group of students to various subcommittees. Each committee is responsible for planning a different aspect of the prom. One committee is solely responsible for administering surveys to the student body. In the spirit of democracy, the polls are designed to determine what the entire student body wants at its prom. A range of detailed questions are asked, such as, "Would you be willing to pay five more dollars for an ice cream bar?" Throughout the development of the prom, decisions are routinely evaluated by the student body. The teachers and administration, while watching over the progression of the prom's organization, rarely intervene in its development. Organizing and experiencing the prom at Stylone provided an opportunity for the school to hook these kids, as members of the cultural and intellectual elite, in relations of ruling by allowing them to actively participate in the "management" of this space. While it is difficult to argue that these relations form a stable and homogeneous class culture at this school, what can be argued is that these relations embed meanings of class in school. Through the distinct activities that define the Stylone prom, students come to understand their experiences and their identities in terms of class and class categories. Many of these students know that their educational experience at Stylone is one of privilege that students at most public schools do not share. Both teachers and students use this class lens to narrate and make sense of this event, and in so doing, reconstitute class relations.

## Responding to the Rules

At a school like Rudolph, where rules pervade all spaces and shape all social relations, how did the kids respond? To assume that kids simply accept the rules would cast students as docile recipients of their control. Of course, kids rarely accept fully the terms of their own governance. How do they navigate what seems to be an endless stream of control?

### Spaces of Trickery

All four high schools had some sort of method to check the kids into the prom. At Stylone, upon entry kids picked up their table cards. Because kids at Woodrow and Hudson were not assigned to tables, they signed their names in a guest book, greeting their teachers as they came into the building. The strategy for "checking kids in" at Rudolph was arguably the most formalized. At the beginning of the prom, the chaperones at Rudolph formed a receiving line in the entry way. Each student was required to greet each chaperone in the receiving line before they could gain entry to the grand ballroom. One of the chaperones told me, as she found her station within the line, that they had had a receiving line at the prom for years, it was a "nice" way to "check in" the kids and also ensure that kids were not under the influence of drugs or alcohol. I stood back and watched as kids were received by their teachers. That the teachers "received" the kids contributed to the sense that the prom belonged to the teachers and not the kids. It seemed emblematic of the direct control the school itself exercised over these kids' lives.

However, many students interpreted the receiving line in a way that radically departed from how the teachers understood it. One young white male student, Chip, provided a creative reinterpretation of the receiving line that developed from his "experience" as a student within a hierarchical school organization. Rather than accept the hegemonic meaning of the receiving line, Chip offered another reading:

AB:    Did you guys go through the receiving line?

CP:    Yeah.

AB:    What did you think about that? I'd never seen that at a prom before.

CP:    You never saw that? You see, I don't know why, because for some reason I liked that so much. Like, I loved doing that. I don't know why, I guess because, um, teachers always expect, like, kids to be, like, drunk or stoned or something but, I mean, like, you're totally not. It's kind of like making them feel stupid. I think just because they think you're gonna be, like, drunk or something or doing something bad but, you're totally not. You're totally sober. They're totally looking to catch somebody and they're just not going to, so it's kind of funny the way you laugh at them a little bit.

Although Chip also perceives the receiving line as an instrument of surveillance and control, the receiving line symbolizes a space in which he can contest this school rule through an inverted reading. Chip's reading challenges the way teachers define students "as always in trouble" and resists the hegemony of particular school practices. Michael De Certeau's work on the culture of everyday life provides theoretical insight into this process. As he explains, "Innumerable ways of playing and foiling the other's game . . . characterize the subtle and stubborn resistant activity of groups which, since they lack their own space, have to get along within a network of already established forces and representations. People have to make do with what they have. In these combatant stratagems, there is a certain art in placing one's blows, a pleasure in getting around the rules of a constraining space . . . even in the field of manipulation and enjoyment."[25] The receiving line emerged as a space of trickery for many kids. Little acts, like jumping on the end of the receiving line and mimicking the chaperones as they greeted the students, represented momentary disruptions of the school's power to manage and regulate the activities of youth. The receiving line, while an expression of power, also signifies a space in which this power is refuted. Destabilizing the ongoing operation of power in schools in this way enables kids to carve out spaces of their own and to make the prom theirs.

### The Dance Floor

> After the prom there was no party so we went from one spot in the woods to another and the cops found us all three times. Finally [we] gave up at around 4 a.m. and came home. A few guys were arrested for being intoxicated but no girls were. (White female student)

Securing privacy and autonomy in school or even outside school can be an enormously difficult task for kids. As the young woman above suggests, students are often required to go to great lengths to find unsupervised leisure spaces, and even then these spaces are never fully secured from adults. At each prom I attended, I watched kids search for and attempt to create makeshift private spaces for themselves within this highly public space. I saw several couples escape off to darkened corners of the room or venture to less traveled areas of the building outside the ballroom to create momentary sites of intimacy in a highly supervised space. Literally ignoring their surroundings, these couples sat close together and kissed and talked. Scores of students at Rudolph's prom, many of them smokers, escaped outside to an adjoining veranda, a significantly less supervised area than inside the ballroom. Whether they smoked or not, many students spent a considerable portion of their prom outside.

Attempts by students to create an unsupervised space can influence the organization of the dance floor; an excerpt from my fieldnotes provides another example of how the dance floor at Rudolph's prom was shaped by kids' struggle to claim a space for themselves:

> When I walked into the grand ballroom where Rudolph's prom was held, many kids had already found their way to the dance floor. Upon first glance, it appeared that they were all dancing. However, on second glance, I noticed several kids standing and talking to one another, rather than dancing. These students came together in small shifting groups, moving their bodies to the music as if they were actually dancing. Off to the side of the dance floor, on the rug, I spotted two older women teachers line dancing in unison. Not once in the evening did I see any teacher dance on the dance floor. (May 1997)

The teachers danced, but not on the dance floor, and the students occupied the dance floor but many of them did not dance. The spatial organization of students' bodies and teachers' bodies seemed to suggest an order to the dance floor, through which it came to be defined as a space for and of youth.

*After the Prom*

At times kids upset the power of schools in more concerted ways. Most of the kids I spoke with had made postprom plans. Agreeing not to drink at the prom, many of the kids at Rudolph postponed drinking until later in the evening. "Nobody I was with drank before the prom but I know after the prom, like, down the shore it was just drinking . . . all weekend," one student reported. For many, drinking at the prom simply was not worth potential suspension, or worse. "It's so enforced and so restricted that like everybody is so worked up and really nobody does it [drinking] before prom," another student offered. Consider this conversation I shared with Chip:

AB:    What about the rules for the prom? I understand there were . . .
CP:    Drinking rules, you mean? The thing they emphasized most is like no drinking, drugs, or anything like that beforehand. Everybody obeyed that one.
AB:    Oh really?
CP:    Yeah, pretty much. At prom, definitely.

At Rudolph, a large group of the kids headed to the beach after the prom for a weekend of freedom and independence from adult supervision. One Rudolph student described the weekend as "a big alcoholic weekend, like for days after, you'd taste beer. It was just awful, I mean, it was a lot of fun and no one got too out of control. No one got sick, no one got alcohol poisoning, thank god." Discussing the politics around drinking, the prom, and the weekend "down the shore," Mitch and Fiona, two white students at Rudolph elaborate:

ML:    People don't really drink that night anyway.
FJ:    The next day is a drinking day.
ML:    Next three days.
AB:    Oh really?
FJ:    Yeah, like everybody. Last year we went, people go down the shore after the prom or they go the next morning. Saturday morning, you still have Sunday night for juniors and then seniors usually have the next day off for senior cut day so they stay down three days. Last year we stayed down Sunday. We had Saturday night so we did. My friends, we stayed at a hotel. All the senior guys, they all stayed at this other hotel. There had to be like forty people there. I remember running into them a couple times; they were down the block and they were like always drinking. All day, all night down the shore and stuff like that.
ML:    Everybody goes down the shore, but not in the same place.

FJ:   Everybody goes down the shore, Wildwood, Long Beach Island.
Everybody goes down the shore, it's kind of known.

At Woodrow High School, as at Rudolph, an entire set of extended activities were organized by the students independent of school. In the students' constant pursuit of unsupervised space, an event once lasting a few hours has been transformed into a series of activities occurring over several days. While the prom itself is identified by students as a school event, the activities to follow exist outside school, beyond the reaches of the school's control. Elise, a biracial student at Woodrow, talks about plans for after the prom:

> Like, a lot of people are going camping, a lot are going to rent a hotel room. And then, like, the people who are doing the hotel thing, like, that's Friday night but Saturday night. You see the prom weekend is like the whole, it's gonna be the whole weekend, so Saturday night we're going camping and Friday night we're doing the hotel thing. They're supposedly renting like a whole—they're going to the Holiday Inn and getting one whole floor, like sixteen rooms.

Some kids who did not go to the prom at Rudolph still participated in the activities after the prom. Sandy, a Rudolph student, told me, "My friends went [down the shore] at like 4:00. A couple of my friends who didn't go to the prom went down and they just started . . ." Another white student at Rudolph related,

> My friend Bren didn't go and Katie didn't go [to the prom]. They are like best friends. They decided they were too cool for the prom this year. They were a bit obnoxious about it. They were like, "Oh you guys are so dumb why are you going to the prom, it's stupid, last year was awful." I was like, "Okay whatever: you guys go to the shore and get started, we're going to the prom." They were too cool this year.

Chip added,

CP:   A few of my friends just didn't go [to the prom]. Like they went to the shore right after school on Friday.
AB:   Why didn't they go?
CP:   Why didn't they? I guess for a couple of them it was like an issue of money to get all the money together for a tuxedo and for the prom bid they'd just rather spend that money on the shore and their hotel and stuff and they'd have a good time that way. I guess just some of them like didn't want to go through the trouble of

finding a date and doing all that kind of stuff. So they just didn't go, they didn't bother with it.

As I spoke with kids at Rudolph, I began to see the redefinition of spaces of importance emerging within their talk:

AB:    So could you tell me a little bit what school was like on Wednesday after the prom? Was there talk about the prom?

CP:    There wasn't really talk about the prom, it was more like, talk about the shore and everything that happened, you know what I mean?

The prom, for many kids at Rudolph, especially, became secondary in importance to the activities that followed the prom. Chip elaborated further:

AB:    The shore, I heard that for a lot of people it was a big drinking thing.

CP:    Yeah, it was awesome. We had so much fun because like, it was kind of like the cliques in my group like really don't hang out, you know what I mean. But like Monday, yeah because Tuesday we had was senior cut day. So, Monday night it was basically just like the senior grade, it was cool because a lot of us haven't just hung out in like two years, you know what I mean? In high school all the girls in our grade go with the older guys and by the time senior year none of us like them. So we really don't hang out so like we finally got a chance to all hang out and have fun together for the first time in a while so that was really fun. I like that a lot. I had a good time.

The idea that the events that followed the prom were somehow better or more important than the prom itself was a theme expressed by students who attended other schools. One student wrote about what she did after her prom:

All the pressure was finally over. Afterwards the group split up and half of the group was driven back in the limo. We all changed at my house and piled into cars. My friend had a cottage on the lake a couple hours away . . . so eight of us drove there. We had driven down a couple weeks earlier and decorated with lights and had prepared food and snacks. Basically we talked all night and watched movies. At 5 in the morning I convinced some of my friends to go row boating with me. We didn't sleep all night and the next day went sailing and ate lunch, played cards and had a great time. Overall I think the prom is overrated. It was too much stress and pressure. Once we got out of our formal wear and hung out, we felt better. I'm glad we went but the after prom was definitely better.

Responding to the students' postprom events, a number of schools have tried to usurp the power kids can assert by providing a supervised postprom party. The organizing committee at Woodrow High School said that their postprom party was intended to provide kids with a fun and safe space to go after the prom. While their concern for students' safety seems genuine, this is also an attempt to manage how kids can experience the entire prom night. Similarly, another school in New Jersey scheduled graduation the day directly following the prom to prevent students from having these several-day "freedom" excursions where reckless drinking and sex were assumed to ensue.

Many students refuse to go to the school-organized postprom events, deciding instead to organize their own activities, while some only go in the absence of available alternatives. "I suspect everybody goes for a little while, or most everyone anyway, those that can walk," one student said about the postprom party at Woodrow. One young man wrote about the postprom party at his school,

> After the prom was really boring. We went to a school sponsored event, but most of us really wanted to go to a party. Nobody was having one.

To enlist kids to attend the Woodrow postprom party, the organizing committee, comprised mostly of parents, promised gifts like microwaves, stereos, and CDs to be raffled, tying kids in direct ways to a culture of consumption. Matt, an African-American student from Woodrow, though originally willing to go to the postprom party because of the possibility of winning some prizes found upon arriving that he could have more fun someplace else outside school:

> After the prom everybody planned to go to the after party but the after party wasn't like everybody thought it would be, like fun. So everybody stayed there for an hour or two and we considered going to breakfast, so we went to breakfast. . . . Everybody was going to Denny's. After that we like just rode around. Some of my friends went to New York City.

The fact that this student preferred "just riding around" to being at the postprom party is suggestive of how kids define this space and its connection to school. Like the prom, this postprom party was a regulated space, governed by rules reflecting the ideologies and authority of the school. Once they entered, kids could not leave and return later. At the entrance stood the principal beside a long table at which several chaperones sat. Each student was required to check in and was warned that if they left they would not be readmitted.

Though many students did attend the postprom party, kids creatively worked this space to their own ends and refused to enter it except on their own terms. One strategy kids deployed to upset the ongoing surveillance by schools was the manipulation of time between leaving the prom and arriving at the postprom party. Students were expected to go directly from the prom to the postprom party, stopping briefly to change out of their prom clothes into more comfortable clothing. Instead, many kids prolonged the time between the prom and the postprom party by stopping at a community diner or college coffeehouse for something to eat. The kids featured in the picture below stopped at a grocery store. So important was their presence in this space, these kids took a picture to record their being there.

Additionally significant is the fact that high school students are usually prohibited from entering public settings. Strict rules around loitering at such places as McDonald's and public parks set limits on how kids are able to interact in public settings; the possibility of their being removed from these spaces is always imminent. On the night of the prom, these kids occupied these public spaces without risk of their removal. As teenagers, they challenged how they came to these spaces. For any onlooker, it was obvious that these kids were coming from their prom; many were still dressed in their prom attire. This is a radical departure from the way kids are typically allowed to enter and occupy public spaces. Samuel, a student from Hudson, reflected on how he spent his time after the prom:

AB:　What was that like, going out to other places?

S:　It was funny, because in the middle of the night everybody was like, "Okay we're hungry let's go out to eat," and then one of the other girl's prom dates, Alex, right, he was like, "Oh, we're going to McDonald's." And he was like, "What will we look like going in there with prom suits into McDonald's, like, let me have a number two" [laughs]. You know, you all dressed up and you're supposed to go to a nice place and Alex was like, "Who told you that lie?" He was joking around, though. And so we was going to go to this diner, we was going to go to the one right here, the one on Second Avenue, Cosmos and then the limo driver said he knew a nice place in Queens that was real fancy and nice and everything and we was like, "Is it expensive?" and he was like "Naw, it's just food." And then, so, we went there and it wasn't that bad. You know, we had fun.

AB:　What kind of restaurant was it?

S:　It was a nice fancy restaurant. It had everything. It had [something] like this high, it had shrimp, hamburgers, cheeseburgers, club sandwiches. It's like a diner, but it had everything in it. Ice creams and everything. So, we sat there and we had fun and we started bugging out and we started talking about the prom, and pictures, and then we went to South Street Seaport and took some more pictures and that was basically it. I liked the diner, it was real nice and relaxing.

Prom night offers itself as a time when kids are allowed to venture to spaces from which they are typically excluded, like upscale restaurants or hotels. They negotiate the meanings of these spaces, redefining them on prom night as spaces of freedom, often finding themselves with more bargaining power in these settings because of the way they are dressed and because they have gathered enough money to buy their entry into these spaces. On prom night they are able to enjoy a type of independence, free of supervision, that they are denied on a day-to-day basis.

### *Reconsidering Rules*

Rules both naturalize and normalize the operation of power in schools in that they are visible but largely taken-for-granted features of life in school. Attending a suburban high school like Rudolph, I often felt overwhelmed by the ongoing sense of being controlled, of being ruled. Like many of the kids at Rudolph, I remember that my days in school were filled with finding more inventive ways to navigate a constellation of rules framing school life and shaping my relationship to a broader project of schooling. A rich layering of disciplinary forms appears in virtually all aspects of schooling.

The regulation and management of social spaces outside of the classroom are significant sites in which the social forms authorized by schools are extended, legitimated, and re-created, enabling schools to control in more encompassing ways how kids engage, negotiate, and contest power inside and outside school. In light of the fact that students often feel constrained by school itself, not only inside the classroom but outside it, we should not take lightly the weight of this control.

In an immediate sense, rules as a text tell us little about the complexities of schooling as a social practice, or about the primary actors involved. But if we look at rules as coming into being through the local, ongoing negotiations of them by students, then we can get at how rules secure and (re)produce specific forms of domination, as well as how kids work within and around them. There is always more to rules than immediately appears; rules around drugs and alcohol regulate the direct action they promise to deter as well as serving to manage an entire terrain of social and sexual relations, as was clearly the case at Rudolph High School.

In addition to exploring the ways rules and ruling shape how youth come to and organize themselves around the prom, this chapter has also concerned itself with how rules and ruling are organized in connection with the (re)production of class and race privilege. An investigation of the underlying ideological workings that give rules shape within specific school sites reveals not only a relationship between youth and school, but makes visible a more complex set of ties that are being shaped and formed between youth and a larger organization of external social relations *through* school. What are the relationships being forged? Both Rudolph and Stylone High Schools are schools that educate upper-middle-class youth; yet, the way each school organized its prom varied in remarkable ways. Expressing a suburban ideology of "safety," Rudolph High School organized its prom to secure heterosexual, class, race, and gender uniformity among its students, thus sacrificing their agency and freedom. To the contrary, Stylone students enjoyed considerable freedom and autonomy. Given that Stylone's curriculum is designed to serve the "the best and the brightest," it is not surprising that students were able to express their agency in myriad ways. What should not be overlooked is that the agency Stylone students were granted resecures their class and race privilege. The organization of the prom in regard to rules at both schools reveals a curriculum embedded in a set of social relations organized to uphold class and race inequalities between schools. In addition to expressing upper-middle-class agendas, the relations organizing these proms embed and reconstitute class and class relations as a meaningful feature of school culture and students' school identities.

# Six

# *The Divided Dance Floor*

## Race in School

> Trying to understand race in the United States is like putting
> together a three-dimensional 1000-piece jigsaw puzzle in dim light.
> Given the vicissitudes of historical amnesia and the elusive quality
> of communal memory, it is unclear if we even have all the pieces to
> begin with. Race is about everything—historical, political,
> personal—and race is about *nothing*—a construct, an invention that
> has changed dramatically over time and historical circumstance.
> From the smallest of gestures—what is packed in a child's lunch box
> or passed on in a smile or a frown—to the largest of historical
> statements—Brown vs. Board of Education, the Vietnam War, the
> Hyde Amendment—race has been, and continues to be, encoded in
> all of our lives.
>
> —Becky Thompson and Sangeeta Tyagi, *Names We Call Home*

The process of "naming" race is no simple one. Few scholars would argue
otherwise. Race operates at so many levels—the structural, the institutional,
the ideological, the terrain of consciousness and self—and appears under so
many guises that it is sometimes difficult to know it when one sees it. This
chapter explores how race, as a set of structural, political, and personal relations (of both privilege and oppression), operates in connection with schooling by examining how a group of students at a racially integrated high school
organized their prom. The question of *how* race works in relation to schooling has been an important one for educational scholars in recent years and
has given rise to a rich body of thinking on the subject.[1] Common to these
approaches is the notion that the complex issues surrounding race and
schooling must be explored on both an educational terrain and a cultural terrain and only can be understood as they intersect with other social relations—class, age, gender, and place. How does race shape kids' school lives?
How are proms racialized sites? How do young people understand and narrate race in relation to school and their identities as students?

### *Visiting Hudson High School: Thinking about Race*

As I approached Hudson High School for the first time, I noticed a group of boys, all of color, gathered at the entryway to school. They stood at the borders between school and street, their laughter lingering in the warm spring air. They barely noticed the two police cars stationed outside the building, feet from where they stood. For me, an outsider to this school, it seemed a strange irony. I walked around them, not wanting to intrude on their tightly knit circle, and into the front hall of the school where I was met by two uniformed security guards who asked me for identification and checked their log book to verify that I legitimately belonged there. I was directed upstairs to the fourth floor to meet the senior faculty advisor, the teacher chiefly responsible for helping students organize their senior prom. Stepping off the elevator, I walked down the sparsely decorated halls, heading for Mr. Stand's classroom. The walls were draped with a dirtied-yellow paint that had begun to peel. A few scattered posters hung on the walls; some were ripped, others hung by a single piece of scotch tape. How remarkably different these hallways looked from those of my suburban, predominately white high school. It took me only a few minutes to realize the chief difference: an absence of lockers. Though their absence initially struck me as odd, I learned later that this city's school district had removed lockers from a number of schools to prevent kids from storing weapons.[2]

I arrived at the senior faculty advisor's classroom and knocked on the closed door. As the door opened, I was greeted by a young Latino student who pointed to an older African-American man sitting at a piano; gathered round him were a group of students. He seemed "cool" with his cane and the small ponytail at the nape of his neck. By the easy way the students joked with Mr. Stand and he joked back, I could tell he was a well-liked teacher. Other students sat at desks in small groups scattered throughout the class; their chatter consumed the room. I walked over to Mr. Stand and introduced myself. Although we already had spoken on the phone, he asked me again why I was so interested in studying, of all things, proms. I replied that I wanted to understand why the prom was such a significant event in kids' school lives. Pausing for a moment, he told me that the kids at Hudson weren't "into" the prom and only a very small group attended. Unsure of what this might mean for my research, surprised because this contradicted what I had found in studying other schools, I asked him why kids at Hudson didn't go. Having apparently given this some thought himself, he responded that it was something about urban kids, a mystery, really. Kids in the suburbs, where he lived, were much more likely not only to go to prom but looked forward to the "big night." I felt reluctant to accept this explanation, largely because 600 of the 700 seniors at Stylone, the other city public school I was observing, attended their prom. (April 1997)

When I began this research, while interested in the different ways kids invest in the prom, I took it for granted that most kids would want to go in the first place. Over and over, I had told school administrators, teachers, and parents that I wanted to understand why the prom was so meaningful to these kids, never questioning that more than a handful of dissidents could feel ambivalent about going to the prom, an assumption arguably shaped by the representations of proms in popular cultural texts and my own immersion in a sort of everyday side banter about proms as this project developed. "Proms are something not to be missed." "Not going is something I'll regret for the rest of my life." "It's a night to remember." These sorts of statements rang as a familiar kind of cultural talk about proms; I had heard them time and time again. As a suburban middle-class white girl who enjoyed attending her prom, perhaps I had even uttered these words myself. More significantly though, most high school students I had spoken with before visiting Hudson expressed their desire to attend; some had been active in the prom's organization, and many, despite initial protestations, were truly excited.

Less than half of the senior class at Hudson was expected to attend the prom.[3] An event traditionally reserved for seniors at other schools had been opened to not only juniors but freshman and sophomores at Hudson for several years because attendance had been so low among the senior class that the prom organizing committee was unable to financially secure a site without these additional students. Why did a compelling number of seniors at Hudson decide not to go to their prom? Mr. Stand's explanation seemed to rely too heavily upon a standpoint generated outside his immediate school setting, an adult standpoint that had the dual function of romanticizing urban working-class kids' marginalization from social institutions and depoliticizing the context in which these kids are differently schooled. If not the reason he provided then, how else can this be explained? What did their absence mean for how the prom at Hudson was then defined and organized? The first part of this chapter investigates what forces were at work in shaping Hudson High School students' lack of investments in their prom. The second part identifies how race and class shaped the context in which the kids at Hudson were able to organize their prom. The last part will connect the particular struggles kids at Hudson faced with broader race and class struggles formed specifically around the prom and, more generally, around schooling.

### Life in School: Exploring Hudson Students' Investments in the Prom

Hudson High School is much like other public schools, with an emphasis on maintaining school order through student discipline and management.[4] Located in the center of a bustling urban hub, Hudson High School is one of the most diverse schools in the school district. Categorically, Hudson is not an "inner city" school; it draws its students from across school districts and occupies the middle stratum of its city's three-tiered school system. The school's curriculum is designed to be academically comprehensive. Talk among teachers and administrators seemed to bolster this understanding of the school; both the senior faculty advisor and school principal repeatedly referred to Hudson as a "college prep" school. Yet in listening to students speak about their schooling, terms like "college prep" rarely emerged. Many of the kids seemed to talk of life in school not only outside an academic rhetoric but as antithetical to it. The official school report also demonstrates this inconsistency—though close to half of the graduating students continued on to college in some form, 48 percent of the students did not graduate in the expected four years. Expressed in countless small ways, the contradiction between how the students I talked with perceived their schooling and the way the school represented itself was striking.

Sari, a recent Israeli immigrant, told me that she had not been to one of her classes in over three months, yet no one had confronted her about her continued absences. (A number of girls had invited me to interview them during school hours; when I expressed my concern about disrupting their studies, they told me it didn't really matter, they wouldn't be doing work anyway.) Whether or not Sari's teachers had actually failed to confront her about her continued absences, or whether I would have been welcomed by school administrators had I shown up during school hours to conduct interviews is only partly the point. What seems more important in understanding the organization of school culture at Hudson is how students themselves articulated meanings of school, narrated their school experience, and how these accounts shaped how they thought about the prom.

As my involvement with the kids at Hudson progressed, I came to see two distinct discourses of schooling operating at Hudson. The first was an institutionally authorized discourse articulated largely by teachers and administrators and some students, many of whom were college bound. The second was a discourse largely generated by the students themselves.[5] Theirs was a discourse in which schooling and ruling merge. The discourse of schooling/ruling (terms used interchangeably here) articulated by many of these students is shaped by a series of small infringements: the police cars parked just yards from their classrooms, the small security force determining the terms of their entry to the building, the metal grates lining the stairwells, and the list placed outside the principal's office each day displaying the names of kids suspended from school that day.

Over time I began to see more clearly how firmly lodged these divergent discourses were within a geography of race and class. Students of color and white working-class students spoke more often about schooling with ambivalence, if not enmity, than white middle-class students. While students of color and working-class students seemed to relate to school as a culture of ruling, many of the white middle-class students did not. For Serena, a young woman of color partly responsible for organizing the prom this year, school was beset with struggle. Serena shared with me a conflict she had encountered with the school's administration. She had been suspended for provoking a fight, which she told me she had not caused. In the following passage, she recounts what she considered to be unjust, partisan treatment by the administration:

When I went in to talk to the dean, he was supposed to give me a piece of paper. He was supposed to say, "Here, bring your witnesses." He didn't tell me none of that. He's like, "Fill this out, write what she called you," and that's it. So, I'm like, "Okay." You know, I knew that I didn't do anything wrong. I come inside the next day and he's like, "You're suspended." And I'm like, "For doing what?" And he's like, "You're suspended. That's it. [You] better leave school premises or I'm gonna call the cops." I'm like, you would think I shot somebody. There are people who do so much more in this school. I'm sitting here and I'm like, I have all 90's because you can't be president with a below 85

average. You can't have that. I never failed a class. I never got into trouble and I'm sitting there. And I'm like, "Why? What are you talking
about? Why am I suspended?" "You better get off the school's
premises." So I go in and talk with the principal. He wouldn't talk to
me. At 2:30 he comes in and he's like, "Tell your mom to call me
tomorrow." So, I said, "You know what, I'm gonna do better than
that." My mom comes in and they like, "We suspended the other girl
too." Liars! She never got suspended. That was a lie because I saw on
the sheet in the hallway. They say the names, when you're suspended,
from what date to what date. My name was up there and her name
wasn't. Liars!

For a number of these kids, like Serena and Sari, school is at best a place to
socialize and at worst, a space of containment. With the ongoing antago-
nisms between the administration and the students, schooling is experienced
as a struggle between "us" and "them."

The white middle-class students with whom I spoke seemed to talk about
school in markedly contrasting ways. Listening to these kids speak, I got a
distinct sense that many of them related to school with a sense of owner-
ship; Hudson was *their* school. One student showed me her yearbook; she
had been on the yearbook committee and spoke in detail about each page,
pointing out the work that went into selecting the photographs. Another
white middle-class girl spoke about her school in glowing terms, ironically
citing diversity and the encouragement of students' creativity as contributing to her positive school experience.

Given the racial fissures between students at Hudson, I began to think
about the refusal to go to the prom in more resistant terms. The prom represented an expression of the school's authority and control over their social
lives. Not going to the prom seemed to be an expression of the general
antipathy and disaffection toward schooling felt by a number of Hudson
students, especially students of color.

As I have argued, proms exist along an indeterminate line between
"school" and "not school." Though schools expect that students will want
to go, prom attendance is not mandatory. Students are able to negotiate the
meanings of the prom, to reject or accept the idea that the prom is an event
in which they should invest. Withdrawing from school sites like the prom,
students at Hudson were able to contest the school's ideological and physical control over their immediate lives, as well as the very idea of schooling
itself. Their unwillingness to go to the prom signified an oppositional stance
they came to adopt because their school, which boasts of being one of the
most diverse schools in the district, had failed them.[6]

But students' disengagement from school only partly explains why so
many kids refused to attend Hudson's prom. Economics also helped determine whether or not they went to their prom, and the investments they ulti-

mately were able to make. For one young Latino man who attended school in the South Bronx, limited economic resources prevented him from attending the prom at his school (this was also true for many Hudson students). Determined to have his "prom moment," he helped organize an alternative prom:

> To be honest, my high school prom must have been the best one that students ever threw together for themselves. My high school arranged a senior prom for us but everything about it seemed too rich for the students. It was a total bust because hardly anyone decided to attend. Only ten couples decided to pay the outrageous price of 250 dollars per couple. The hotel that was chosen was meant to hold all 260 seniors and their girls, but 250 dollars was too rich for the seniors. Almost every senior wanted to be part of it, but no one could afford the price. Fifty of us decided to throw our own prom, so that is where I decided to go with my girl. It only cost me 20 dollars to get in the party and it was just as nice as the prom my school decided to throw. It was not a fancy hotel, but the room was big enough to hold the people that went. There were no limos or fancy foods, but being with all your friends and my girl made it special. If I had a chance to choose what prom I would go to I still think I would have gone to the party we threw. My school must have been out of their minds if they thought all the seniors were going to pay an arm and a leg for the prom.

The economic reality of students, combined with the school's unwillingness to organize a prom that reflected this reality, led to their collective disengagement and organization of an alternative, student-hosted prom.

For a number of kids at Hudson, the prom was a waste of time and energy; it was expected to be a disappointment. As one girl saw it, "Well, everybody is telling me that it's really *boring*. They say you just go in the prom and take your pictures and you dance, and show off your dress, and strut some stuff, and that's basically it." Their ambivalence, some reported, had been shaped by the way other students had talked about their previous proms. One student offered,

> Last year's prom, I heard it was worse. It was like, Mr. Stand started letting in freshman and sophomores because they had like fifty people going. And I don't think it was in the same place. It was like a restaurant and everybody was like, "Okay."

Highlighting the contradictory position many students come to occupy in relation to school-organized events, Samuel, an African-American student, reported,

I know a lot of people that missed it, well they didn't miss it, they just didn't want to go and I was like, "Why not? This is like so exciting for you." And they're like, "Ah, same ol' same." I know one girl that didn't even go to her graduation or prom, none of the senior stuff, and I'm like, "Why? If you're gonna miss all this stuff." And I was like, "You're gonna regret it later in life. You should have went. That's a once in a lifetime opportunity." What do you have to lose, you know?

Having limited resources to finance the night's activities and the expectation that the prom could be just another "boring" school event may explain in some ways why kids don't go to the prom, but this can also conceal a more complicated set of relations patterning students' investments and ambivalence. It is not uncommon for high school students to define school events as "boring," as many students did at Hudson; there are typically a host of rules to follow and intense supervision; school events rarely get "rowdy." But when articulated within the context of a school where racial struggles are not only observable to an outsider but named by insiders, "boring" may be a term carrying racial significance.

At the prom, the racial split among students attending appeared to be roughly 50 percent white and 50 percent of color, which in itself is significant considering that over 75 percent of students at Hudson are of color.[7] For many African Americans and Latino/as at Hudson, proms seemed to be coded as "white." Part of this can be explained by the fact that dominant representations typically depict white suburban kids at the prom: prom magazines typically target white middle-class girls, seldom featuring girls of color; the key prom players in most prom films (one exception being the 1999 release *Trippin'*) are largely white; and local prom advertisements rarely include kids of color.

But the idea that proms are a school activity reserved exclusively for white kids is not simply reproduced through the wider economy of images; the local organization of proms within particular school settings also helps to define these events through a lens of race. In previous years, the Hudson prom had been chiefly organized by a group of white students who, I was told, rarely consulted the larger, more diverse student body while planning the prom (an issue I will address later in the chapter). The construction of the prom as a white activity, shaped here by concrete social relations between students, was heightened by the fact that this school, while officially integrated, was not only racially segmented but was, for many students of color, a site of ongoing struggle. Talking about school life more generally, one African-American male student from Hudson offered,

Okay, um, everything is so mixed, so everybody gets along with each other but sometimes people crack heads. Sometimes it's territory space. Either you have problems with each other, like a look, you know? Everybody wants to claim their own territory. It is, okay, like when I first came there, I hung out with my certain group and I knew my certain friends and then I got into my Urban Rights class and we had everybody in there. Like a whole mix and so they made you talk to this person, work with this person, work with that person and then you started liking this person and trusting this person and by the end of the year they had us closing our eyes and falling back and catching us. You know, and somebody you never expected to do that and that brought everybody together. There are only certain classes that do that but other than that if they don't have that class that person will stick to their little group. Nothing really makes this group go with that group and mix in all together.

Though not explicitly named, race is clearly an important force that can prevent students from coming together.[8]

When considering these racial tensions, the use of the term *boring* by students of color seemed to be one strategy used to disengage from an event that simultaneously upheld the ideologies and practices of white culture and erased those cultural practices specific to communities of color. The prom was an event where kids of color already felt excluded.

After considerable deliberation and encouragement from his mother, Samuel, a young African-American man, decided that the prom was not to be missed. Despite the possibility of boredom, that the prom might not be "all that," his words provide further insight into why such a significant number of kids did not attend the Hudson prom:

> AB:    A lot of kids from your high school don't go to the prom.
> SB:    Yeah, I don't know why, they just don't want to. They find it boring. They'd rather go to a club theyself or sit home and do nothing.
> AB:    What do you think about that?
> SB:    I think it's bad, but maybe if the prices was less, you know, and they do a guaranteed have-fun thing, you know, or maybe even longer, maybe they would go. But there's no guarantee, you know, and the prices is so high, it's like if I don't have fun, throwing away money, you know. For eighty dollars I can go to this club, buy this suit, you know, do this and that.

What emerges from Samuel's narrative is a clear sense that it is not poverty that prevents kids from attending the prom; instead, as consumers these students are able to choose how to spend their money. As has been previously discussed, youth have increasingly been incorporated into the folds of mass consumerism. They have experienced not only a new sense of authority and control as buyers, but have been propelled into more public avenues (streets, dance clubs, department stores) to fashion, and express a range of cultural identities that often are limited in school. When students at Hudson were faced with a decision between going to the prom and spending their money elsewhere, many passed on the prom, conferring little importance on the event. Significantly, they refused to read the prom as a special night, as students at other schools had. For the students at Hudson, the prom was just one among a range of possible ways to spend their Friday night—not unlike going to the movies or a dance club. Their reading of the prom is a significant departure from how proms have been conventionally read.

Ongoing racial struggle, economic constraints, and the greater sense of autonomy kids experience in spaces outside school patterned in varying ways how kids came to understand and invest in the prom. None of these forces singularly caused the Hudson students' refusal to attend their prom. Though each provides some insight, these forces worked in concert, as interdependent layers structuring the meanings students attached to the prom. What were the consequences of their disengagement from the prom? How did this disengagement by a large number of students shape the context within which the Hudson prom was then organized and defined by those students who were invested in the prom? Given that race and class shaped how students came to understand the prom and its relevance to their school lives, were race and class also relevant as students organized the prom?

### Organizing Proms: Sites of Struggle, Reading for Race

The students at Hudson organized their prom within a context of waning school support. Serena, a student of color and the senior class president, told me that the school administration and a group of students had been hostile to her as class president and for the greater part of the year failed to support her and the activities she organized. They had attempted to remove her from her seat on student government several times. For her first two years in high school Serena had been defined as a troublemaker by the administration; she often cut class and got into fights. I wondered if her hip-hop style of dress, heavy eyeliner, and use of street slang had somehow contributed to how she was treated by the largely middle-class school officials. When she decided to run for class president she told me that several teachers and administrators had actively tried to dissuade her, suggesting that a student with her reputation as a fighter poorly represented the interests of the school and student body, in spite of the fact that she earned good grades and was well liked by most of the more diverse student population. Serena also faced severe scrutiny by a number of white students who had participated in student government during their years in high school and had already cemented an alliance with the school administration.

While Serena may have been an unlikely candidate for class president, she won the election and told me that throughout the year she had struggled to demonstrate her competence as a school leader. A central dimension of her work was to better represent the needs of a large segment of the diverse student body against a student-teacher alliance whose attempts to undermine her were both vigilant and unrelenting. Serena saw herself as a class president who actively worked to minimize the racial marginalization of many students that was sustained by white students and the administration.

Guiding me through her tumultuous experiences as senior class president, her narrative expresses not only the daily conflict she faced, but revealed the ongoing forces that operate to exclude racially marginalized kids at integrated schools from exerting control over their school lives. As Penelope Eckert has argued, the organization of schooling itself often produces and maintains these divisions, which are heavily embedded within race and class relations, between students.[9]

For Serena and her friend Katy, organizing the prom was embedded within these racialized struggles. Because the school administration and this group of young white women who had organized the prom in past years viewed them as incompetent and expected Katy and Serena to fail, organizing a successful prom took on particular significance for these two young women:

> KT:    You know, one thing I don't like about this school is that they try and do whatever to you, and you see. And they think you're stupid enough to take it. You know, like, they think we don't know.
>
> SF:    Yeah, that they're smarter and older, they're teachers.
>
> KT:    Some of them, I'm not going to say all. Some of them. But, they think that because you're young that you stupid and you gonna take everything. I don't like that.
>
> SF:    It's hard especially at this school, and when people don't like that, especially higher authorities, like everybody was waiting for the prom to fall under.

Reflecting on the difficulties she faced as she tried to organize her school's prom, Serena added,

> SF:    Those kind of people [read: *white*], they always exclude other people. And that's why, when I got elected president, that's why nobody wanted me. *They* were like, "Hey, she's not from our bunch. She's gonna reveal everything we're doing." And I was. I had teachers who didn't like me and I didn't even know them. And I wasn't a part of *them* so that it got to the point and, you don't know this, when I went to school for two years. I didn't know that this was going on and so all of a sudden you're put in

a room where everybody is looking at you and you want to do this and they're telling you, "No! you can't do it." And you're sitting there and you're like, "Why?" Why are they excluding me? Why are they, what did I do to them?" And then you see everything that's going on and then you see everything that they did undercover and then you see that you're, like, "Oh that's it, they didn't want me there."

AB:    So, who are these kids?

SF:    These are the kids you see in the yearbook over and over and over.

KT:    This is a group of Caucasian females.

SF:    And that's who they are, just female Caucasians.

Recognizing that musical styles are racially organized, Serena expressed to me and to students and teachers the need for all racial groups to be represented at the prom, whether that be through salsa, rap, or Asian techno music. She asked students of different racial groups to come forward and request the music they wanted to be played at the prom. She added later that she chose the DJ because he allowed listeners to bring their own music and would play it at the prom. But her efforts to create a racially democratic space were met with resistance by some students. Serena elaborates,

As I told them, you can't take away from other people. The Asians brought in their techno songs and people got mad. I said if you want to hear songs to be played, bring in a tape. You can't run after everybody and say, "okay this is it, you, this is it, this is it, this is it." You know, so, the Asians knew about it and they bring in their tape and I'm not going to deny you because it's Asian music.

Despite Serena's efforts to make the music reflective of the racial diversity of the school, a group of white girls intervened. They secured the song they wanted—sung by white French-Canadian pop singer Celine Dion and titled "Because You Love Me"—as the last song of the night.

The problems Serena and Katy encountered in selecting the dance music represent a much larger struggle over expressions of cultural and racial identity shaped by the conflicts over multiculturalism in education reform. The discussion of the music is ultimately about a struggle over space, how the space of the prom gets defined, and who gets to define it. In the articulation of racial identity, individually and collectively, music emerged as a means to debate and to make visible the taken-for-granted privileging of whiteness as the social norm. [10]

Significantly, while these racial fissures were noticeable to Katy and Serena, the administration seemed to have little awareness of these tensions. Consider a conversation with Hudson's principal that I recorded in my fieldnotes:

I had seen the Hudson High principal earlier in the night; at 10:30 I decided to go over and talk to him. He talked about the coming together of all these different kids and how at other schools they often have separate proms for different groups. I asked if he was talking about race groups and he said, "Yes, you often have the Black kids' prom, and the Asian kids' prom, the Latino prom and the white prom." He said they were "lucky" they didn't have to do this. He went on to talk about how this is a safe space for these kids and that when they leave school they face a rude awakening. He said integration in the classroom is one thing but colleges just aren't willing to accept integration in social spaces. The prom, he said, was "the ultimate celebration of togetherness." But I couldn't prevent feeling conflicted about his statement, because while these kids come together to share this space, it still remained spatially segmented and racially divided. White students on one side of the room. Students of color, separated by the dance floor, on the other. (June 1997)

Relations of race and class structured Serena's struggle in a range of ways. The ongoing, underhanded practices she identified by one group of white girls who sacrificed the interests of the larger, more racially diverse student body to secure their own is an expression of the racial hierarchies that shape life at integrated schools like Hudson. The administrative support these white middle-class girls received, from what Serena suggests, provides some indication of how unequal race and class relations can be institutionally legit-imated and maintained through daily school practices.

It is difficult to know why students of color at Hudson decided to seize the prom as a space to address race. Perhaps the administration's inability to see the relevance of race to the prom forced students of color to take mat-ters into their own hands; they could not count on the administration to support them.[11] What is clear is that Serena's and Katy's struggle in advocat-ing and implementing a policy of racial inclusion was visibly painful. The two had to convince students that the prom was a space for *them*—that the prom was not just a space for white kids. A vision of "fairness" (undoubt-edly shaped by her consciousness of race and class) guided Serena as she worked to create a prom in which all students would be able to find its rel-evance to their immediate social realities, to simply enjoy their prom, and to not feel that this, too, was a site where they had to confront race. It is worth noting that Serena's and Katy's efforts to make the prom available to students of color were rewarded; sixty students more than were initially anticipated went to the prom. Yet to define this as a success story in which students inspired by a multicultural vision battled against the pernicious forces of racism and emerged victorious would be naive. While the struggles to create racially democratic schools are ongoing, there is more at stake here. In addition to the tenuous relations among students and between students and the administration, broader institutional constraints based on relations of race as well as relations of class helped shape the prom and how it was organized at Hudson High School by these two young women.

### Me&Ms and Fashion Shows: Organizing Prom Night

The first time I met Serena and Katy was in the school cafeteria just a few weeks before the prom. They sat with a group of four or five other women of color at a long table in the entry way to the cafeteria. Behind them stood a TV. Muffled dance music emanated from its small speakers, and on the screen a crowd of high school students, all white, danced under a ceiling of colored balloons. From what they were wearing I surmised that this was a commercially produced "prom video." I walked over to the table where these girls sat and noticed several different commercial pamphlets on the cafeteria table. After introducing myself, I asked them what these pamphlets were and they responded, "Prom guides." "What is all this for?" I asked. They told me they were trying to get kids to sign up for the prom. The video, balloons, and pamphlets were intended to ignite a sense of excitement about the upcoming prom. Much to their dismay, they were having little success. Last year, attendance had been low—in part, Serena reported, because it had been held in a renovated warehouse. The decorations were sparse and the food bland, Katy added. "It was terrible, and everyone had a really boring time. The DJ wasn't even that good," another girl chimed in. I asked to see the signature list of kids who planned to attend. They had only collected forty signatures and the prom was just a few weeks away; one woman commented that they needed a total of one hundred signatures to financially secure their prom site.

The weeks before the prom seemed to be touch and go. Serena and Katy experienced great difficulty collecting the twenty-dollar deposits from those students who had committed to going to the prom, contributing to a sense of urgency. As the prom approached I began to wonder if these girls would be able to pull off what began to look like an insurmountable feat. I never shared with them this concern, though it's likely it wouldn't have fazed them; these girls knew, somehow, that the prom would come together. But how did the organizing committee get students to go to the prom? What did this involve for these two women? To get a larger number of students to attend the prom, the Hudson High School prom committee promoted the prom as a site at which students could consume a range of goods and services. I first noticed this in the talk generated about the prom during school. The discussions were organized around the selection of food that would be served, the remembrance gifts to be given, the luxury hotel where the prom would be held, and the video and light show that the DJ was guaranteed to provide. Even the seniors' advisor had commented to me that the prom had to be really "sold" to get these kids to attend.

As noted previously, today schools have to compete against other leisure spaces (McDonald's, movies, shopping malls, video arcades, and dance clubs) organized within commodity culture because youth often prefer these commodity-based leisure sites over school-sponsored social spaces. Though schools have a vested interest in supervising the spaces where kids socialize, this has become increasingly attenuated in the wake of eroding resources. The continued decline in local and federal funding for schools directly impacts how schools are able to organize proms, or other sites of the extracurricular, which is admittedly pronounced for those schools, like Hudson, with limited resources.[12]

Recognizing the often competing currents of school and consumption, Hudson's prom committee knew they had to host the prom in a place that was desirable to the students, while also maintaining a strict budget. The key issue was money: being able to have a prom hinged on being able to secure enough money to do so. For Serena and Katy, this meant they needed to have more students attend than had in the past:

AB:    The last time I saw you guys you had forty names. People signed up and it looked like there were probably 160 people at the prom. So, what did you guys do? How did you get everyone to go?

SF:    Talking to them.

KT:    More like, yeah, it was basically, like, word of mouth because last year's prom was so whack and whatever.

SF:    Yeah, so everybody thought this year's was going to be like that and it was hard.

KT:    And plus, it was the money also. So, a lot of people wasn't able to get it until the last minute.

SF:    So, they didn't know whether they were or whether they weren't [going]. So, if you keep counting them and running after them, they came through.

AB:    So, did you guys do that a lot, just keep going after people?

SF:    Yeah, showing them pictures. Telling them, like, talking it up.

In addition to the work of producing emotional investments in the prom, students must also raise enough money to cover a range of expenses: the DJ, the hotel, decorations, invitations, and remembrance gifts. Most schools rely on local fund-raising activities to finance the prom. These fundraising activities depend largely upon the availability of resources in the community and the economic situation of the school. With eroding educational funding, schools often find themselves dependent on local and community resources to maintain the ongoing operation of school; the consequence, of course, is the re-creation of huge disparities in not only the resources available in the classroom but in other school spaces, like the prom.[13]

Rudolph, a white upper-middle class suburban school, followed the trend

in a number of suburban schools and sponsored a fashion show two months before the prom, charging a ten-dollar admission fee at the door.

At the fashion show, students modeled clothes donated by local merchants and large retail chains like The Gap and The Limited. Students from Rudolph canvassed local merchants asking for donations (a dinner for two at an upscale restaurant, gift certificates from expensive specialty stores like Tiffany's, plants and housewares) to be raffled as door prizes. As one white student remarked,

> The junior fashion show is I guess supposed to take away the cost of the prom. That's why we have the big junior class fashion show. The more money they raise the less the prom bids will be. I think they were more expensive last year, the prom bids.

Kids at Rudolph also depended upon the energies and material resources of their parents, mostly mothers, to help them raise the needed funds and organize the fund-raisers. The following fieldnote account of my initial impressions of the fashion show at Rudolph is suggestive of how deeply embedded these differences in social and economic resources are in the everyday operation of school and community life:

> As I walked into the high school building along with a group of others, I was immediately relieved I had decided not to wear my jeans and to stay in my slacks from work. Looking around at the others as we entered the building I noticed that I was not overdressed, as I thought I might be; almost everyone was dressed

nicely. I danced passed the opened doors giving a quick nod to the kids collecting $10 admission tickets; I was looking for the principal. The hall was overrun with students and adults, mostly women milling about, engaging in small talk. All were white. A large array of geraniums lined one wall. Other walls were encased by large tables draped in white table cloths piled high with gifts donated from local merchants. These gifts were to be given away as door prizes. Well-dressed women in conservative sweater sets and gray wool slacks, which I have always recognized as markers of upper-middle-class suburban life, stood behind the tables, busying themselves with last minute details. In that moment, it struck me that this event was not only an important student event but a community event as well. This was later confirmed for me during the intermission when well over two hundred people, ranging from the youngest, who looked to be about two years old to older gray-haired men and women, filed into the school cafeteria to enjoy desserts and pastries donated by the local bakeries and, of course, prepared by the students' mothers. (March 1997)

In addition to differences in parental involvement, there also seemed to be an observable difference in teachers' involvement in organizing the prom at the two schools. At Rudolph, a large number of teachers were active during the planning stages, while at Hudson, Mr. Stand appeared to be the only teacher involved in the prom's organization. These extended resources, which typically are available to the middle class only, both express and sustain social inequalities between schools.

The kids at Hudson were unable to access a local community of merchants or demand the sort of time from their parents that middle-class kids could. To raise funds, students at Hudson sold boxes of M&Ms at two dollars a box on the street and in school, an individual rather than collective strategy. Almost one case had to be sold, one girl told me, to raise enough money to pay for the eighty-six-dollar prom bid for each student at Hudson. Living in New York City, I had come to recognize that selling boxes of candy is a fund-raising practice distinctively used by groups with limited resources; I had bought several boxes of M&Ms from young kids, typically of color, to benefit community youth centers, local basketball camps, and church organizations. Students at Hudson were also responsible for raising enough money to cover the additional cost of the five chaperones required by the school to supervise the prom, a cost absorbed by the collective fund-raising activities at the other schools.[14] Because of Rudolph's successful fundraising, the significant financial safety net provided by the community, and the work of teachers and parents, the school was able to reduce the cost of the prom to eighty-two dollars per couple, less than half the cost of Hudson's prom. Stylone's prom is another story, however.

Stylone, another public school but with significantly better resources, held its prom in one of the city's oldest and most exclusive hotels, located within one of the largest concentrated areas of wealth. The main ballroom, where most of the prom took place, was an enormous room encased by a wraparound balcony. The room's decor included wall sconces, moldings, draperies, and window treatments that dated back to the 1920s and contributed to a feeling of opulence and elegance, all of which was underscored by the fresh flower arrangements and silver service on each table. The prom, lasting about five hours, included a cocktail hour and a five-course sit-down dinner which was followed by dancing. Over six hundred of the seven hundred seniors attending Stylone were in attendance. Theirs was arguably the most extravagant of proms.

To afford this gala event, Stylone sponsored a school performance produced, directed, and acted by the students. Despite their successful fund-raising efforts, the prom cost almost one hundred dollars per student. Stylone does not receive any federal support because it does not offer programs in special education or English as a second language, which means that it actually has less money available to sponsor events like proms than other schools within the school district. As a result, if students wish to go to the prom they must pay their own way. However, gathering the needed amount of money individually was not difficult for the larger group. For those classmates unable to afford the price of the expensive prom bid, the administration at Stylone was able to fully subsidize the cost, unlike at Hudson. The Stylone administration, aided by the parent-teacher association, maintained a discretionary fund so that "no student would be denied going to their prom because they were poor," the senior faculty advisor told me. Stylone would never be able to provide this financial support if the greater part of the student body could not afford the high-priced prom ticket.

If we recognize that proms, for better or worse, are a central part of a larger process of schooling, in which kids make sense of who they are and where they are, what then does it mean if some schools are unable to afford to organize and host a prom and must rely on individual student campaigns for money when others are able to easily host their prom while also reducing the significant costs for students? Limited resources at Hudson created an especially tenuous situation for the young women organizing the prom. The racial struggles at Hudson, identified earlier in this chapter, were complicated by these institutional constraints, and may also explain why so many kids refused to attend their prom. The situation there exemplifies the ongoing struggles schools with limited resources face, just as Rudolph and Stylone express the taken-for-granted privileges embedded within middle-class schools. What emerges here is an expression of the vast economic inequalities between schools, their students, and the communities in which they reside.

### *Struggles Beyond Hudson*

The events surrounding the organization of Hudson's prom do not exist in isolation. Rather, the relations formed around race and class identified at Hudson High School are expressions of a larger set of structural relations shaping the process of schooling today. Students of color are forced daily to mediate and negotiate their racialized identities within the context of broader institutional constraints. Consider the following prom narrative, written by an African-American student who attended a predominantly white, affluent private school. For her, as for Serena, race is a central factor structuring her relationship to school and the prom:

> My memories of my prom are not horrible but I wish I could do it over again at another school. I went to a predominantly white, afflu-ent private school. At my prom as well as through most of high school I felt very isolated from most of my classmates, as well as under great scrutiny by a great deal of the administration who did not know me personally. So even though the preparations for the prom were fun and wonderful I was excluded from the pre-prom and post-prom activi-ties because of financial and personal restrictions. In all honesty, I only went to my prom because I felt if I didn't go I would regret it years later.

For this girl, material constraints punctuated by the continued assault on her sense of racial self by school officials made her feel alienated at the prom.

For a number of students of color in this study, the prom was fundamen-tally about race. "Since my school was a predominately white high school, we felt that it was our duty to represent the 'black race,'" one African-American student wrote. The connection between the prom and race *and* class was especially apparent during an interview with a young African-American man, Sadah, who came from a poor inner-city community to attend Rudolph's prom with his African-American girlfriend, who was one of Rudolph's few students of color. A significant portion of Sadah's discus-sion centered on a comparison between his school's prom and Rudolph's. He spoke at length about the differences in music and dress, emotional investments in the prom, and the disparate realities that gave rise to these differences:

> When you go to a prom, well, at Rudolph you just go to the prom and you meet up at a place. You say hello and dance, have fun. When you go to, well, this is how it is at most black schools for their prom. It's just a big deal. They like to go up to the school, show off their cars. They get their Lexuses for the day or the Mercedes, their sixteen-seater limousines. That's what we had. You show off. I don't think they

[white kids] show off too much. They come with their sneakers on and their tuxedos. They get there. The first thing they do is kick off their shoes and start running around. From the first dance everybody's hair is falling out. They don't really care. They make their appearance and that's it.

Underlying Sadah's efforts to distinguish his school's prom from Rudolph's is his struggle to demonstrate a race/cultural identity independent of this white middle-class community.[15] His struggle stems from the taken-for-granted forms of racism and classism he and his girlfriend encountered at her prom. Sadah attempts to articulate a local identity that places him outside the nexus of social relations that organize life at Rudolph High School and in doing so affirms the social practices that organize his racial community.

Sadah also makes visible how white middle-class entitlement was partially responsible for the ambivalence that the Rudolph kids expressed toward the prom. Unlike his community of students, who define the prom as a meaningful space in which to articulate the pride and dignity of a racial self, for the white middle-class kids at Rudolph the prom lacks that kind of overt resonance. It is simply another occasion to dress up.

Race and class remain invisible to these white students. Yet, of course, race and class are relevant. This became particularly evident when I asked kids at Rudolph about the issue of diversity. Most kids talked about diversity in terms of divisions based on social grouping (popular kids, geeks, jocks, and burnouts) and made few references to any racial meaning.[16] In contrast, kids at Hudson and Woodrow recognized the term "diversity" as a code word for race. These kids were well versed in the discourse of multiculturalism.

The ability to evade race, to not see race as a fundamental feature of self-identity and day-to-day social relations stems directly from the discursive systems through which "whiteness" gains currency.[17] Ruth Frankenburg, in her book *White Women, Race Matters,* elaborates the meaning of whiteness in relation to self-understanding and social context, explaining, "Whiteness, as a set of normative cultural practices, is visible most clearly to those it definitely excludes and those to whom it does violence. Those who are securely housed within its borders usually do not examine it. The same is true of 'Americanness' in relation to those whom it marginalizes or excludes, and of the privileged class attitudes in relation to those who are not privileged. In addition, white American individuals are most able to name those parts of themselves and their daily practices that are least close to the center of power, least included in that which is normative."[18] For white students, to acknowledge race means to acknowledge a set of taken-for-granted privileges based on race. The privileges derived from living as a white person in contemporary U.S. society are so embedded within everyday life that they are almost impossible to identify by white students unless the issue is forced by students of color, as it was at Hudson.

This explains why when it comes to music few conflicts emerged at Rudolph. Little consideration was given to how race might differently influence students' music preferences; however, as two African-American students who attended the Rudolph prom, Sadah and his prom date Ondre, suggest:

> OL: The only thing is just going to a predominately white school, the music difference. But compared to last year's prom the music improved a lot. Like I'm not, I listen to a lot of R & B, like rap type of music, which is what you would call "black music." But it improved from last year to this year so, I enjoyed it. I had fun. I knew what to expect just from being at the prom last year and the dances, all the high school dances and stuff. So I'm basically used to it.
>
> AB: [addressing Sadah] How about for you, what did you think of the music?
>
> SD: The music, um, it was different from last year 'cause I went to her junior prom but, still it was. . . . They tried to be improved, but it was still phony because they started. . . . They knew they were gonna have people there that like different songs and music so they tried to play the rap and hip-hop but, the thing they was playing was, um, from when I was like six years old. They were playing the older music.
>
> AB: Oh, so it was dated?
>
> SD: So, they tried to just though, something like, you gotta like this and you gotta like that. Just playing it to play it. If they really wanted to. . . . They didn't really know what to. . . . They just wanted to make it seem a little better than what it was last year because. . . . An example, if you came to my prom, we wouldn't play rap music we would play like, club music or the club music we listen to like in your school they like that discotheque stuff, right? So they tried to throw in a little something for, I guess, the black students.

Sadah reads the attempt by Rudolph's prom committee to incorporate musical expressions located outside white culture as not only insincere, but as an expression of their very whiteness. When I asked him if anyone ever voiced concern for the race/music question, his response was "No," adding, "They never ask, either." His articulations seem to resonate with a larger struggle over music. In 1992, a group of black students protested their Georgia high school by organizing an alternative prom because the music they played each year was rock, which is typically coded as white kids' music.

The difficulties Katy and Serena faced in organizing the prom at Hudson and racial tensions articulated by Sadah are not entirely unlike what students at other integrated schools face as they struggle to claim a space for themselves within the context of a racialized school program. What happens when racially marginalized kids decide the prom should be as much theirs as it has been for white kids? The much publicized prom of Wedowee, Alabama in 1994, another site where struggles for racial justice were particularly intense, reminds us of the pervasiveness of such struggles. The trouble started during a school assembly when Hulond Humphries, the school's principal, threatened to cancel the prom if students continued to date across race lines. Outraged by Humphries's blatant expression of racism, students, parents, and community members took swift action. Students withdrew from the public high school to attend community organized freedom schools; a series of demonstrations and community marches followed. When the county school board reinstated the principal, thereby condoning his public condemnation of interracial dating among the schools' mixed-race student body, the National Association for the Advancement of Colored People (NAACP) and the Southern Christian Leadership Conference (SCLC), along with Alabama's black community, held a protest prom. Attended by twenty students and several community members, the protest prom became a political space, making visible the ongoing racial injustices embedded within the school.[19]

When I think about concrete strategies to make school sites racially just and integrated, I now think of the prom. I think of Katy and Serena and their struggles to claim the prom as theirs. I think of the difficulties they encountered in organizing the prom and how these difficulties ultimately led to their politicizing the space. I think of all those kids at Hudson who did not go to their prom, where they were and what they were doing while I, ironically enough, *was* at their prom. In our culture, in thinking of proms we often see them as peripheral to "real" school. An important dimension of school life, proms become sites at which students negotiate the meaningfulness of race, racial democracy, and economic inequality. The material in this chapter underscores the need, in envisioning a notion of a just school, to reconceptualize what counts as "school" to include spaces central to kids' understanding of school life.

# *Seven*

## *Breaking Rules*

### Contesting the Prom

> People resisting domination can only fight in the arenas open to
> them; they often find themselves forced to create images of
> themselves that interrupt, invert or at least answer the ways in
> which they are defined by those in power.
>
> —George Lipsitz, "We Know What Time It Is"

> As lame as school dances can be, there's always that one moment.
>
> —*Dawson's Creek*

The prom is a deeply conformist scene. Yet even though it is laden with
pomp and circumstance, it is still possible for kids to find ways to resist the
traditional trappings of the event. At its core, their resistance reflects a struggle for kids to make the prom a site both relevant to their lives and in agree-
ment with how they define themselves within youth cultures.[1]

What possibilities for resistance exist in this site? Some kids, like those at
Hudson High School, resist the prom by just not going. For the students at
Hudson, their not going becomes a way to disengage from school and from
the ideologies of whiteness that frame life in integrated schools. But what
about those students who do decide to go? Can students participate in the
prom and still resist it? What does resistance look like in this setting? To
what extent can expressions of resistance at the prom disrupt or alter its
organization and the social and material conditions it secures?

This chapter identifies two forms of resistance that emerge at the prom.
In the first portion of the chapter I explore the significance of cultural style
and the various ways kids use a politics of style at the prom to define this
event and their identities in this space. The second portion of this chapter
considers the recent emergence of "gay proms" and the ways in which queer
youth have challenged conventional readings of the high school prom as an
event that upholds and restores the hegemony of heterosexuality. More
broadly, this chapter considers the struggles of youth to construct their iden-

tities as contestational identities and the limitations and contradictions of these identity projects within this cultural scene.

### Setting the Scene: Reading Style

Dress is both a social practice and a system of signs ordered by a complex set of relations of domination that correspond to histories of class, age, race, and gender.[2] Bound to a system of class, dress styles reflect and uphold dominant ideas of what it means to be male and female.[3]

Looking at changing patterns in clothing styles at the prom sheds light on how these shifts in style parallel shifts in cultural ideology while also providing a contextual frame to understand the particular resistant expressions kids use in this setting. Take, for example, the light blue tuxedo and the frilled tuxedo shirt, favorites in the 1970s. These can be read as an indication of the emergence of a "softer" masculine form resulting from the arrival of the feminist movement and the salient critique of masculine domination that it provided.[4] The 1980s, a period fraught with a reactionary politics, brought the return of a more conservative and uniform male dress style reminiscent of the 1950s mode of middle-class male dress embodied in the gray

flannel suit.[5] During the 1980s, creative variations in male prom attire were confined to clothing accessories: the cummerbund and bow tie. Typically, boys wore black tuxedos with colored or patterned cummerbunds and bow ties. Though different combinations of cummerbunds and bow ties were common, usually the black tuxedo and white shirt remained intact. This "conservative" style reflects a more conservative political era and was secured in part by the reassertion of a more rigid and traditional masculinity—epitomized by then president Ronald Reagan.

In contrast to the 1980s, the 1990s is a period in the history of fashion marked by its incorporation of "difference" into the commercial retail market.[6] A significant number of today's young men opt not to wear the traditional black tuxedo. Instead, a range of styles, from white dinner jackets to vests or waistcoats, can be worn. Several boys wear the Mandarin- (or Asian-) styled tuxedo, which is identifiable by its collarless white shirt and the replacement of the traditional bow tie with a simple black button. A number of boys now wear brightly colored shirts (purple, orange, or pink) with their tuxedo jackets, in place of the conventional white shirt. Instead of the traditional single- or double-breasted lapelled tuxedo jacket, some boys wear boxy black jackets, substituting a large gold medallion for the black bow tie.[7] Such variations can be read as expressions of individuality or even rebellion, though it should also be noted that such expressions may be a consequence of the commercialization and exploitation of multiculturalism (masked by a commitment to individualism) and an indication of the fashion industry's commodification of and expansion into masculine dress.

### *Dress Codes and the Politics of Dress: Conformity and Resistance at the Prom*

Though embedded within the ongoing politics of school, the prom differs in radical ways from the everyday routine of school life. Today, high school proms are often held in  luxury hotels; if they are held in a school gym, the space is transformed to look nothing like the school gym. The organization of physical space, the decor, and music come together to create a narrative of fantasy and spectacle. This highly playful space, in which many of the rules governing school practices are loosened provides an occasion for kids to forge identities that distinguish them from who they are at school. While many kids enjoy the prom as an occasion to appear as well-dressed grownups, to reveal their class location, their skills at conspicuous consumption, or an astute knowledge of the intricacies of gendered refinement,[8] other kids actively seek to position themselves on the borders of this cultural scene through what they wear. Drawing upon the resources available in the commercial market of style and trend, kids craft their identities as cultural "resisters" and not "conformers."[9]

The institutional context in which proms come together shapes the sort of expressions kids offer through dress. The prom is a supervised space organized by a set of regulations around admittance, activities, and attire. Kids at the prom are expected to dress up in formal clothing, and they are familiar with these dress codes, codes that reflect cultural definitions about social function and the management of social spaces.[10] Definitions of appropriate dress, whether loosely or rigidly imposed, order our actions and determine how we relate to others within different social settings. These requirements of dress and decorum take shape within a discourse of social class and culture.[11]

During an interview with Erin, an African-American student at Woodrow, I inquired about how she knew what forms of dress were expected. She replied,

> Um, tradition, 'cause, you know, it's every year and you have to get a formal dress and a tuxedo. So, you know what's expected to wear, what you're expected to wear. That's what I think. It's just tradition. 'Cause you know it's always formal, you have to look really nice and conservative. You don't just come in, like, it's not a house party or nothing. It's a formal dinner. But you know you have to come in and look nice. You can't just come in anything you would regularly wear off the street.

Terms like *conservative*, *tradition*, and *formal* function as code words designating a specific set of behavioral rules defined by the middle and upper classes. By imposing a dress code of formality at the prom, schools socialize kids to a middle-class fashion aesthetic whose purpose is to regulate how kids act in addition to how they look.

For Samuel, an African-American student, the prom emerged as an occasion to gain in "class" status that seemed to be denied to him in his day-to-day school and street life as a city kid. He accomplished this feat by dressing up:

> Everybody was saying, "You look so different, you dressed up, you look nice like that." And I was, like, "Thank you." And I seen other people and I'm like, wow, dressing up makes a big difference. You, like, the people you see in school, you may think they look like hoodlums or like, you know, how they dress, or whatever, baggy pants and baggy shirt, but you know, when they dress up, they look sophisticated, they like job material and they just like, wow. It's just like a drastic change that makes people look good.

Yet kids do not uniformly embrace dominant styles nor the class logic to which they are attached because these rules limit how they may express themselves. The construction of the prom as a middle-class space leaves some students feeling excluded and out of place. As one girl explained,

> A lot of limousines showed up . . . I didn't have much fun. The place and the environment seemed to be reserved for high class. I don't really like the environment. The place was friendly but somehow I felt uncomfortable.

Some students interpreted the formal dress code as an example of the superficiality and pretentions schools imposed, as another attempt by their schools to make them into something they were not. Consider the following comments from Scott, a white male student from Woodrow:

> I'm thinking about not wearing a tuxedo, maybe, maybe just wearing a suit, some type of suit because, I don't like the way they [tuxedos] look. They look good on James Bond and the president, but, uh, well, maybe not *this* president, but ah, people of presidential and Hollywood type. They look good on them because, they're supposed to wear them. But you get some disproportionate kids with, you know, acne and bad hair and it doesn't work.

Erin, an African-American student, told me that at Woodrow's prom the previous year, a group of kids were sent home by the principal because they were dressed in shorts, sneakers, and T-shirts:

> I think it was kind of ridiculous because, you just don't come to the prom with everyone dressed up but you got sneakers on. You know, I didn't like that. That's what I have a problem with. But he [the principal] wouldn't let them in. He said it was inappropriate, so I think. I don't know if they deserved it because, they did pay already but, they knew what was expected so I think they kind of set themselves up for that.

The enforcement of rules by teachers, administrators, and sometimes other students shape kids' self-expressions. In this instance the students dressed down as a demonstration against the authority and control that schools exercise.

How kids fashion themselves, the styles they wear, are often used to respond, to reject, to "talk back" to dominant culture.[12] The metaphor of "talking back," which I borrow from bell hooks, is a particularly useful way to understand the meaning of style in this particular cultural setting.[13] "Talking back" locates these expressions within the play between power and opposition to power, recognizing both control and defiance. In reading these prom styles, I often felt as though students were talking back to school, to adults, to history, and to mainstream culture. Kids use style as a vehicle in which to locate themselves on the cultural fringe, and to challenge how they have been narrowly defined by those who control them—adults. They use style as a resource to express their individuality in a scene that is often conformist, trifling, and, most of all, "uncool." "I wore a cowboy suit to my prom. I knew everybody else was gonna have a Chinese tux. I had a cowboy hat and a guitar," one student offered. Fashioning identities that located them on the periphery of school, kids actively constructed themselves as "resisters." They went to the prom, but did not "buy into" the idea that it is an event to be taken seriously.

One white student from Woodrow wore an oversized seersucker suit, which I learned he had bought secondhand for two dollars and fifty cents. "It was the right price," he said. Throughout the evening he walked around the prom sucking helium from the balloons that covered the ceiling (and thus speaking in a squeaky voice). He carried in hand a clear plastic baggy full of carrots, which he offered to other promgoers, to me, and to chaperones. Explaining why he had chosen to wear what he had instead of a tuxedo, he offered, "Some people say like it's [the prom] some type of rite of passage. Into what? This is not what adult life is like, you don't wear tuxedos all the time and spend all kinds of money. It is just another event!" His rejection of how the prom is defined by age-specific codes is symbolized in what he wore. Through dress, he contests the very idea that the prom is an important coming of age rite; for him, it is "just another event."

Students wear a range of styles, many of which express an unwillingness to take the prom seriously, to accept how the prom has been defined by an adult ideology. At Hudson's prom, one white student wore goggles on his head and a floral print shirt beneath his cream-colored linen suit, a Latino student bleached his hair specifically for the prom, and a young white woman wore a canvas army camouflage full-length halter dress. (Over the dress, she wore a cream-colored, cropped, secondhand 1950s angora sweater with little pearl buttons and white fur trim on the collar and sleeves.) Such attire is an indication of not only how she defines the prom, but also how she relates to dominant constructions of gender. The little pearl buttons, the fur lining, and the soft fabric of the sweater are signifiers for an idealized femininity. The addition of army fatigues, typically associated with rugged masculine physicality, can be read as a subversion of the way feminine and masculine identities are inscribed within a gender binary.[14]

Through dress, some girls reject the idea that the prom is a place to solidify their feminine identities; they reject the prom as a feminine space. Some girls wear tuxedos instead of the expected prom dress, thus enabling them to locate themselves outside a feminine culture but firmly within a youth culture, one that is dominated by masculine symbols and codes.[15] One white girl from Rudolph styled her hair into a rather exaggerated "beehive" bun, a symbol of middle-class femininity embodied in images of the 1950s housewife. Instead of bobby pins, which are typically used to hold the beehive in place, she used little fabric bumble bees. The significance here is difficult to miss: the girl is using hair as a site in which to provide social commentary on women's roles in society. Her modern reinterpretation of the beehive can be read as a form of mimicry that parodies the feminine forms that have historically confined women.

The culture of youth is often defined by symbols that express ideas of newness and progress, in addition to a blatant disdain for history.[16] Wearing secondhand clothes or emulating popular styles from other historical moments provides a ground on which kids playfully mock previous generations of adolescents who now govern and regulate their lives. In so doing, these acts redefine the prom firmly within the cultures of today's youth.

At the proms I attended, some kids creatively worked between youth subcultural styles and the styles prescribed by adult culture to exaggerate and expose the tensions between the two. A number of boys wore traditional tuxedo jackets and pants in ways that expressed a more confrontational youth style. Several boys wore oversized jackets, with their tuxedo pants worn on their hips so that they were baggy in the back. This style, typically associated with the urban street style of hip-hop, presents itself as an alternative to the clean cut middle-class style expressed in clothes tailored to fit the body.[17] Although both white kids and kids of color, from both city and suburban schools, wore their tuxedos in this way, this style expresses different and in some measure contradictory meanings for the different groups. For boys of color, this style could be read as an articulation of their

racial identity and urban location. For white middle-class boys, resistance has a distinctly urban face. The emulation and appropriation of dress styles emerging from working-class youth communities and communities of color enables them to participate in an alternative youth subculture in ways that middle-class clothing styles prevent.

Some kids more actively resist adult supervision. At each prom invariably there were kids who wore sunglasses. While wearing sunglasses at night could be dismissed as a silly gesture of adolescent's preoccupation with coolness, I think the significance of sunglasses is more complicated. Teachers at the prom are responsible for monitoring kids and ensuring that they do not engage in illicit actions like the consumption of drugs and alcohol. Wearing sunglasses invites teachers' suspicion, as if prompting the question, "What has she got to hide?" But if wearing sunglasses could stir so much direct attention, why would a student wear sunglasses to the prom? I would suggest that it is not an attempt to conceal something illegitimate (glassy or bloodshot eyes), but is a symbolic act: an explicit gesture of defiance, laden with social meaning. Dick Hebdige sheds some light on the significance of such acts, saying, "The tension between dominate and subordinate groups can be found reflected in the surface of subculture, in the style made up of mundane objects which have double meaning. On the one hand, they warn the straight world in advance of sinister presence—the presence of difference and draw down upon themselves vague suspicions. . . . On the other hand for those who erect them in icons, who use them as words or as curses, these objects become signs of forbidden identity sources of value."[18]

To wear sunglasses to the prom, a school-sanctioned event, is a statement that one is implicitly refusing to be supervised, a dramatic statement that gains its meaning less from how adults respond than how other students interpret the action.

Dissension expressed through style, however, is not equally celebrated by all students. Often these confrontational stances are met with open hostility by kids who are invested in a more conventional prom. Consider the following discussion I had with one young woman from Woodrow:

ER:    Some people came last year with their jockey outfits, like the horse riders, like the knickerbockers pants up to the knee and they had on high socks. They want to be different. I mean they came in like the big ruffly shirt, like . . . you ever watch the movies where they had the men in the light blue tuxedos, the real ugly tuxedos?

AB:    Oh, from the seventies?

ER:    Yeah the ruffled shirts. They came in those. I mean it was just, um, everything. Then the girls had like, tie-dyed dresses on. It was real crazy.

AB:    What was the reaction to them?

ER:    Everyone couldn't believe it, I mean. A lot of people had, like, attitudes. They didn't like it cause they were like, "How are you gonna mess up your prom by wearing something like that to your prom?" You are supposed to look nice for them. I didn't have a problem with it, if that's how they want to be remembered, you know that's how they want to look. You have fun. You can't get mad at them because they probably saying the same thing about us. Why are we dressing so plain and conservative?

The more dramatic forms of dissension displayed through style undermined the way some students ultimately defined the prom within adult systems of meaning. Some of these students saw these "resister" students as "posers," imitating alternative styles that were not "authentically" alternative. Their comments and critiques point to the ongoing tensions and fissures between students who experience life on the margins and those at the center.

Not all alternative expressions were met with disapproval. The more tempered expressions were often received by adults with not only tolerance but outward approval, suggestive of the contradictions in constructing alternative styles at the prom. Increasingly, these gestures have been incorporated into the consumer market and adult strictures of acceptability.[19] In a cultural moment of rampant individualism, many adults accept these transgressions as creative assertions of individual identity. Wearing Doc Martens boots to the prom provides one such example. Doc Martens, once radical symbols of British working-class youths' cultural disengagement, are now part of a category of contained youthful experiments that are applauded by adults and exploited by the market. I watched two teachers praise two young men's choice to wear Doc Martens with their tuxedos. For shoes that were once in relative obscurity, the fact that these teachers knew that they were called Doc Martens is a cogent reminder that resistance always operates under the imminent threat of incorporation by the powers that be.

### Being Kids: Irony and "Adolescence"

The prom symbolizes one of the few spaces authorized by adults in which kids practice being adults, though in class-scripted ways. They are allowed to dress up, sit down for a formal dinner, and are able to interact with teachers on a more symmetrical social plane than they are typically permitted to at school.[20] A range of practices and symbols contribute to the sense that this is a more sophisticated and adult-like event, but the rules imposed remind students that there are limitations on how adult-like they may be.

The remembrance gifts given to students at the prom, usually an engraved wine glass or champagne glass, express schools' ideas about how kids should behave as adults. While alcohol's association with adulthood is significant, wine glasses and champagne glasses also carry rich social meaning about middle-class refinement, "polite" adult cultures of taste, and restrained consumption.[21] Consider the following comments from one white male student who is profoundly aware of the meaning the wine glass carries:

> The wine glass you got at the prom, you're so dignified. It's a wine glass. Wine is dignified, professionals drink it. You know, just a fancy, fancy business kind of thing. Ah, you know I'd like to get a mug out of it.

Alternatively, beer mugs—which are, rarely (if ever) given as gifts at the prom—convey a different meaning about consumption. Beer mugs are typically associated with working-class beer brawls and fraternity keg parties. The selection of the wine glass over the beer mug suggests that proms are structured to sustain particular social forms, while also socializing kids to a particular type of adulthood that corresponds to a class system of meaning.

While socializing kids to adulthood, proms are also thought to exist outside the serious (adult) world of responsibility, belonging instead to an apolitical space where insignificant and childish struggles over who is more popular take shape. As I discussed in chapter 4, students were profoundly aware of how the prom is defined as a frivolous and superficial activity. Both celebrated and subject to considerable contempt by adults, its location in culture is a precarious one. One student articulated this paradox succinctly, explaining that "people always look down on high schools and proms. They tend to think it's a very immature thing." For many students, the contradictory location of the prom produces a tension for them between being an adolescent, wanting to reject adolescence, and challenging the way culture defines adolescence as inferior. Consider one girl's comments, which reflect her struggle to make sense of the prom against the way it is typically constructed within adult discourses on adolescence:

> I don't know, I haven't put a lot of work into my dress and I don't have a limo. We're not going to go in a limo, we're going to probably go in a big van. We're getting a whole bunch of people together and half of us with a date and half of us, um . . . we're going to go out to dinner just because we want to show off our stuff not because it's the thing to do. We're just going to go around town and stop at various places and, "Look we're all dressed up" and it's going to be more of a fun thing than, "Wow, we're so cool, we're so mature."

Many kids playfully manipulated the conflicting definitions of being an adult and not being an adult by importing objects that contradicted the "adult sophistication" of the prom. One young man wearing a tuxedo blew large bubbles while chewing his bubble gum as he checked into the prom. At Stylone High School, many kids at the beginning of the evening carried around backpacks over both shoulders. (Having become such important symbols of youth subculture, backpacks have been prohibited from some schools.) At the Rudolph prom, I watched four girls walk to the bathroom hand in hand; beneath their dresses, they were adorned with brightly colored athletic socks. One young woman at the Woodrow prom gave her date a boutonniere made of two bright red radishes instead of the expected carnation or rose. These creative attempts to position youthful symbols or, in the instance of the radishes, lowbrow culture, beside the sophistication and "reserved elegance" of prom night expose the prom as a moment of irony. An excerpt from my fieldnotes at Rudolph's prom provides another example of this mocking playfulness many students embraced:

> It was about 11:15 and the sophistication and high glamour present at the beginning of the night had been replaced by a sort of playful childishness. At least half the kids by this time were wearing—either as necklaces, bracelets, or hair bands—glow sticks, the sort of sticks often found around every child's neck at Fourth of July fireworks

celebrations. The sit-down dinner was completed with a hot fudge sundae bar and most of the kids had taken off their shoes and the boys their tuxedo jackets. Many of the guys now wore baseball caps. The night was winding down. (May 1997)

Students use irony as a rhetorical tactic to disrupt, expose, and resist the adult meaning systems through which the prom is defined. They often use these rhetorical strategies because few other resources are available to them as resisters. Students' playful use of irony is highlighted, almost mockingly, in the picture below.

These four promgoers are outfitted in the standard prom regalia; all are wearing boutonnieres, and significantly, the girls are dressed in tuxedos. In the picture they are sitting in a Burger King, smoking, having just finished dinner. Traces of their dinner remain: an empty Whopper box, tattered ketchup packets, and paper cups with the Burger King logo. But they have brought with them a table cloth, a candle, place cards and a small vase of white daisies. They intentionally pair the opposing and contradictory symbols of the commercial marketplace and base culture (epitomized by Burger King and McDonald's) with symbols of middle-class refinement (a table cloth, fresh flowers). The act is especially meaningful because it is expected that, on the night of their prom, kids would prefer to dine at an elegant, upscale restaurant. Additionally significant is the class subtext shaping this calculated play of irony. These four kids, all of whom are middle-class, use the knowledge they have of their own class signifiers to reject the prom as an event organized by a middle-class logic of taste and style.

Students' resistance to the prom and the meaning through which it is defined is expressed not only through dress and how they fashion their bodies, but also through their use of other symbols, like cars. While many students rent limousines to transport themselves to and from the prom, other students reject the limos, because the limo carries meanings about class and "sophistication" that they find problematic. In an article in a student-run teen magazine, *HJ*, a student explains why she and her friends decided to drive her friend's father's station wagon to their prom, saying, "For my three comrades and me. . . . We're going in a two-tone woody, you know, one of those station wagons with fake wood panels? The kind of car parents love and kids hate to be caught dead in? . . . We decided we'd wash and wax the woody the morning before the big day . . ." Their plan was to drive the woody to the prom, "blaring disco from the radio, and attaching a surfboard to the top." Again, irony is used to disrupt the meaning of the prom. These kids appropriate a symbol not only associated with parenting, but with teen angst about self-image. The subversive value of this act depends upon the fact that being seen in a woody by friends would normally be considered embarrassing. The key point is to disrupt the idea that youth are image conscious and insecure about how they are perceived by their peers. Yet their plan was foiled; as the writer explains, "I was actually looking forward to the prom. But a group of saboteurs were out to get us. When news of our prom transportation got around people started thinking that was pretty cool . . . we heard someone else thought going in a woody was a great idea and they'd bring one too. We declared war."[22] If other students also drove to the prom in their parent's station wagon, the woody's subversive meaning would be lost. No one would know they came up with the idea first; they would be lost among a crowd of teen "conformists."

### Gay Proms: Resisting and Redefining Sexuality and Youth

In 1980, a gay student named Aaron Fricke sued his Rhode Island high school for the right to attend his prom with his boyfriend. In his 1981 autobiography, *Reflections of A Rock Lobster*, Fricke offers a painful tale about growing up gay in a white middle-class suburb, about suing his school and ultimately attending his prom with a male date. Fricke's narrative exemplifies the difficulty and hardship queer students encounter within an institution that not only actively promotes and naturalizes heterosexual practices but pathologizes being queer.

Most of Fricke's tale suggests that the prom is a site at which students' sexual identities and practices are closely disciplined; rarely are students able to come together at the prom in ways that transgress these boundaries. Yet as Fricke suggests, kids can come together in radical ways, even if only momentarily. Recounting an important memory of dancing at the prom, he writes, "'Let's Rock!!!' bellowed from the speaker and to my surprise when

I looked up Paul [his date] had disappeared. In his place was Bob Cote. I looked around: several other guys were dancing with each other, and girls were dancing with girls. Everybody was rockin' everybody was 'fruggin'. Who cared why? Maybe they were doing it to mock me and Paul, maybe they were doing it because they wanted to, maybe one was an excuse for another. . . . I didn't know and I didn't care. It was fun. Everyone was together. Eventually Bob and I drifted away. I danced with girls, I danced with guys, I danced with the entire group."[23] In most cases, however, gay, lesbian, bisexual, and transgendered kids who do go to their high school proms are forced to conceal their queer identities. The prom, like school, is rarely a welcoming space for queer students, most of whom are forced to remain on the fringe throughout much of high school.

High school proms exist within (and sustain) a normative order of heterosexuality, their very organization working to manage students' sexual relations and socializing them toward heterosexuality.[24] The crowning of the prom king and queen, the social and informal rules around dating, and the images of proms in films and texts often secure the exclusion of queer students from their proms.

However, while the prom is coded in dominant culture as a heterosexual space, in recent years proms have taken on special significance within queer youth communities. A number of GLBT (Gay, Lesbian, Bisexual, Transgendered) proms have sprung up in several cities—Los Angeles; Columbus, Ohio; Syracuse and Ithaca, New York; Miami; and New York City, among other places—so that queer kids may experience going to the prom *as* queer kids. A youth group in Northern California organized its first gay prom in 1995.[25]

I spoke with twenty-year-old Arnie, who attended the second annual Project Now gay prom in Miami with his boyfriend. When we first spoke, Arnie told me he had originally intended not to go to the gay prom because he did not want to go with anyone other than his boyfriend Tom, and that he and Tom had been having difficulty in their relationship. However, two weeks before the prom, Arnie asked Tom if he would go with him; Tom agreed, under certain conditions. "No sex" was one stipulation. "Tom didn't want to do any of the things that normally happen at the prom," Arnie told me. As with many straight kids, plans began with deciding what to wear to the prom. The gay prom, Arnie explained, is not as formal as school proms. "No one should feel obligated and decide not to go if they don't have a tux," Arnie said. By making the event less formal, this space became more accessible. Overcoming the range of barriers that keep people out is an important strategy because this prom, unlike the typical school prom, is a strategic site of political action. A central strategy of the early gay liberation movement and more recent queer political action (most notably ACT UP! and Queer Nation) has been making queer presence more visible in settings typically regarded as "straight."[26]

## The Second Annual
# Rainbow Prom

Did you miss your High School Prom?
Didn't Get Invited?
They refused to let you bring your
best Gal or Guy?

Well, then have we got an EVENT for you!
Grab your best Gal, Guy or Pal and come DANCE, FEAST and
just have a ball at the First Annual Alternative Prom.
Music    Hors D'Oeuvres    Finger Foods    Desserts    Cash Bar
**Saturday, June 3, 1995**
3:00 p.m. - 12:00 a.m.
The West Hill Country Club

Arnie and Tom finally decided on tuxedo tops and blue jeans. The night before they both tried on their outfits and decided to wear the tuxedo jackets with their shirts out. Tucked in, the shirts looked awkward and too formal. It reminded me of the lesbian couple in Virginia who wore lavender cummerbunds and bow ties with tuxedos to their high school's prom to remind their straight school of their presence as lesbians.[27] Arnie had ordered two boutonnieres, one for himself, the other for Tom, and the day of the prom was spent together getting ready and taking pictures.

A little nervous about what to expect during the night, Arnie told me, he and Tom were "edgy," but that the tension quickly dissipated once they got to the prom. The rules that Tom had laid down when he agreed to go, Arnie confided, "were thrown out the window. . . . Something was in the air," he added. While Arnie alluded to some sort of magical force, it is likely that he was responding to the fact that the prom was a safe and authenticating space in which to be queer. Amid an environment of mutual friends, Arnie and Tom were completely at ease.

When I asked Arnie to tell me about this prom's significance, he spoke with cogency. Queer kids, he argued, are often forced to exist in an adult social world to be "out":

It was nice to enjoy something that had to do with how old you are. It made me feel a part of society, part of it, part of everyone else, where I wasn't judged or evaluated. Being not normal was just not an issue because nothing got more normal. The word *normal* is not even a question. It was a fun environment. The chaperones were gay couples. There were guys and guys and girls and girls and weird outfits—well, not weird, but different, like drag queens. You would never see drag queens at a straight prom.

Arnie spoke in detail about the issues queer kids face when forced to participate in normative heterosexual practices, like those comprising daily school life. Jerry, another young gay man who attended the same prom, also addressed this issue, noting, "Few spaces are available for gay kids to be out of the closet." Schools and football fields, which are typically regarded as spaces for teenagers, are not readily open to queer kids. Instead, many queer kids go to dance clubs to be with other queer kids. Yet dance clubs, both Arnie and Jerry told me, are part of an "adult world." Kids, Arnie argued, "lack adult tools to deal with the environment." Propelled into a world of responsibility and adult-occupied social spaces like dance clubs, queer kids are often denied the chance to identify themselves as simply "kids."[28] GLBT proms provide kids an opportunity to reclaim aspects of their lives as youth that are denied them because they are *queer* youth, and to redefine the prom outside an organization of sexuality in which heterosexuality is dominant.

While different in many ways, the gay prom looks a lot like a high school prom. Similar kinds of cultural discourses are at work in this setting: the prom is again thought of as an important coming-of-age rite, and the scene is infused with romance. In this way, the gay prom reinscribes the prom's cultural significance. Many gay kids see attending the prom not as a political act but simply as a night to have fun. Writing about a student who was the first to attend his prom with his boyfriend in his central New York community, one journalist offered, "They left their matching 'freedom rings'— a rainbow of metal some gays wear around their necks to symbolize diversity among homosexuals—at home. They didn't go to the prom to make a political statement."[29] Whether intentionally politicized or not, making an event whose very history is tied to a project to secure heterosexuality open to queer youth is subversive. The gay prom is perhaps the most deliberate attempt to both politicize and resist this cultural scene.

In both playful ways and more conventionally, GLBT proms are politicized spaces. Obviously, there are significant differences between "prom queen" and "drag queen." The gay prom is an inversion of the straight prom, a cultural scene infused with playful parody and mockery. The GLBT prom is used as a forum for community education: HIV/AIDS skits are sometimes performed, and information is distributed. Gay proms, unlike straight proms, typically generate community tension. They are almost always protested by the Christian Coalition or other antiqueer organizations, and are usually attended by the press.

Gay proms also face the ever-present threat of heterosexual assimilation. To work against this, queer youth communities intentionally use symbols and meanings that belong specifically to a queer politics. The metaphor of the "closet" is a significant one in this space. In Miami, the fourth annual GLBT prom held by Project Yes was "Beyond the Closet and into the Sunflowers." For decor, oversized hangers and sunflowers hung from the ceiling. Gay proms, then, are like and unlike straight high school proms. Kids get dressed up, bring dates, promise to not drink, and are chaperoned by "trust" counselors. Yet instead of crowning a prom king and queen they have performances by drag queens, and catwalks on which the "biggest dyke" or the "cutest boy" parade. Camp, a style historically tied to the queer community, pervades in this space.[30]

Homophobia and heterosexual mandates make life for queer youth difficult, dangerous, and painful. Queer writer James T. Sears summarizes the issues queer youth face as they struggle to claim their sexual identities within a context of heterosexuality supremacy, where those youth who do not extol the virtues of white middle-class heterosexual life are forced to exist at the cultural, economic, and political margins. As Sears notes, "Few public schools or social agencies in the South provide support services for queer adolescents, and gay bars or social activities within the gay community are generally age-segregated. Thus, teens of the nineties, like those of generation past, must largely re-create communities of difference and construct sexual identities from cultural materials available to them."[31]

Queer proms exemplify a political strategy to take a cultural resource belonging to heterosexual society and use it to expose its tyranny, to challenge its hegemony. In so doing, queer proms capture the struggles of the disenfranchised to resist and subvert cultural practices that normalize and naturalize heterosexual romance.

### Reading Resistance

In this chapter, I have traced two forms of resistance that emerge at the prom. Both forms are tied centrally to the body, youth identity, and the politics of style. Cultural style is an expressive form symbolically deployed as a response to cultural hegemonies.[32] An expression of refusal, resistance, and transgression, cultural style enables students to display more confrontational stances toward the adult structures of control that have defined them and the prom in limited and patronizing ways. Theirs is a fight largely over social meanings. The meanings these kids create express a struggle to define themselves within this space in ways that do not undermine how they define themselves as part of youth culture.

The prom is a site in which kids engage in a range of cultural practices and struggle to make these practices relevant to their lives both inside and outside of school. Kids read cultural style within the space of the prom in a range of ways. This chapter has focused on the ways kids construct oppositional readings of this scene, and subsequently of themselves within it. Kids' use of style reflects an attempt to expose the prom as a moment of irony—adults may continue to define the prom as an important coming-of-age rite, but not all kids will. Both straight proms and queer proms are full of ironies; these ironies may be expressed not only in what straight kids wear to their proms, but in how queer youth communities have appropriated the prom to challenge heterosexuality as an institution.

This chapter also demonstrates that just as the gay prom serves to destabilize the heterosexual imperatives upheld through the prom it also works to restore this event as a culturally important one for youth. Similarly, kids' stylized acts of resistance and nonconformity at school proms maintain the idea that the prom is "a special night"—even if kids seek to undermine this very logic. The prom is a deeply conformist space, and clearly a number of youth conform to its edicts—even those who worked to disrupt them by generating alternate meanings of the scene. There is an ongoing tension here. Many kids seek to express their individuality through what they wear. The notion of individualism is not in the least subversive; to the contrary, it is firmly in keeping with mainstream cultural ideology. Kids' relationships to the prom are complicated; as they may both accept and reject this event. There is a clear sense that students cannot resist or reject the prom fully insofar as they still confer importance on this event. What is clear is that kids use proms as sites to fashion and display identities that undermine the discursive controls adults use to contain them.

The prom is fraught with political potential, where the hegemony of middle-class life can be contested, heterosexuality resisted, and adolescence redefined. But kids' direct challenges to these social forms seem to exist largely at the cultural periphery of this scene. Most students do not resist the prom, though they may negotiate many practices within this space. Queer youth may go to queer proms, but they have been largely unable to disrupt the heterosexual controls that continue to operate within straight proms. The structural limits kids come up against as they struggle to claim the space of the prom and define it on their own terms are powerful, though not seamless. Kids use the cultural resources immediately available to them—irony, parody, and mimicry—to work within these institutional and ideological constraints, not necessarily to disrupt them entirely but to make life within such constraints tolerable.

# Eight

# Conclusion

## Learning to Listen

In high school I attended three proms, the first with a boy I hardly knew. I had initial hopes that our affections might be ignited by our attending the prom, but romance never materialized between us. The second prom I attended with my high school boyfriend. The promise of romance accompanied us both to the prom. Yet as often happens with promgoers, we fought about everything: how many times we would dance together, to which songs, and how long we would stay. By the time my senior prom rolled around, romance and the other more conventional pleasures of the prom seemed remote. I even debated whether to go at all, but I went, again with the same boyfriend.

I remember my senior prom differently than the first two proms I attended. I don't remember spending countless hours looking for the perfect dress as I had for the first two; in the end I wore a dress I already had. While I still thought it important that I had a date for the prom (I don't remember anyone going alone), I remember refusing to sit for the professional photographs taken that night. I also remember not wanting to wear a corsage; in fact I was adamant that my boyfriend not get me one. I had become increasingly ambivalent about the prom, particularly its connections to the project of becoming feminine (though I certainly had not fully abandoned this project).

Not entirely unlike the kids whose accounts have been provided here, I felt the tensions around the prom, that it was not to be taken seriously, that it was silly and "uncool"; yet, I still wanted to go. These tensions have everything to do with how youth experience life as youth in contemporary American culture, as well as with our culture's unwillingness to take seriously the tensions and struggles that are specific to young people. Studying proms and their significance to these kids' lives has required that I take seriously the struggles youth engage in and the tensions they feel. More than that, studying proms has required that I recognize kids' struggle to articulate what the prom means to them as a struggle to fundamentally understand who they are and where they are, and the broader structural and discursive constraints that frame those understandings.

This study takes a cultural scene that at first glance appears to offer little promise for critical insight as a site at which to make broader connections about identity, the ongoing production of cultural life, and structural limits. Proms are ideal sites for exploring these complex connections. The discourses that frame proms not only tell us something about their cultural significance, but also about how those who have the power to define discourse (adults, in this case) will make it serve their own interests. Most often the prom is discursively constructed as a domain of the trivial. After viewing the many sites at which images of the prom are presented, it is clear that young people have little control over the production of these representations (though kids certainly struggle to make sense of them in relation to their own realities as they interpret them).

The findings of this study reveal a different picture of the prom and its attendants than the narratives provided through these media representations. I have argued that proms are key places at which kids make sense of school, where they forge a politics rooted in their experiences as "youth," where they contest forms of authority and control, and where they work through the difficult process of becoming men and women.

Kids' relationships to proms are as varied as the youth themselves. Gender, sexuality, race, and class are key social relations defining this space and kids' investment in it. These social forms differently influence the meanings kids construct in this setting and the resources they use to make sense of themselves as young people in American cultural life, as students in public schools, and as consumers and producers of culture. How kids organize themselves in relation to school or against it reflects their emerging understanding of themselves not simply as youth, but as middle-class youth, white youth, working-class youth, queer youth, racially marginalized youth, and gendered youth.

This project has been developed from a line of feminist inquiry that seeks to unmask local forms of domination by taking seriously the everyday struggles against it. In this sense, this study reflects a broader project to theorize the shifting ground in which power—which is always contradictory—is locally produced, and the diverse ways young people actively participate in both the production and disruption of that power.[1] In this way, this book is less about social control than it is about how youth negotiate that control.

Understanding the investments kids make in the prom means understanding the larger cultural and historical context in which these investments are shaped. Making visible the structural limits in this scene required that I use a methodology that would enable me to connect what kids had to say about the prom with broader social themes: authority and social control, the relations of state and market, schooling and race and class conflicts. I studied proms drawing upon a range of materials for analysis: participant observation, narrative analysis, in-depth interviewing, and the analysis of contemporary films and historical documents. I have drawn upon a rich body of cultural studies literature to understand the dynamics of this control and to identify the struggles against it. I have used the practice of "reading," whereby everyday life is treated as a text to be analyzed and deconstructed.[2] Every action and every utterance can be read as meaningful. I listened carefully to what students said, attentive to the codes and cues they offered that indicated they were talking about a larger set of social processes shaping how they had come to define the prom. Because these social forms are usually taken for granted, they were often difficult for students to articulate; nevertheless, they were always embedded within their talk. Combining the tools of an ethnographer with the theoretical perspectives of cultural studies I was able to inquire into the wider terrain through which the social meanings mediating proms are formed as I examined how these meanings are articulated, interpreted, and negotiated by kids within and around this setting.

This study contributes to a more concrete understanding of the processes through which "culture" is made, shared, and contested within a setting that youth may occupy, but are unable to wholly determine or define for themselves. The meanings kids create and the practices they privilege help to define the prom's continued cultural significance, yet these meanings do not exist in a vacuum; they are patterned by history and context. Proms exist along a murky line bordering "school" and "not school." While filled with youth symbols and meanings, proms are organized by (middle-class) adult ideologies that secure adult interests and express adult agendas. Because of their contradictory organization, proms are particularly useful sites at which to explore how power and domination are secured through cultural life, as well as the attempts by marginalized groups to manage, evade, and contest these forces.

## *Youth, Schooling, and Popular Culture*

Proms are multifaceted: they are part of school institutions, expressions of commercial interests, and repositories for the formation of youth cultures. Proms originated as a space of social management within schools. Enlisting youth to participate in a middle-class ritual like the prom, schools attempted to subordinate sexuality to romance, and the subcultural practices of youth to the cultural practices authorized by the middle-class adult world. Proms sustain the circulation of hegemonic cultural meanings and work to secure kids' consent in dominant social practices. Proms are institutionally linked to schools; their organization expresses the ideological and pedagogical commitments of modern schooling systems. They are embedded within the same set of economic and social conditions that structure school classrooms and curricula. On a very basic level, proms are a reflection of the enormous disparities that continue to exist within schools and the educational system.

In addition to being sites organized by the ideologies of school, proms are also part of a growing consumer market directed toward youth. They testify to the explosive force of consumerism in society today and highlight how youth have been shaped into a distinct consumer group. Like other leisure activities of youth, the prom has been "discovered" by the market as an untapped niche for capitalist expansion.[3] Those commodities considered necessary for a successful prom thirty, or even fifty, years ago have evolved in dramatic ways to include a wider range of commercial resources. Limousines, luxury hotels, expensive dresses, appointments at hair salons, and long weekend excursions are now an important part of the prom for many students.

As much as the prom's organization reflects the ideologies of school and the economic interests of the market, this is a negotiated space. Kids read the prom in varied ways. Some draw upon conventional narratives to make sense of this event, suggestive of their deep investments in the discursive and social forms that frame American culture. For many kids the prom is an essential coming-of-age ritual, an iconic event in American cultural life. Constructing the prom as an all-American teen rite embeds firmly in the schools' notions of what America and American adolescence are. While helping to define what counts as American schooling, events like the prom also operate as filters through which young people then understand their identities as students, citizens, and youth within a narrow range of possibilities. Yet, some kids read the prom in alternate ways; they reject the logic of coming of age. While not fully undermining the prom's importance to American culture (many of these students still go to the prom), their readings of this event force a space in which American cultural life can be problematized, debated, and, quite possibly, reworked.[4]

Kids have taken up the prom, often without the support of educators, as a space in which to enact social change. Gay kids have sued their schools for the right to attend the prom with same-sex dates. Kids of color have engaged in local struggles over multiculturalism and taken those issues most relevant to the prom as opportunies to counter the silencing of marginalized students' voices and to make visible the daily operation of whiteness. These events not only tell us that kids define the prom as a meaningful space, but more important, that kids exert agency in this space. They do not simply accept how the prom is packaged by the market, by school, or by adults; they define it in relation to their everyday realities and the meanings that arise from within *their* youth cultures.

Some students refuse the trappings of commodity culture and they evade, disrupt, and sometimes resist the ideologies and practices authorized by schools. Some kids don't go to the prom, in order to disengage from this scene. Many of those who do go find creative ways to demonstrate their opposition to the authority of school through the clothes they wear, the resources they import into this setting, and the meanings they make. Kids have made postprom events like weekends at the shore and unchaperoned hotel parties as significant as the prom dance itself, if not more so. Such acts should be read as attempts by kids to redefine for themselves what the prom is outside the perimeters of school.

Using cultural resources immediately available to them, kids have taken the prom as a site at which to counter schools' control over their lives and self-expressions. Irony is an important tool in this space. Through irony, kids create and articulate a series of meanings and images (often on their bodies) to "talk back" to a culture that has defined them through an adult lens—that has reduced them to something less than adults.

Proms get taken up by kids to address much larger issues that penetrate their school and social lives; cultural meanings about politics, school, and youth are waged and contested at the prom. The difficulty Katy and Serena encountered as they organized the prom at Hudson High captures how everyday racial struggles emerge around what might appear to be insignificant school decisions like selecting music for the prom. While focusing their discussion on music, Katy and Serena were responding to something much more fundamental about the social and racial organization of integrated schools in general. Connecting the struggles they articulated to a larger discussion about multicultural education and racially democratic schooling enables us to consider first, a range of factors that shape the school lives of students of color, and second, those issues *they* define as important to their overall school experience.

Highlighted in the recent emergence of the gay prom, proms are often sites at which young people work against social forms that oppress them. Responding to homophobia in schools, lesbian, gay, bisexual, and trangendered youth groups have organized gay proms to enable queer kids to experience the prom without fear of harassment or physical harm. Yet gay proms signify much more than this; proms have been taken up by gay kids as spaces to solidify their queer identities, to narrate queer history, and to contest heterosexuality as a taken-for-granted cultural practice. Although the prom is conventionally bound to normative ideas about heterosexuality and gender, the gay prom relocates the prom within a discourse of political disruption and in so doing challenges the prom as an event through which heterosexuality is normalized, naturalized, and institutionalized.

I have argued that proms are sites at which kids negotiate the terms of their schooling and struggle to make sense of their own location in history and in social life. We will fail as adults to understand the messages they offer if we are unable to recognize that the relations kids form, the symbols they use, and the resources they bring into this space are meaningful attempts to shape the everyday processes through which culture and identities are made.

## *Power, Pleasure, and the Prom*

While this study demonstrates that the relations of control and domination that organize proms are not seamless, I also want to make clear that the ideologies organizing this space are powerful. In chapters 3 and 4, I discussed the prom in connection with gender and heterosexual controls. I identified how the promise of romance and the promise of making a statement work to gain girls' consent to a set of gendered social relations that prevent their claims for equality.

Largely designated as a feminine space of spectacle and pageantry, the prom emerges as a place where girls announce themselves to their immediate social world, make a dramatic statement about who they are. The discourses of pleasure, beauty, and consumption I discussed in chapter 3 operate to secure girls' investments in both "body work" and "body talk" and in doing so sustain the social organization of gender as a critical force structuring girls' experiences in school. [5]

Yet dressing up also provides an occasion for these young women to express alternate identities to those they perform on a daily basis in school, and to respond to how their schools define adolescent femininity. Many girls challenge their schools' emphasis on modesty and propriety in both dress and sexual expression through what they wore. Ironically, while they may provide a different presentation of themselves as "adolescent" girls at the prom, they do so within the prevailing organization of gender and heterosexuality. As much as these girls work to challenge the codes of femininity patterning their lives, they also resecure them.

In addition to producing feminine subjects by harnessing girls' pleasure in a project of self-transformation that centers on the body, proms sustain

an organization of gender through the celebration of heterosexual romance. The promise of romance becomes a powerful ideological tool in winning young men's and young women's consent to the operation of gender. The ideology of romance reproduces the hegemony of heterosexuality as kids make sense of themselves as young men and women.

Because girls are central players in the production and organization of both the actual prom and the systems of meaning through which the prom comes into being, boys often express less of an investment. Many define the prom as a homosocial setting to assert their manhood, while few define the prom in connection with romance. While girls' investments in heterosexual romance (particularly because of its connection to their feminine identities) force many to forfeit their claims for equality in this space, boys' disinvestment enables them to perform their masculine identities. This gender division not only reinforces but legitimates the notion that these differences are fundamental to the process of becoming men and women.

As these chapters demonstrate, proms highlight the more general dilemmas about the continuing influence of dominant gender meanings on young men's and women's lives. They not only tell us something about the broader terrain in which femininity and masculinity become meaningful, but also about the pleasure that is needed to secure a normative organization of gender and heterosexuality. It seems especially important that we continue to theorize the role pleasure plays in securing dominant social forms and practices—particularly its service in stabilizing normative ideas about hetero-sexuality and gender.

I have resisted the idea that culture is created from above and works downward, focusing instead on how culture is created from below.[6] I have argued that culture is contradictory, demonstrating through an examination of proms that the sites in which culture is made are contested sites. The cre-ation of culture is an ongoing process of constructing meanings that reflect and structure our everyday lives.[7] People gain pleasure from their invest-ments in dominant discursive and material forms even as they feel con-strained by them.[8] The production and circulation of dominant culture depends upon the pleasure actors gain from their engagement with particu-lar meaning structures.[9] Power and pleasure are enmeshed. Understanding the tension between the pleasure individuals derive from participating in the processes of culture making on the one hand and their subordination by ide-ological and structural forms of domination on the other is key to under-standing why cultural actors continue to participate in practices that sustain their own subordination.[10]

## *Teaching Proms: Cultural Pedagogy and the Literacy of Change*

As a feminist sociologist concerned with social change I have spent a lot of time thinking about proms. Most people want to know whether I am for or against them; I have intentionally refrained from taking such a definitive position. Had I only examined the prom as a practice that secures the ideo-logical controls that maintain cultural and institutional dominance—had I not examined the struggles and negotiations that occur within this setting—I might have arrived at the "against" position. Had that happened, perhaps I would have been able to provide a clear set of recommendations as to how proms should be reenvisioned. What would it mean to no longer have proms? Should proms simply be changed so that fewer students will feel excluded? If they are changed, what will they look like? Would this change be the work of teachers, administrators, or school boards? What about the students who attend these proms; what role would they play? The recom-mendations I offer, as I conclude this chapter, do not include what might fall under the rubric of "institutional reform." (Chances are, students would be excluded from such decisions in the first place.)[11]

Most of the radical intervention work that takes place at the prom has been the work of students and probably will continue to be. I would argue that this *is* the work of kids. The work of teachers, cultural workers, and school administrators is to help carve out a space so that sites like the prom can be more readily politicized, so that more kids can more easily identify and fight against the ideologies of control that pervade this space and beyond.

While I have little hope that "prom reform" will successfully erode the hierarchies or cultural tensions that permeate the space of the prom, I do want to advocate for a pedagogy that would "center" proms (given that political struggles have increasingly shifted to a cultural terrain). Proms are ideal places for students to explore the connections among power, pleasure, and cultural life *as students*. Educators and cultural workers need to continue developing more critical pedagogical strategies that encourage young people to take up issues in their everyday lives to explore how ideological and material forms organize the institutions where youth reside.[12]

Undertaking this critical pedagogical work seems particularly important at this historical moment—the cultural climate in which youth are forced to live has become increasingly hostile to them. In the aftermath of the Columbine High School shooting, schools have become increasingly difficult places to be. And as kids occupy public space outside school they must navigate a mine field of control that is especially attenuated for working-class kids, urban kids, and kids of color. As they ride subways, board buses, hang out at shopping malls, or walk to school kids are confronted with a culture that does not like them, that has given up on them. In a context where conservative calls for a return to a moral education that stresses "character building" seems to be the most convenient answer to a set of structural problems with no simple answers, we face the risk of mistakenly naming the issues that directly impact youth and their immediate realities.[13]

Students also need to find new ways to articulate their social selves. This process must begin with a critical examination of how their own identities are socially and historically constructed and mediated.[14] An investigation of the prom could be used to help teachers and students explore the social organization of school, and to connect in more concrete ways commodity culture and globalization, power, and domination to the formation of student identities.[15] Additionally, a pedagogy of proms would enable teachers to use the local knowledge students have as the basis to examine the larger social patterns and processes that frame their lives.[16] Kids need to analyze their own pleasures and desires in different social forms, and to find a more critical framework in which to identify and think through those conflicts that pattern their understanding of school and cultural life and the relationship between the two.[17] Kids need also to be able to make connections between their immediate and local social experiences and larger patterns of economic, historical, and social change so that they can better understand the forces that shape who they are and where they are (particularly in connection to oppression and privilege).[18]

This means that educators, as they take up questions of multiculturalism, feminism, and politics, must look to and understand the ways kids themselves have taken up and made sense of these political forms in their own lives.[19] What are the key spaces in which kids address these issues? Clearly, the issue of music choices for the prom has broader implications for how we envision racially just schools. It is important that educators understand the meanings that spaces like the prom provide for kids, and to use those meanings as a way to map a pedagogy of liberation.

Educators need to take seriously the sites kids invest in, while they must also identify the underlying social and political forces that structure kids' investments in these sites. As Henry Giroux and Roger Simon argue, "By ignoring the cultural and social forms that are authorized by youth and simultaneously empower and disempower them, educators risk complicitly silencing and negating their students. This is unwittingly accomplished by refusing to recognize the importance of those sites and social practices outside of schools that actively shape students' experiences and through which students often define and construct their sense of identity, politics and culture."[20]

A principle task for schools should be to create a place where dissenting, marginalized, and historically silenced voices can be articulated, and at the same time to critically analyze larger patterns of global change and how these changes structure symbolic and material shifts in local settings.[21] We find ourselves living in an increasingly multicultural society, yet difference, and those people who signify difference, are repeatedly under attack. *How* we teach about difference, and the pedagogical strategies educators use, matter. Admittedly, our culture seems more willing to talk about issues of diversity and teachers are more likely to integrate multicultural themes into classroom curricula than they had been in the past, but there has been a general reluctance to address how these differences structure material life. All too often the meaning of difference has been depoliticized. What emerges is a portrait of celebrated individualism; gender, race, class, sexuality, nationality, power, and age lose their salience as key determinants of identity and experience.[22] In teaching about difference and multiculturalism, we need to recognize how the macrorelations of capitalism have harnessed difference to increase consumerism, and the paradoxical ways difference has been rhetorically used by the powerful to reassert economic domination.[23] bell hooks, in *Black Looks: Race and Representation,* speaks pointedly about the importance of examining the discourses and actual practices through which difference is constituted, noting, "Within current debates about race and difference, mass culture is the contemporary location that both publicly declares and perpetuates the idea that there is pleasure to be found in the acknowledgment and enjoyment of racial difference. The commodification has been so successful because it is offered as a new delight."[24] Taking a politics of difference seriously means developing a more complex understanding of how gender, social class, age, race, and sexuality shape school practices differently and unequally.

There is much we can learn by listening to the kids who participated in this study.[25] The struggles they raise address many questions relating to the subordination of youth; the dynamics of gender, race, sexuality, and social class; the workings of schools; and the formation of youth identity that deserve ongoing consideration. If we are unable to learn the lessons kids are offering us, it is likely our efforts to effect change in schools will be thwarted.

# Appendix A: Methods

## Beginnings

This study began as a project concerned with the self-organization of youth in settings connected to school. I began by collecting narratives from college students about their memories of their high school proms. The decision to collect written narratives stems from my interest in identifying those discursive codes used in everyday talk to distinguish among a range of social practices (such as choosing a prom dress or selecting music for the prom). In examining how narrative themes are patterned by race, class, gender, and sexual relations in high school, we can understand how meanings of these relations organize our memories.

Collecting written narratives allowed me to gain an understanding of students' experiences that cut across specific school settings. Students who wrote narratives came from rural, suburban, and urban public schools, as well as private and parochial schools. In their narratives, I looked for thematic continuities that told me something about school and youth culture in general and examined the differences in their narratives to understand how different social contexts pattern prom experiences.[1]

From these narratives, two central issues emerged: first, the prom provides an occasion for kids to talk about much larger issues that penetrate their school and social lives; and second, the term *prom* operates as a code word for students talking about other activities and spaces connected to the actual prom dance. Their narratives suggest that these other events are not ancillary to the dance, but are central to how the prom as a whole is defined and experienced. Without understanding the relevance of these other spaces to students' prom experiences or the connection between the prom and the larger issues they raise about schooling, I could not really understand the prom.

This rather simple observation led me to study proms by drawing upon a range of theoretical traditions, and a heterogeneous mix of research strategies and materials for analysis. I wanted to make sense of the prom, its place in culture and in the lives of high school students. To do so required that I study not only kids' perspectives on the prom but the complex relations that framed these perspectives.[2]

In analyzing these narratives, I relied on cultural markers to designate class relations and practices.[3] I looked closely at the different ways students used concepts like *taste*, a heavily coded class term. I also examined the different ways kids talked about their consumption, their educational histories, their schools' resources, and their family and community lives. This focus is most closely associated with cultural capital theories.[4]

While deeply concerned with the material conditions of *class*, this study places greater emphasis on unraveling its symbolic dimensions: how specific class practices gain cultural currency, the institutional expressions of class ideologies and symbols, and how kids relate to them in the context of preparing for and attending the prom.[5] I looked specifically at how class organized kids' talk and their social interactions, and how kids made use of particular class codes. I deliberately avoided relying simply on how students talked about the resources (e.g., money) they had available to them to determine their class location. Many students who are poor or working-class spend as much money on the prom as those from the middle- or upper-middle classes.

Students wrote with candor more frequently about particular gender, sexual, or class practices than they did about race. I was usually able to recognize the significance of race only when it was explicitly stated. Those narratives that did focus on race defined it in terms of the racial discrimination students of color encountered at school. The fact that a number of these students were white is arguably significant. Most whites take for granted the significance of their own race position and define their realities as though race were unimportant to who they are.[6] Yet the inability to get at race, to make whiteness visible, has as much to do with the limitations of research. Qualitative sociologists are just beginning to develop tools to draw out how race operates on a symbolic terrain, while tools for "excavating" the symbolic dimensions of gender and class as "everyday" phenomena are considerably more developed.[7]

### Prom Texts

In the written narratives I collected, students frequently drew upon cultural meanings outside their immediate setting to define their proms. The frequent statements made by students such as "The prom is a night not to be missed," or that it is "a night to remember" suggested to me that their local interpretations of the prom were shaped by particular codes operating within a representational field that cut across local sites.[8] These comments occasioned my investigation of cultural documents relating to the prom. I examined five different types of prom documents over a period of four years: girls' fashion/beauty magazines, local newspaper clippings, popular culture films and television shows representing high school proms, archival illustrations and photos dating back to 1930,[9] and several prom websites.

Television sitcoms and films in particular provided a useful avenue to understand how proms are constructed culturally. I was surprised by how frequently television commercials, news reports, situation comedies, and dramatic films referred to the prom. I recorded countless references. These texts enabled me to gain a sense of how proms are defined from adult ideological standpoints. Though there was considerable historical variation, these documents packaged proms in particular ways. The promise of romance was a dominant theme in these texts, most pronounced in girls' beauty/fashion magazines and popular prom films. An assumption of gender difference also organized these texts; it was simply taken for granted that boys and girls thought about their proms differently and occupied separate social spheres. One local newspaper provided "to do" lists for the day of the prom: one list for girls and another for boys. As a recurring theme, gender difference mediated how other themes, from conceptions of romance to dressing and dancing, were presented.

Though not the primary source of my data, these prom documents occupied my thoughts as I analyzed my data and wrote this book. These prom texts informed how I thought about and made use of the term *local*, how I distinguished between students' and adults' standpoints (most of these texts are constructed by adults, with the exception of a few of the prom websites), and how I understood the ongoing production of social meaning. These texts, though often dismissed by kids as we spoke, were fundamentally a part of the process of their constructing local meanings. Kids are profoundly aware that the cultural definitions of the prom created in these texts come from adult perspectives and not their own. The tone of many of these texts is patronizing, which many students resent. Many kids spoke about their prom in ways that tried to either undermine or counter the legitimacy of these texts. Sometimes they made fun of these texts by referring to them as jokes; other times they spoke bitterly about the portrayal of high school kids and high school life in these texts.

## The Interviews

In the spring of 1996 I began conducting in-depth interviews with high school students about their proms (appendix B). My aim in conducting interviews was twofold: first, to understand proms from the perspective of kids, and second, to examine how cultural struggles formed around competing definitions of authority, schooling, identity, and politics were embedded within their talk about the prom. I was interested in connecting those local struggles they addressed, such as decisions over music, dress codes, dating, and school rules, with larger ones.[10] I explored how conceptions of schooling, issues around multicultural education, and the schools' management of youth shaped students' sense of everyday life as they prepared for and attended the prom.

Whom I interviewed was guided by a concern for uncovering layers of meaning, and understanding how these heterogeneous meanings are created, shared, and contested. Students were selected with attention to their race, class, gender, and sexual biographies. Though I was less interested in drawing broad conclusions about high school kids, I was interested in understanding how students in different social groups thought about, experienced, and talked about their proms. My aim was to specify how race, class, gender, and sexuality worked together differently in the formation of student identities and how this shaped students' investments in their proms.

In 1997, I returned to the field to conduct more interviews. Like those conducted in 1996, these interviews lasted one to two hours and were conducted either at school or in students' homes, with the exception of one interview that was conducted at a McDonald's.[11] In total, I conducted twelve individual interviews and five group interviews. These individual interviews allowed for more in-depth inquiry into how individual students related to their prom, their school, and local social groups. Group interviews enabled me to observe how students constructed their sense of social selves through talk.[12] They often facilitated more relaxed discussions and required less direction from me as a researcher because students were able to build from and elaborate on each other's responses.[13] Their talk often opened up an entire field of extended relations and practices in school that shaped the prom. While I initially saw these directions as counterproductive and often struggled to bring students back to my line of inquiry, over time I began to see how their talk about school and social life provided me with a much larger context in which to interpret the prom and thus broadened my scope of analysis.[14]

The questions qualitative researchers ultimately want answered are never the questions we ask our respondents. Accordingly, in conducting the interviews, I avoided broad questions, like why they thought the prom was meaningful. I tried instead to uncover meanings from their talk about specific events and practices that emerged around the prom. I chose this interview strategy because of how I came to see the prom as a collection of relations, practices, and spaces, and because I wanted to move beyond a conventional discourse of the prom as "a rite of passage" that might deflect consideration of concrete and specific practices.[15] Choosing to focus on particular practices and actions enabled me to read for local, shifting, and contrary meanings generated around the prom.

I worked with a flexible interview style, focusing more on the nature of the kids' talk. I set the prom in the context of their ongoing lives; the questions I asked depended on the context.[16] I listened for subtle clues that indicated when students were talking about race or class, even if they did not name race or class explicitly.[17] During an interview with an African-American student who attended the prom at a predominately white middle-class school in the suburbs (but was a student at a lower-income, predominately black school in the "inner city"), I paid close attention to how he spoke about these schools differently. In this segment of the interview, he never explicitly connected his discussion about the schools with race (though he named race at other times during the interview), but from the subtle distinctions he made between his own school's prom and the other school's prom, it was clear he *was* talking about race.[18]

Sometimes students had difficulty even talking about the prom in the first place. This was immediately apparent during an interview with a young bisexual woman who planned to attend her prom with another woman. She answered my questions with *yes* or *no* responses with greater frequency than any other student I interviewed (certain death for a qualitative sociologist); mostly her comments sounded more like platitudes than thought-out responses. It became clear to me that talk about the prom is embedded within particular assumptions about heterosexuality and gender that made it exceedingly difficult for her, as a bisexual, to find a space to speak about the prom. Many of the questions I asked assumed particular investments in dominant gender constructions. When I asked her to describe her dress, she told me its color. These questions did not pique her interest or elicit more in-depth dialogue, as they had for the other young women interviewed. Midway through the interview I changed my research trajectory; I asked her to speak to her experiences as a bisexual student. This opened up the interview, allowing us to move in more creative directions, but silences persisted.[19] The interview was plagued by the silences that heterosexual schooling enforces and that I may have even inadvertently reinforced with my questions.[20]

Race, age, and class structured interviews in countless ways. Students deployed language in ways that constructed and sustained my identity as an outsider and a white middle-class woman. This was apparent during an interview with two young women of color from Hudson. Throughout the interview, these girls translated for me certain words like *down*, *dope*, and *bomb*, assuming I did not understand. Consider the following translation provided by one of the girls:

> We shout them out [she pauses and begins her translation] . . . like, show their true colors.

I saw these acts of translation as a way to solidify their racial and age identities and my own. Ironically, little translation was needed. Like these girls, I am a reader of popular culture, and these idioms, although originating from urban street culture, are in wide circulation. They have been taken up and appropriated as signifiers of youth (sub)culture within dominant culture.[21]

As an adult interested in studying youth cultures and kids' lives in school I continually felt the burden of my age, my identity as a researcher, and my affiliations with a university. In the context of studying kids' lives and often befriending them, this identity sometimes became a source of conflict. I often felt the tug of my social identity. Not wanting to conceal it and often unable to, I struggled to find a place within the social organization of school culture as an outsider.[22]

### Observations in Prom-Related Settings

To broaden my understanding of how proms work, I observed several prom-related settings: one girl's bedroom, where a small group of white middle-class girls prepared for their prom; a hair salon where many girls from one school had their hair done for the prom; a prom fashion show sponsored by *Seventeen* magazine at an upscale department store in an affluent, predominantly white community in New Jersey; a school-sponsored fashion show in a white, middle-class community (Rudolph); and a school-organized postprom party at a midsized city school (Woodrow).

In the spring of 1996, I observed a group of five girls from Woodrow High School getting ready for their prom. I listened to them talk about other proms they had attended, and their expectations for this prom. These girls spoke with ease and a frank openness about boys and girls, cutting school, sex, and clothing styles that seemed to be determined by the context—they were talking within the privacy of a girl's bedroom.[23] On one level, they spoke as though they had forgotten I was observing them, yet on another, I was aware that they were deliberately attempting to impress upon me a particular understanding of them as students and as young women.[24]

In March of 1997, I observed a fashion show sponsored by *Seventeen* magazine held in an upscale department store. During my observation of the actual fashion show, I listened to how the show's emcee (a young woman brought in from the New York City corporate offices) represented the prom clothes featured in the show. I was also interested in examining how girls sitting in the audience talked about the featured clothes, the models wearing them, and the music. I listened to ongoing conversations among girls sitting around me, many of whom sat with their mothers. After the show ended, I walked around the teen section of the store as girls browsed through the dresses on clothing racks, many of which had been worn by the models. I trailed behind small groups of girls as they walked around the store, many of whom I later approached to ask their opinions on the dresses worn by the models, the fashion show, and what they thought they might wear to their prom. I visited several more department stores after this initial visit.

Two weeks later, I observed a fashion show at Rudolph High School, a predominantly white, upper-middle class school. This fashion show was held in the school's auditorium two months before the actual prom dance and was strikingly different from the show sponsored by *Seventeen* magazine in a number of ways. The glitz and glamour that pervaded the other show was scaled down significantly. The music was more tempered, the outfits less outrageous and the models less made up and more fully clothed.

The auditorium was packed with students, parents, and teachers producing a sense of excitement comparable to that of the other show. During my observation, I paid particular attention to how the student emcees talked about the prom and how they described the dresses and tuxedos. I observed how the students in the fashion show walked on stage and recorded the responses they received from those students seated in the audience. I also talked with students, parents, and teachers before the show began and during its intermission. Studying this setting pushed me to question how other schools raised money for the prom, how activities like this one connected kids' school experiences to commodity culture, and how these types of preliminary events figured into the ongoing development of the prom's importance in schools.

I also observed Woodrow's postprom party. It was held at a recreation building a few miles from the site of the actual prom dance, and lasted into the morning hours. I spent a considerable amount of time talking to the kids about the prom they had just attended. I inquired about their thoughts on this postprom party and their plans for the rest of the weekend. I also talked with some parents working as chaperones about the origins of this postprom party and how it was sustained from year to year.

Observing these settings allowed me to explore aspects of the prom I would never have been able to understand by simply attending the dance. I visited hair salons, floral shops, and tuxedo rental stores, observing and talking with countless people. Observing in department stores and a girl's bedroom brought into clearer view the work girls do to prepare for the prom, and enabled me to gain an understanding of how their work is ordered by the social organization of these spaces.

While in these sites, I conducted informal interviews with a number of kids, teachers, parents, and retail workers. These were considerably less structured than the in-depth interviews. Originally, I had been reluctant to include these informal discussions as part of my research strategy because they did not fit neatly into the categories of conventional research practice. I had no interview format—we just talked—nor did these discussions always occur during the times I had officially designated as "research times." On one occasion, I found myself engaged in a long conversation with a sales woman in a department store about her daughter's prom. The story she told me was significant and I included it in my analysis. I often found myself collecting data in the most unexpected of places. Many of these conversations I wrote up in my fieldnotes; others contributed to my overall understanding of the prom.

As my investigation deepened, the tidiness I had managed to maintain in the early stages of my research began to disappear. I came to associate my research design with a model of research Deborah Gordon refers to as the "whatever it takes" model. This methodological approach, increasingly utilized in feminist and cultural studies, provides an expanded lens with which to explore how the personal realities of those studied are organized by a highly complicated set of structural, temporal, and contextual factors.[25] As this study evolved, I uncovered a rich layering of meanings that previously had not been visible to me. Yet, I continued to struggle against the logic of standard empirical research procedure. I wanted to include these conversations as an important part of my research because there was a level of depth to this data that could not be overlooked.[26]

As a feminist sociologist rooted in a tradition of cultural studies, I am deeply concerned with the production of culture and cultural meanings as they emerge within the most basic everyday relations—those that are spontaneous and less scripted (which sometimes taped interviews can be). I resolved to include these informal interviews in my research design not as supplementary material, but as a central aspect of the research project. These conversations enabled me to analyze the role of peripheral players in the production of the prom and address key issues that emerged from my interview data with a broader base of students.

### Observing the Proms

In the beginning of my research, my emphasis centered on kids' talk. I was concerned with examining how kids' local accounts were ordered by cultural discourses on gender, race, and class, and how these discourses mediate the ways they talked about different aspects of the prom. I was also concerned with finding patterns in their talk that told me something about becoming masculine and feminine, the ways this process was refracted by race, class, age, and sexuality as they understood and talked about the prom.

As this study progressed, I began to focus more on the actual organization of social space.[27] I wanted to understand the lineaments of social space, the concrete social relations that gave these different spaces meaning, and how particular practices gave rise to expressions of identity. As a result my attention shifted from the kids and what they could tell me about their identities to their (inter)actions. I saw these kids' identities in production and I wanted to document the particular practices and interactions through which they displayed a sense of their social selves.

In the spring of 1997, after I had observed Woodrow's prom in 1996, I observed three more schools. By this time I had developed a much deeper interest in observing those specific practices that frame kids' understanding of the prom—such as dancing—and decided to concentrate more on observations of these practices. Observing these three proms, I made mental notes about the dance floor, when kids danced, and how they danced. I committed to memory the organization of the spaces around the dance floor. I took notes on the spatial ordering of kids and teachers, when they came together and those times when they were apart.

My observations differed slightly at each school I studied as my inquiry continued to develop and shift during the different stages of data collection. In the early stages of my project, I had little regard for how high school proms exist within the social organization of schools. During my field research at Woodrow, I barely noticed how the institutional context of schooling organized the planning of the prom or the actual event and I rarely mentioned the term *school* in my fieldnotes. Concerned largely with the social processes that (re)produce kids' sense of raced, classed, and gendered selves, I rarely related to these kids as "students." Reading back through those first group of interviews, several months later, I was struck by the rich narratives many of the kids provided about their lives in schools, despite the fact that I rarely asked students to talk about them. While I may have located the high school prom outside the context of schooling during my initial work, the kids who shared their stories about their prom never did. For many of them, their prom was a fundamental part of their school experience; how they experienced their lives in school profoundly shaped the way they thought of their prom. Schooling emerged as a dominant theme directing my research when I returned to the field in 1997 to study the prom at three additional schools.

The three key sites of observation at the prom were the girls' bathroom, the front entryway, and the ballroom. I moved between these places frequently, sometimes just sitting and observing, other times initiating conversation. I spent time observing in the girls' bathroom because this was a space where a lot of girls congregated. I wanted to compare how they demonstrated their feminine identities in this private/public setting with how they acted and interacted on the dance floor and in larger groups of both sexes. The girl's bathroom also functioned as a space for note jotting (unless it was too crowded). In these instances, I sought more private places to jot notes and sometimes ran into young couples stealing a moment of privacy. Often these accidental run-ins would lead to conversations about the prom. Gaining distance from the actual ballroom, kids were more likely to reflect upon the event. Some kids, whom I had interviewed previously, approached me to expand upon a statement they had made earlier. These students acted as my main informants, providing me with background information about different social groups and teachers.

## Going Back to High School

Observing school settings often evoked memories of being a student in high school. I sometimes felt intimidated by school administrators, as if I were still a high school student rather than an adult researcher, and often felt that my continued presence was contingent on how well I "behaved." Sometimes this fear consumed me in ways that hurt my research. At Stylone's prom, I was not allowed to initiate conversations with the kids about the prom because of the arrangement made with the school administration. Every time I tried to talk to a student, I felt distracted by the possibility of getting caught. Like the students, I shared the feeling of being under the gaze of authority.

As a student, I had always deliberately evaded school administrators. As a researcher, I often found myself furtively wanting to undermine their authority. At Rudolph's prom, I "bummed" a cigarette from a student and smoked with him and his friends outside.[28] At Hudson, a young woman borrowed a cigarette from me and sat and talked with me while she smoked. On two occasions, I asked if I could sit down and join a group of smokers. I treasured the opportunity to connect with these kids, allying myself with them against the school by participating in this taboo activity. Smoking with them enabled me to develop a rapport that minimized my identity as an adult and a researcher. Sharing this space with kids also invited several inquiries as to my purpose in being there; most had assumed I was a chaperone.[29]

Yet sometimes I felt a little guilty participating in activities I knew school administrators would not condone. I had entered these settings through school administrators, and in some ways was indebted to them. Some administrators, like the principal at Rudolph, expressed genuine interest in my topic and wanted to support my research. New to the school, he had been treated as an outsider by the students, many of whom opposed the changes he had implemented. Additionally, he had been treated as an outsider by other administrators and teachers. He expressed to me a concern with the way teachers treated the students at his school that produced for me a sense of understanding for him. Mr. Stand, a teacher from Hudson, was another who supported my line of inquiry. I had watched him interact with students and it was evident that many of the students respected him and that he respected them.[30] I had repeatedly seen flocks of students gather around him. He often facilitated an easy rapport with students by introducing them to me. School administrators had allowed me to come to their school and often treated me like a member of their group.

Nevertheless, I actively avoided conversations with administrators and teachers at the proms (with the exception of Stylone); I wanted to minimize my associations with them to avoid being excluded from kids' social groups.

## Identity Work and the Politics of Research

Through these interactions with kids and adults I saw my identity in construction. My authority as a researcher and an adult in the eyes of kids sometimes worked counter to my research aims. During Rudolph's prom, I approached a girl to ask if we could set up an interview; I thought I had overheard her say to her friends that she was leaving and I wanted to interview her. Afraid I would lose the chance to talk with her later I rushed up to her, asking if she was leaving. Incensed by my abruptness, she told me she was not leaving. I felt like a spy and an intruder. Barrie Thorne, in her research on the production of gender meaning and elementary schooling, expressed a similar dilemma that emerged from her contradictory stance as researcher and adult, saying, "Schools are physically set up to maximize the surveillance of students, with few private spaces and a staff who continually watch with eyes that mix benign pedagogical goals, occasional affection and the wish to control. Kids sometimes resist this surveillance and I wanted to observe and document their more autonomous collective moments. But in the very act of documenting their autonomy, I undermined it, for my gaze remained, at its core and in its ultimate knowing purpose, that of a more powerful adult."[31] Like Thorne, I often felt like I was undermining their attempts to resist control when I tried to participate in their conversations or enter spaces where few adults were present (like the veranda outside at the Rudolph prom). Sometimes kids' responses were guarded: from their perspective, I was an adult. Consider the following comments in my field-notes:

> I was getting bored watching the kids dance and decided to go outside. I hadn't been outside all night and was a little nervous about going out into this space. I felt like I was invading a space for kids. There were no chaperones out there, only the two cops guarding the exit from the terrace. I walked outside and there must have been about thirty kids outside, mostly smoking. Many of the girls were wearing their dates' jackets, probably because it was cold. I walked over to a group of kids, mostly boys, and asked if one of them would give me a cigarette. I was given a cigarette and I asked how they were enjoying the prom. Most gave the blanket response, "Fine." A girl asked me if I was a chaperone and I said no that I study proms. A guy asked me if I get paid to do this and I said, "I hope one day." They seemed to think it was pretty neat and talked with me a little. I asked what they were doing after the prom and they said going down the shore for four days. I asked what they were going to do. My question was met with silence by some and laughter by others. I interpreted that as a cue; they were not going to tell me any specifics because I was an adult. They did talk about their sharing rooms. This was a conversation I observed but was not invited as a participant. I thought it was interesting because the kids from the city school were so much more open about their alcohol consumption, while these kids deliberately tried to hide it. It was not said, just understood. (May 1997)

The kids at Hudson and Woodrow (both racially integrated schools) generally seemed more willing to talk with me than the students at the other two schools. I spent considerable time in the bathroom with a group of young women at Hudson talking with them about their dresses and the time they spent getting ready. One young woman asked me to help her replace a hair comb that had fallen out of her hair before she returned to the dance floor. I found that when I offered this kind of help or when I shared some of my memories from my own prom, the girls were more willing to talk openly (they often asked if I had attended my high school prom). (In this instance, acting as a dispassionate researcher seemed to work against my research aims. This provided an interesting example of how graduate students internalize particular rules of the trade; I had been immersed in feminist research questions for sometime, had read several feminist texts that offered compelling critiques of the detached researcher, yet despite this, how I constructed my research persona was in some measure still dictated by the need to be objective.[32])

I had also developed a similar rapport with the girls from Woodrow that I observed in the one girl's bedroom. The fact that I was an older woman (but young enough that they felt they could relate to me), one who could offer suggestions about getting ready, seemed to facilitate an easy entry into the space of their talk. One of the girls and a friend who was helping her seemed to be having difficulty with styling her hair. They debated for a few minutes whether or not to re-wet it and just start over, but they were running out of time: their dates would be arriving soon. I decided to make a suggestion about how they could fix her hair without starting again, which, to my surprise, they welcomed. I had been hesitant because I feared my interference might "spoil" my findings. From that moment, I was on a completely different footing with the group. They offered me some of the food they were eating, and one girl asked if I would help her do her nails. My status as a woman worked to my advantage. They perceived me as someone who had knowledge of feminine/beauty work that might help them. But as a feminist I felt conflicted. By helping them to achieve a particular feminine ideal through beauty work, I was reinscribing the idea that a girl's appearance matters, which is an idea that I have always resisted.[33] Yet on the other hand, how they looked on prom night *did* matter to them; this was their prom, they wanted to achieve an idealized image of feminine beauty, and I wanted to respect their decision to do so.

While these kids constructed an identity for me, I had also constructed them in particular ways. I saw these kids largely through a maternal lens and this patterned and limited how I spoke to them. For example, while I was in the girl's bedroom it would have never occurred to me to ask them for advice on my appearance, though I was willing to offer advice. I wanted to learn about their local setting and their lives, but largely as a researcher. I was very conscious of my age and theirs. While the rapport I developed with the students was comfortable and open, I never related to them in a way I might with a person in my age group; I related to them in a way a teacher might relate to her student or a therapist to her client. I was patient and helpful, sometimes consoling; while I was a good listener, I very rarely related to them as intellectual equals. At Stylone, a student I knew invited me over to his table to talk with a group of his friends while they ate dinner. I told them I was studying the prom, and they launched into a series of questions I was largely unprepared to answer. Most of their questions were analytical and specific. They wanted to know exactly what my line of inquiry was and why I had decided to study the prom. They seemed unimpressed with my more rehearsed responses. Because I had not anticipated such in-depth, conceptually driven, and sophisticated questions from them, I was poorly prepared to intellectualize the prom with these kids. Again I was forced to deal with my being an adult researcher, and to question its limitations.

Though I feel confident in the data I collected, in how I conducted this work, I also continue to feel an uneasiness, as do many adults who study kids, about doing this kind of research. This uneasiness sometimes made me feel unsure about the analysis I was developing. I had authorized myself to speak for kids and felt conflicted about doing so. The ongoing tension I felt and continue to feel even as I write led to my returning to the field in 1999 to seek out kids, not to collect more data, but to share with them how I was thinking about this work, about proms, about their lives in school. I routinely shared parts of my analysis with the students I taught, asking them for their feedback. I am indebted for their comments, their affirming nods of "uh-huh" and their assurances that I was on the "right track."

## *Conclusion*

My aim in this study has been to specify how proms work in different social contexts, considering the complex set of practices, activities, spaces, and events that give proms meaning. Combining ethnography and textual analysis provided a level of depth to my analysis that would have been difficult to achieve through a single method of inquiry. Narrative analysis enabled me to generate many of my research questions and provided a conceptual base from which I could pursue these questions using other research strategies. In-depth interviewing allowed me to better understand students' perspectives on the prom and to explore what the prom meant to those students, while document analysis provided a ground on which I could examine how proms gain currency through a wider cultural terrain. I studied a range of settings peripheral to the actual prom dance through observation and informal talk to understand how these related sites support and make meaningful the actual prom.

Looking at a range of settings and sites enabled me to create a rich, multilayered conceptual field to do interpretive analysis.[34] Not bound to a single method, I felt free to address a range of questions in detail, many of which may have remained unanswered had I selected one method of research. Utilizing several research strategies provided an opportunity to theorize the complex intersections of identity formation and larger structures of constraint by bringing into closer view the taken-for-granted forces that mediate growing up today, and the complex connections among youth culture, commodity culture, and schooling. I was also able to examine the intricate processes of becoming masculine and feminine and the ways in which these processes are mediated by school practices and ideologies, as well as how those sexual, class, and racial tensions that are so central to understanding contemporary American educational institutions play themselves out at the prom. From interviews, scores of informal conversations, observations, and narrative analysis I am left with a complicated picture of the prom—not only what it is and what it means to students, but its centrality to how kids define school, participate in cultural life, and make sense of who and where they are.

# Appendix B: Interviews

*Woodrow High School (9)*
(3) European-American middle-class female students
(1) African-American working-class male student
(1) European-American middle-class male student
(1) European-American/Malaysian middle-class male student
(1) African-American middle-class female student
(1) African-American working-class female student
(1) European-American/African-American middle-class, bisexual female student

*Stylone High School (1)*
(1) European-American upper-middle-class male student

*Rudolph High School (6)*
(1) European-American upper-middle-class male student
(1) European-American upper-middle-class male student
(1) European-American upper-middle-class female student
(1) European-American middle-class female student
(1) African-American middle-class female student
(1) African-American working-class male student (attending a predominately black city school)

*Hudson High School (3)*
(1) African-American working-class male student
(1) African-American working-class female student
(1) Latina working-class female student

*Gay Students who attended Gay Prom (2)*
(1) Latino gay male student
(1) European-American gay male student

*Gay Student who attended High School Prom (1)*
(1) African-American middle-class gay male student

# Appendix C: Written Narratives

Seventy-three narratives were collected from three sociology courses: one lower division sociology course comprised entirely of first-year students and two upper-division sociology courses, in which few first-year students were enrolled.* Narratives were between one-half page and one and one-half pages in length. These narratives were collected in two stages: forty-five narratives were collected during 1995, and twenty-eight in 1996.

*Female students* (58)

European-American (42)
African-American (9)
Asian-American (5)
Latina(2)

*Male students* (15)

Asian-American (2)
Latino (1)
African-American (2)
European-American (10)

*The narratives written by students from the lower-division course were significantly longer and more detailed than those written by students in the upper-division course, which may suggest shifts in the prom's importance and the meanings students derive from attending as students become adults. For first-year students who attended their senior prom less than six months earlier and may have been still struggling with the transition from high school to college, the prom appeared to have a more significant place in their memory and their lives. In contrast, for students attending college for at least two or three years, the prom seemed a distant memory. This demonstrates that while proms may be of little consequence for adults who are removed from high school life, for young adults whose lives are largely defined by the practices and politics of high school culture the prom is a meaningful event.

# Appendix D: Prom Films

High School Films Organized around the Prom
or with Scenes Organized around the Prom

Feature Films
*American Pie* (1999)
*She's All That* (1999)
*The Rage: Carrie 2* (1999)
*Jawbreaker* (1999)
*10 Thing I Hate About You* (1999)
*Trippin'* (1999)
*Never Been Kissed* (1999)
*Something About Mary* (1998)
*Grosse Pointe Blank* (1997)
*Romy and Michele's High School Reunion* (1997)
*Angus* (1992)
*Encino Man* (1992)
*Buffy the Vampire Slayer* (1992)
*She's Out of Control* (1989)
*Born on the Fourth of July* (1989)
*Heathers* (1989)
*Hairspray* (1988)
*Can't Buy Me Love* (1987)
*Pretty in Pink* (1986)
*Peggy Sue Got Married* (1986)
*Lucas* (1986)
*Just One of the Guys* (1986)
*Back to the Future* (1985)
*Teen Wolf* (1985)
*Footloose* (1984)
*Valley Girl* (1983)
*Fast Times at Ridgemont High* (1982)
*Prom Night* (1980)
*Grease* (1979)
*Carrie* (1976)

Documentary Films
*The Last Dance* (1989)
*Street Talk and Tuxes* (1999)

# Appendix E: Prom Magazines

*Your Prom* (1995)
*Your Prom* (1996)
*Your Prom* (1997)
*Your Prom* (1999)
*Young and Modern* special prom edition (1995)
*Young and Modern* special prom edition (1996)
*Young and Modern* special prom edition (1997)
*Young and Modern* special prom edition (1999)
*Seventeen* (1995)
*Seventeen* (1996)
*Seventeen* (1997)
*Seventeen* (1999)
*Sassy* (1996)
*Allure* (1996)
*People* (1996)
*People* (1999)
*HJ* prom special (1996)
*HJ* prom special (1997)
*HJ* prom special (1999)

$\mathcal{N}otes$

**Chapter One**

1   Throughout the term of her pregnancy and in the few hours that followed her giving birth, no one, with the exception of her boyfriend, knew she was pregnant.

2   Gaines, 1990; Lefkowitz, 1998; Salinger, 1995; Silverstone, 1997.

3   The emergence of these texts has much to do with the moral panic stemming from the changing structural conditions that have altered the lives of the white middle class.

4   The one exception is Michelle Fine's (1997) analysis of the events that developed around the prom in Wedowee, Alabama.

5   Castells et al., 1999; Daspit and Weaver, 1999; Giroux, 1997, 1994; Molner, 1997; Steinberg and Kincheloe, 1997; Trend, 1995.

6   Cancian, 1987; Illouz, 1997; Ingraham, 1999.

7   Ingraham, 1999.

8   With the rise of industrialization and urbanization, however, a steady flow of available adult immigrant labor arrived in the United States. With this surplus of employable adult labor, rules governing children's participation in the labor force were rigidly imposed; by the end of the nineteenth century, children had been steadily pushed out of the labor force. Schooling became possible for a growing population of kids who were now considered by the state to be ineligible for work. Mandatory schooling laws and sanctions against truancy were created around this time. See Gettis, 1998 and Mitchell, 1995.

9   Fiske, 1989a.

10  Palladino, 1996.

11  Kett, 1977.

12  Odem, 1995.

13  I borrow here from the arguments provided by Michael Messner in his important book on masculinity and the social institution of sport, *Power at Play*. Early in his analysis he discusses the rise and expansion of recreational sports in connection with attempts by the upper classes to control the underprivileged by socializing them to the ethos of democracy. According to Messner, "By the turn of the century, historians have argued, the expansion of sports into widespread 'recreation for the masses' was seen by the upper classes as a means of integrating immigrants and the growing industrial working class into the expanding capitalist order where work was becoming routinized and leisure time was increasing" (1992:11). Though his discussion centers on sport, it is a useful one for understanding the general shifts in leisure and the organization of class cultures and class divisions. Maureen Montgomery (1998) has similarly written on the shifts in leisure, though her discussion focuses on the ways in

which the upper class organized itself and the importance leisure time played in securing a bourgeois elite.

14   Fiske, 1989a; Montgomery, 1998; Palladino, 1996.

15   Jane Addam's work at Hull House is an exemplary case in extending the notions of democracy so that the working class could participate in the American political system.

16   Fiske, 1989a.

17   Graebner, 1990.

18   Montgomery (1998) argues that the "popularization" of the debutante ball is in part a consequence of the expansion of print media. With the development of print media and newspaper publicity, the social practices of the elite, which had once been hidden from the public gaze, were now subject to public viewing. See also her in-depth examination of the debutante ball.

19   Montgomery, 1998.

20   The compulsory boarding schools for Native American youth are exemplars of these socializing projects. John Bloom (1998) and K. Tsianina Lomawaina (1994) both provide extensive accounts of the organization of Native American boarding schools. Both argue that these boarding schools were central to U.S. efforts to socialize native youth to Christian life, American democracy, and middle-class standards of bodily comportment. The compulsory practices in these boarding schools worked to obliterate native culture and cultural identity while also securing the disenfranchised as docile citizens.

21   John Fiske (1989a) discusses the ways in which working-class pleasures were disciplined through a class-based reorganization of leisure. For example, the carnival or fair was replaced with the official observance of national holidays. Working-class beer halls were replaced with reputable middle-class dance halls. Social outings organized by companies for their workers flourished after the turn of the century. According to Fiske, work and leisure are ideologically linked.

22   This historical sketch identifies the broader cultural currents that have shaped proms discursively and materially. While this discussion highlights the social and political forces that gave rise to proms, it does not address the ways in which the prom may have operated as a space of social contestation in the past. Examining how proms have historically worked as sites of struggle would no doubt be an interesting undertaking, but unfortunately requires a far more extensive discussion than space allows here. It should not be concluded by this omission that the prom only recently emerged as a site of struggle. There is little question in my mind that proms have always been places where cultural forms are both secured and resisted. The analysis I provide here is pieced together from archival research conducted at the New York Public Library's Picture Collection and social analyses provided by a number of important scholarly works. I relied on historical analyses developed by Graebner, 1990; Fiske, 1989; Kett, 1977; Mitchell, 1995; Montgomery, 1998; Odem, 1995; and Palladino, 1996, to form this historical analysis.

23   Gettis, 1998.

24   Adult-organized activities primarily stressed "character building" and the

virtues of good grooming (Palladino, 1996). See Gary Alan Fine's (1987) discussion of "character building" in connection with the ethos of Little League baseball as an example.

25  Devlin, 1998; Kett, 1977; Gettis, 1998; Palladino, 1996.

26  Grace Palladino (1996) and William Graebner (1990) are two who provide an extensive look at these activities and the underlying agendas that gave rise to them. Palladino discusses the emergence of the National Youth Administration during the depression, which was a program initiated under Franklin Delano Roosevelt's New Deal reforms in 1935, to train and educate "troubled" youth through work. Palladino argues that what underlies this program was a fear that disaffected youth, without proper means to channel their energies, might be inclined to social revolution (much in the same way the Hitler Youth were).

27  Palladino, 1996.

28  Brumberg, 1997; Palladino, 1996; Schrum, 1998.

29  Palladino, 1996.

30  Graebner, 1990.

31  These activities helped solidify class and race divisions as well as maintain cultural notions regarding appropriate masculinity and femininity. Grace Palladino (1996) asserts that these activities usually were organized along neighborhood lines to prevent mixing among different race and class groups. William Graebner (1990) argues that the sock hop was an event largely attended by white middle-class girls and was designed to protect this group of teenagers from the activities organized within working-class, black, and male youth cultures. Its conservative undertones, especially the selection of music played at the sock hop, kept many youth, whose musical tastes were rooted in youth subculture and not in the adult-sanctioned youth culture, away. The history of these programs as they relate specifically to race, gender, and class undercurrents is too extensive for adequate attention here. For an examination of the different ways in which ideas about race, class, and gender shaped projects to socialize youth see Austin and Willard, 1998; Graebner, 1990; and Inness, 1998a.

32  Devlin, 1998; Gettis, 1998; Graebner, 1990.

33  Graebner, 1990: 112. Of course, rock n' roll did intrude upon the space of the prom, often to the dismay of school officials and parents.

34  Connell et al., 1982; Devine, 1996; Eder, Evans, and Parker 1995; Foley, 1990; Irvine, 1994; Lesko, 1988b; Proweller, 1998; Swaminathan, 1997; Thorne, 1993; Walker, 1987.

35  Devine 1996; Eder, Evans, and Parker, 1995; Fine et al., 1997; Fine and Weis, 1993; Giroux, 1995; McRobbie, 1991; Torres, 1998; Walkerdine, 1990.

36  Feminist scholars have been particularly instrumental in bringing those sites and activities conventionally thought to be trivial to the fore of critical cultural work (Thompson, 1995; McRobbie, 1991; Lesko, 1988; DeVault, 1991; Luke, 1996; Radway, 1984). Concerned with expressions of broader class and gender inequalities organizing young women's everyday lives, Carrington examined graffiti written by working-class girls in public bathrooms. Leslie Roman explored girls' participation in punk rock to understand how class politics mediates the formation of a gender politics among young middle-class and

working-class women. Hair salons, beauty contests, and kitchens have also been examined as critical sites at which pressing cultural issues are shared, reworked, and most often upheld (Cohen, Wilk, and Stoeltje, 1996; DeVault, 1991; Cimlin, 1996; McDowell, 1999; Radway, 1984). "Centering" those aspects of culture traditionally considered outside the realm of the political, feminist projects of this nature have exerted a significant influence on how we define cultural life, and the tools we use to "excavate" those cultural resources necessary to its ongoing production (DeVault, 1999; McRobbie, 1991).

37   Anyon, 1997; Apple and Weis, 1983; Castells et al., 1999; Connell, 1987; Daspit and Weaver, 1999; Davies, 1992; Eckert, 1989; Fine and Weis, 1993; Giroux, 1983; Kozol, 1991; Lesko, 1998a; Luke and Gore, 1992; Jones and Mahoney, 1989; Mac an Ghaill, 1994; McCarthy and Crichlow; 1998; Sadker and Sadker, 1987; Sennet and Cobb, 1972; Smith, 1987; Spring, 1994, Willis, 1977.

38   Giroux, 1983; Giroux and Simon, 1989; Gilbert and Taylor, 1990; Christian-Smith, 1993; Roman and Christian-Smith, 1988.

39   A number of scholars have begun to rethink the connection between popular culture and schooling by tracing the diffuse ways students carve out their place in school and culture through their participation in popular cultural practices (Giroux, 1995; Proweller, 1998; Roman and Christian-Smith, 1988). Focusing on romance readership among high school girls, Linda Christian-Smith (1993) examined how girls negotiate the process of becoming feminine within a relatively "fixed" school terrain. Nancy Lesko (1988a) explored the symbolic currency conferred upon smoking and girls' dress styles, and their connection to the sexualization of girls' bodies in a private Catholic school. Hip-hop and rap also have been analyzed as critical practices through which an everyday politics of race has been forged within black "ghetto" youth/school culture (Allinson, 1994: Dyer, 1993; Gray, 1993; Neal, 1999). The intersection between popular culture and schooling is an area of scholarship that has flourished in recent years. See also Despit and Weaver, 1999; Unks, 1995; Steinberg and Kincheloe, 1997; Torres, 1998; and Voss, 1996.

40   Hebdige, 1987; Skelton and Valentine, 1998.

41   Grossberg, Nelson, and Treichler, 1992; Halle, 1993; Harrington and Bielby, 1995; Ross and Rose, 1994; Skelton and Valentine, 1998; Thomas, 1993.

42   Inness, 1998a, 1998b; Whiteley, 1997.

43   Graebner, 1990: 9.

44   See Daspit and Weaver, 1999; Hebdige, 1987; McRobbie, 1991; Radway, 1984; Roman and Christian-Smith, 1988; Skelton and Valentine, 1998; and Willis, 1977.

45   One of the key aspects of this study is to examine the prom from the perspective of those who experienced it firsthand. In doing so, it is important to not reconstitute ideological standpoints of adults in talking about youth. So often youth, their relationships, identities, and thoughts are understood through an adult lens that reduces them to "adults-in-the-making" (Thorne, 1993: 3). Seeing kids simply as developing adults and not as social agents who actively participate in cultural life, scholars and educators reproduce those very forms of power that we seek to understand and alter. The language we use to write about youth conveys and constructs them, and their realities, in particular ways. This raised important questions for me in terms of how I referred to those who populate

this book. I wanted to find ways to represent those I studied that did not deflect from the complexity of their experience, did not disempower them by glossing over the local knowledges they had acquired, and did not dismiss those axes of struggles that are central to their lives. With this in mind, I tried to avoid using the terms *teen*, and *teenager* (although I did fall back on these terms occasionally) because these are terms tied directly to the commercialization and commodification of youth (Palladino, 1996). The term *adolescent* was equally unappealing. The term is tied to developmental models that often deny "adolescents" agency and fail to see the process through which we are socialized to culture as an ongoing process (Thorne, 1993). Only rarely did I refer to those I studied as *students* because I wanted to avoid defining them entirely by their relationship to school; their lives outside of school figure considerably in shaping their school lives, and thus the prom. Mostly, I refer to them as *kids*. I use the term *kids* to capture the sense of their unity as a group and because their age was always relevant, shaping how they experienced other factors mediating their identities like gender, sexuality, race, and class. Referring to them as *kids* as opposed to as *students* or *teens* also enabled me to convey my allegiance to them, an allegiance rooted in a shared sense of rebellion (whether fictional or real). The term *kids* has always reminded me of the way "stodgy" older folks refer to those who are dismissed as "misunderstood," those who move through daily life without the legitimate status that the term *adult* confers. Though *Prom Night* seeks to shed light on the realities kids face in school, I also realize that to be "misunderstood" is part of what it means to be young in culture today. As Andrew Ross and Tricia Rose observe, "Youth craves recognition but does not necessarily want to be understood by adults" (1993: 13). That space of misunderstanding has more than symbolic currency; it is a concrete space of being where kids carve out a politics that is not always intelligible to adults and that is part of its disruptive power.

46  The names of the schools have been changed to protect the privacy of my informants. Additionally, I have not identified the precise location of each school for the same reason.

47  Devine, 1996: 22.

### Chapter Two

1  Equally significant is the possibility for multiple readings. I am not arguing here that these texts only can be read in one way. There is always the possibility for oppositional readings (Daspit and Weaver, 1999).

2  For more extensive analyses on teen films see Bernstein, 1997; Lewis, 1992.

3  Steinberg and Kincheloe, 1997.

4  Phillips, 1998: 75.

5  Shepard, 1972: 299–301.

6  "Dance Fever," 1996: 42.

7  Kett, 1977; Lesko, 1996; Steinberg and Kincheloe, 1997.

8  That a prom is held for homeless kids further supports the argument I make here. Implicit is that this is an event that all youth, regardless of the conditions under which they live, should experience.

9  The analysis I offer here focuses on the ways in which this film sustains a narrow construction of the teen; however, the film can be read in a number of dif-

ferent ways (some of which will be identified later in the book). It also provides a rich, gendered narrative on what constitutes youth romance. In other ways, the film offers an alternate reading of femininity. It is clear that Laney in some ways is developing a feminist consciousness as she struggles to make sense of her newfound popularity. At the prom she is not elected prom queen. Surprisingly, she isn't crushed by her defeat. My purpose in making this point is to highlight the varied ways in which this film can be interpreted.

10    Significantly, two popular teen horror films, *Carrie* and *Prom Night*, center on the prom.

11    Of course, this image is racialized. Mary's presentation as "a dream date" is convincing in part because she is the embodiment of white purity (for more on this notion, see hooks, 1995).

12    In the course of researching this project, I heard scores of stories by adults about their proms. Adults were eager to share with me their tales (of disaster— most were horror stories), often unsolicited. The number of times I heard "Have I got a prom story for you" are too numerous to count. And there is more: a friend of mine was invited to a bachelorette party for a bride to be, for which all guests were requested to wear their 1980s prom dresses. I also learned of a self-help group that hosts a prom for its members. What underlies this adult event is the idea that participants can revisit their prom and rewrite its story in any way they wish.

13    After kids decided on their photo package, they then wait on line to have their photographs taken with their dates. Prom photos are constructed as standardized, idealized images in which the photographer, not the students, has total control over production. Pictures are typically taken outside of the actual room where the prom is being held. In this way, a disconnection is created between the image recorded in the photograph and the actual prom event. At Rudolph, all table shots were taken at a table outside the ballroom that was cleared of any evidence of food. The effect of the standardized photos is a false sense of continuity in the experience and narrative of the prom. When viewed as an image (the photo), little variation is noticeable.

Photos of dates are staged events that attempt to capture and reproduce normative conceptions of gender and heterosexuality. At Woodrow's prom, couples stood before a white canvas backdrop. Typically the boy was positioned first. Once in position his date was placed beside him. Each girl was directed by the photographer to position herself at an angle, so that her full body was not in view. The girl was then told to place her feet in a T formation with her left hand, bearing the wrist corsage, resting on her thigh. Her head was slightly tilted to the side by the photographer, to express feminine deference and sexual innocence. Her other hand was hidden behind her date's back. His right hand was also hidden. His left hand was then placed (again by the photographer), in his pocket to convey ease and a relaxed masculine confidence.

This arrangement can sometimes be upset by the kids. At Woodrow's prom I watched two sets of girls have their photos taken together. The significant rearranging of their bodies, required by the photographers because they were two girls together, is indication of the extent to which standard photographic text at the prom relies on heterosexuality as the normative order. The photographer

could not very well place the two girls in the same formation as he would a heterosexual couple. It was important to position the girls together in a way that
made clear they were just friends and not dates—together but apart.

14  For an interesting analysis of wedding photography see McCoy, 1995.

15  www.proms.net.

16  Vinitzky-Seroussi, 1998.

17  For many of these kids, leaving high school is accompanied by greater "adult"
responsibilities and the possibility for greater freedom and autonomy (at least
in some measure). Many youth feel conflicted about finishing high school.
Though schools exercise enormous control over their lives, for some kids
schools also serve as sanctuaries. This seems to be especially pronounced for
white middle-class kids, whose adolescent experience is structured largely
around securing their protection from an external world (Gaines, 1994).

18  Stoeltje, 1996: 15.

19  For more information on popular culture, *what* it is and *where* it is, see Daspit
and Weaver, 1999; Fiske, 1987a, 1987b; Roman and Christian-Smith, 1988.

### Chapter Three

1  Griggers, 1997.

2  "Discover Your Perfect Prom Look," *YM* special prom edition, 1997: 37.

3  Roman and Christian-Smith, 1988: 4.

4  Berger, 1977: 46.

5  McRobbie, 1991; Montgomery, 1998; Willis, 1990.

6  See West and Zimmerman, 1987, for a discussion on how gender is actively constructed and reconstructed through day-to-day relations.

7  Bordo, 1993: 166.

8  Carrington, 1989; Craik, 1989; Clark, 1987; Fiske, 1989a; McRobbie and Garber,
1981; Radner, 1995, 1989; Radway, 1984; Roman and Christian-Smith, 1988.

9  Hillary Radner (1989) suggests in her work on femininity and consumption
that women find pleasure in the consumption of beauty culture because it provides a space in which women can be the agents of their own desire. Radner
develops a compelling analysis of how feminine pleasure in the production of
appearance is tied to beauty and culture industries. In the 1980s, she argues,
these industries recognized the influence of women's struggle to articulate an
autonomous self-identity on women's patterns of consumption. In so doing, the
market repositioned beauty work within a discourse of self-pleasure; the focus
shifted from making oneself over for others to doing it simply for oneself.
Beauty work at this particular historical moment not only is rooted in the discourses of heterosexual desirability, but in a discourse of feminine desire (e.g.,
"I'm beautiful and I'm worth it").

10  Brumberg, 1997.

11  Jones, 1994: 297.

12  Mercer, 1990.

13  See Bourdieu, 1984, for more on this notion.

14  "Big hair," often associated with shopping mall culture, is a signifier for a class-
specific femininity that is very much a part of our cultural imagination. "Big
hair" is tied to a series of other class/ethnic (Italian-American, Latina) signi-

fiers: Camaros, tight acid-washed jeans, high-heeled boots, and heavy eyeliner. For examples, see movies such as *Working Girl, Jungle Fever, My Cousin Vinny*, and *The Wedding Singer*. These films, with the exception of *My Cousin Vinny*, depict women with "big hair" as either deferential, sexually loose, dependent on their boyfriends, consumed with beauty culture, and/or as especially loud.

15   "Don't Break the Bank," *HJ* prom special, 1996: 16.

16   Bourdieu, 1984.

17   Blackman, 1998; Dwyer, 1998; Inness, 1998a, 1998b; Leadbeater and Way, 1996; Leonard, 1998; Nava, 1987; Sato, 1999.

18   See Fiske, 1989a, for a more extensive discussion of how consumers use the market in ways that disrupt its power.

19   Lesko, 1988a. See also Fine, 1993; Inness, 1998a, 1998b; McRobbie, 1991; Tolman, 1994; Walkerdine, 1990.

20   This may be especially pronounced for middle-class girls because the prom may represent for them a momentary chance to abandon their concerns with sexual respectability (Tolman, 1994).

21   Carrington, 1989; Fine, 1993; Krisman, 1987; Leahy, 1994.

22   Fine, 1993; Tolman, 1994.

23   See Clark, 1987; Haug, 1987; Lesko, 1988a, for more on this notion.

24   Angela McRobbie and Jennifer Garber (1981) argue along a similar line that working-class girls often embrace conventional feminine practices like wearing makeup and talking about boys in the classroom as a way to contest schools as middle-class organizations.

### Chapter Four

1   Cancian, 1987; Illouz, 1997; Ingraham, 1999.

2   Relegated to the realm of feeling, romance is thought to be private, intimate, and above all else, outside the contested terrain of politics; in this way it conceals the very political workings of domination it serves.

3   Eder, Evans, and Parker, 1995; Ingraham, 1999; Leahy, 1994; Radway, 1984; Tolman, 1994.

4   Linda Christian-Smith (1993) has argued in her research on romance readership among girls that many girls derive pleasure from reading romance novels precisely because they do *not* mirror their actual lives.

5   "Romance: Your Mushiest Prom Night Moments," *YM* special prom edition, 1996: 6.

6   Leahy, 1994.

7   William Graebner writes, "Even sexuality, or more properly attitudes toward sexuality, was a function of class . . . middle class sexuality was supposed to be: dreamy, fraternal and mediated by commodities" (1990: 74). While silencing girls' articulations of their own sexual desire, this discourse also functions to uphold the good girl/bad girl divide, which is critical to the ongoing operation of gender domination. What is striking is that this sentiment continues to pattern girls' thoughts and actions despite feminism, girls' pursuits for greater autonomy, and changing sexual relations.

8   Connell, 1987, 1985; Lorber, 1994; Messner, 1992, 1997; Mac an Ghaill, 1994.

9   Ingraham, 1999: 161.
10  "Twenty-five Ways to Get a Date—We Promise!" *YM* special prom edition, 1996: 46.
11  Holland and Eisenhart, 1991.
12  This also is formed within a context of social class. Often, middle-class girls have the most resources available to them to be feminine.
13  For more on this notion see Holland and Eisenhart, 1991.
14  For more on the issue of sociability and romance see Thompson, 1995.
15  Hudson, 1984: 47.
16  See Fine, 1993, for a more extensive discussion of how girls silence their own desire.
17  While many of these young men actively worked to distance themselves from the prom and its romantic framings, some boys (as I discussed earlier in the chapter) viewed the prom through a lens of romance. Boys read the prom in varied ways as they attempt to make sense of themselves as masculine.
18  Willis, 1977; McRobbie, 1991; Connell, 1995; Walker, 1987.
19  Mac an Ghail, 1994: 102.
20  "His Secret Thoughts about Prom: Find Out What He Thinks about the Big Night," *YM* special prom edition, 1995: 36.
21  While girls' narratives focused considerably on securing a date for the prom, few references to finding a date were mentioned in narratives written by boys. In the interviews, boys talked in more animated ways, providing more detailed descriptions of what they hoped the prom would be. This suggests that masculinity is demonstrated not only in the prom site but in these narrative reconstructions.
22  Connell, 1995; Mac an Ghaill, 1994; Messner, 1992; Morgan, 1996; West and Zimmerman, 1987.
23  See Mac an Ghaill, 1994; Connell, 1995, for more on the ways men regulate masculinity.
24  Hughes, 1994.

#### Chapter Five

1   "Forget Drugs, Drinks: Have a Natural High." *HJ* prom special, 1997: 20.
2   Ibid., 21.
3   This is an exemplary case of Michel Foucault's work on self-surveillance and the daily operation of power forces. Theorizing power as it emerges from below and works "upward," Foucault writes,

> Although surveillance rests on individuals, its functioning is that of a network of relations from top to bottom, but also to a certain extent from bottom to top and laterally; this network "holds" the whole together and traverses it in its entirety with effects of power that derive from one another . . . it is the apparatus as a whole that produces "power" and distributes individuals in this permanent and continuous field. This enables the disciplinary power to be both absolutely indiscreet, since it is everywhere and always alert, since by its very principles it leaves no zone of shade and constantly supervises the very individuals who are entrusted with the task of supervising; and absolutely "discreet" for it functions permanently and largely in

silence. Discipline makes possible the operation of relational power that sustains itself by its own mechanisms and which for the spectacle of public events substitutes the uninterrupted play of calculated gazes (Foucault, cited in Rabinow, 1984: 192).

4   This is an important distinction that Sari Knopp Biklen, in her 1995 book *School Work: Gender and the Social Construction of Teaching*, makes. She argues that the critiques of teachers by educational scholars reflects the gendered organization of teaching; it is largely women who teach. She points out that teachers are often subjected to a similar set of controls as students as they work in schools.

5   Spring, 1994.

6   Connell et al., 1982; Eder, 1995; Fine and Weis, 1993; Fiske, 1989; Hall, 1981; McRobbie, 1991; Smith, 1990a.

7   Bowles and Gintis, 1976; Giroux, 1995; Proweller, 1998.

8   Given the nature of this research—that this research centers on proms—it is impossible for me to speak to the everyday enactment of Rudolph's cultural curriculum as it occurs specifically in the classroom. What I am interested in demonstrating through this chapter is how the pedagogical aims of the community and school become embedded within the prom's organization. How does the community and school envision education as it is undertaken in this setting?

9   In 1980, the Rhode Island Supreme Court—after Aaron Fricke, a gay student sued his high school—ruled it was a violation of the First Amendment's protection of free expression for schools to prohibit same-sex couples from going to the prom (see Fricke, 1981).

10   See Silverstone, 1997, for more on this notion.

11   Cameron McCarthy and Alicia Rodriquez argue that the underlying logic of suburban fear is the fear of the "encirclement by difference" (1997: 232). Their concept, the "encirclement of difference," is particularly useful in understanding the imposition of rules at Rudolph's prom.

12   The concept "outsider on the inside" that I employ here is discussed at length by Patricia Hill Collins, 1990.

13   Fine, 1997.

14   See Giroux, 1995, 1997, for more on this issue.

15   Additionally, I would argue that the need to secure these class interests through educational capital takes shape within a context in which the relative promise of middle-class security has been eroded by the broader shifts from an industrial-based economy to a service-based economy. These local and global economic changes have resulted in the growth of new employment categories rooted in service work and significant management downsizing. The consequence of significant corporate restructuring in the 1980s and 1990s has meant a less predictable future for many young members of the middle class (Proweller, 1998).

16   See Ehrenreich, 1985; Proweller, 1998; Smith, 1987, for further discussion of how middle-class communities shape the organization of school.

17   This is an important distinction that I came to realize after I had met with the school principal several times. More than once he expressed his dismay with

the influence parents and the community had over the organization of the school. He was troubled by the ways in which parents pushed these kids and felt that the community's commitment to "success," which he suggested was measured solely by the number of students accepted to Ivy League colleges, undermined the education of these students. Eventually I came to see that the control the teachers and school administrators exercised was a consequence of the community control they felt.

18  Proweller, 1998: 59.
19  See Giroux, 1995, 1997; Proweller, 1998, for more on this issue.
20  Sapon-Shevin, 1992.
21  Of course, not all students at Stylone were equally invested in the rhetoric of gifted education or its hidden class codes. I spoke with one student who was enormously critical of the school and its students. Talking with him, I sensed that his critique was a class-based critique. He spoke with what felt like an almost-contained rage about the elitism assumed by other students. It was clear he felt alienated from the class practices at Stylone.
22  Biklen, 1995, discusses at length how teachers talk about their work.
23  See Chalmers, 1997; Sapon-Shevin, 1992, for further discussion of how privilege organizes school space.
24  Connell et al., 1982; Proweller, 1998, for more on this issue.
25  De Certeau, 1984: 18.

### Chapter Six

1  Anyon, 1997; Connolly, 1998; Dilg, 1999; Fine and Weis, 1993, 1998; Giroux, 1995; McCarthy and Crichlow, 1993; Proweller, 1998; Pruyn, 1999; Schofield, 1989; Torres, 1998a.
2  Devine, 1996.
3  Of the 650 students that comprise the senior class, only 160 attended the prom.
4  Spring, 1994; Tozer, Violas, and Senese, 1993.
5  Glassner and Loughlin, 1987.
6  See also Anyon, 1997; Giroux, 1995; Kozol, 1991; MacLeod, 1987.
7  At Woodrow High, another integrated school studied, there was also a noticeable absence of Southeast Asian students, a group that comprises roughly 20 percent of the student population, at the prom.
8  Equally significant is the fact that the kids at Hudson responded positively to this teacher's effort to take up the subject of race and to establish trust across different racial communities.
9  Eckert, 1987; Anyon, 1997; Schofield, 1989.
10  For more on this issue see Cummins, 1993; Cohen, 1993.
11  Gender also seems relevant here. As argued earlier, the prom is constructed as a feminine space. This gender organization structures girls' investments in this event at which they solidify their feminine identities. Significantly, organizing the prom is often the work of girls. Given this, it is worth considering that the race struggles I have identified here prevented these girls from participating in an event in which they are supposed to be deeply invested *as* girls. Katy and Serena name race; they do not identify gender. I would argue that this has less to do with the fact that gender is impertinent and more to do with the fact that

race carries such force in this setting that it overshadows gender. The specific gendered organization of the prom as it intersects with race here is overlooked.

12  Anyon, 1997; Fine and Weis, 1998; Giroux and Simon, 1989; Kozol, 1991; Spring, 1994.

13  Smith, 1987.

14  Hudson was also the only school that did not automatically waive the fee for me to attend the prom. Luckily, it was eventually waived because I promised Mr. Stand I would not eat any food. As a graduate student, coming up with the eighty-six-dollar fee would have been difficult.

15  See Cohen, Wilk, and Stoeltje, 1996, for an interesting exploration of the formation of cultural identity in relation to beauty pageants.

16  Penelope Eckert has argued that these delineations between students, like "jocks" and "burnouts," are in fact embedded within class relations and operate as code words for class divisions.

17  A growing body of race literature focusing specifically on whiteness as a category of identity has made visible the ways in which race hierarchies depend on the invisibility of whiteness as a position of privilege. See Frankenburg, 1993; Fine et al., 1997; Delgado and Stefancic, 1997; and Wray and Newitz, 1997, for a more elaborate reading.

18  Frankenburg, 1993: 228–29.

19  Michelle Fine (1997) provides a critical reading of the events surrounding the school board's decision to reinstate Humphries.

**Chapter Seven**

1  Brake, 1985; Fiske, Turner, and Hodge, 1987; Graebner, 1990; Hebdige, 1979; McRobbie, 1991, 1993; Ross and Rose, 1994; Roman and Christian-Smith, 1988; Skelton and Valentine, 1998; Whiteley, 1998.

2  Barthes, 1983.

3  Benstock and Ferriss, 1994.

4  This analysis is informed by the creative work of Anne Hollander, *Seeing Through Clothes* (1975).

5  This analysis developed from different sources. I spoke with many people who attended their proms in the 1970s and the 1980s; I viewed films from those decades; and I examined others' personal photos.

6  Fiske, 1989a, 1989b; Nava, 1991.

7  These creative variations were more common at the racially diverse schools than at Rudolph.

8  See Hebdige, 1979; McRobbie, 1991, for discussion of the relationship between style and youth identity.

9  See also Nava, 1987, for an extensive discussion of the intersection of commodity culture, youth culture, and style politics.

10  Bernstock and Ferriss, 1994.

11  Bourdieu, 1984; Halle, 1993.

12  Hebdige, 1979.

13  hooks, 1989.

14  For more on this notion, see Bornstein, 1994; Butler, 1990.

15  See Blackman, 1998; Leonard, 1998; McRobbie, 1991; Roman and Christian-

Smith, 1988; Whiteley, 1997, for discussion on how gender and youth culture interrelate.

16  Graebner, 1990.

17  In my personal communications with Project Advance teachers, two of them explained that their students wore this pant style because it derives from the uniforms that prisoners wear. Prisoners, they argued, are not allowed to wear belts, so their pants hang very low on their hips. Although I am unsure of the validity of this claim, I think it is worth reflecting on why some students might identify with prisoners in this way.

18  Hebdige, 1979: 2–3.

19  Ross and Rose, 1994; Fiske, 1989b; Fiske, Turner, and Hodge, 1987.

20  At Stylone's prom I observed a young man approach a teacher and greet her by her first name. She quickly corrected him. I view this interaction as a type of negotiation in which the young man is "feeling out" and determining the boundaries of appropriate interaction. He enters the interaction with an awareness that the rules of standard conduct have changed at the prom.

21  I learned from teachers that some schools have replaced these glasses with other gifts, like picture frames, because of the alleged promotion of drinking. This year was the first year that Rudolph stopped giving out these glasses.

22  "Getting There Is Half the Fun," *HJ* prom special, 1996: 20.

23  Fricke, 1981: 101.

24  Butler, 1990; Jennings, 1998; Pinar, 1998; Unks, 1995.

25  "May we have this dance?" 1995: 20.

26  Rodriquez, 1995; Scott, 1992.

27  Cunningham, 1992.

28  Miceli, 1997; Sears, 1998.

29  Hirsch, 1994: BB7.

30  See Walcott, 1998.

31  Sears, 1998: 184.

32  Dwyer, 1998; Hebdige, 1979.

*Chapter Eight*

1  DeVault, 1992; Luke, 1996; Mac an Ghaill, 1994; McRobbie, 1994; Roman and Christian-Smith, 1988; Rose, 1994; Smith, 1987; Thorne, 1993; Enloe, 1989; Nicholson and Fraser, 1990; Seidman, 1992; Smith, 1987; Willis, 1996.

2  Fiske, Turner, and Hodge, 1987; Smith, 1989a.

3  This analysis is informed by Joseph Schumpeter's sociology of capitalism, cited in Collins (1986). Schumpeter argues that what drives capitalist expansion is this process of developing undiscovered market niches and capitalizing on them. These niches function at first as monopolies but are then incorporated further into the market; supply increases and profits decline. Schumpeter's central argument is that these monopolies, although short-lived, sustain the circulation of capital.

4  Let me illustrate with an example. The crowning of the prom king and queen, a practice that is often regarded as "a popularity contest" bound by normative ideas about heterosexuality and gender, was made into a site of popular culture when a group of students from one school in this study successfully organized

their entire Honors English class to vote for two unlikely candidates—two "brainy kids" who typically would not be seen as embodying idealized masculine and feminine identities (an absolute requirement for the throne). What makes this particular instance significant has less to do with the act itself and more to do with students' references to their efforts as "grass-roots organizing." The meanings these kids created to narrate their actions, while they capture a sense of the political and social salience of these contests in sustaining unequal relations along gender and sexual lines, highlight the malleability of these social forms as they take shape in local settings.

5 Bordo, 1993; Connell, 1987; Brumberg, 1997; Gilbert and Taylor, 1991.

6 Fiske, Turner, and Hodge, 1987; Lavenda, 1996; McRobbie, 1993, 1994; Radway, 1984. For an excellent discussion of this process see Fiske's "The Jeaning of America," in Fiske, 1986b.

7 Fiske, 1989a; Gilbert and Taylor, 1991; Hall, 1981; Roman and Christian-Smith, 1988.

8 Giroux and Simon, 1989; Fiske, 1989a, 1989b; Fiske, Turner, and Hodge; 1987; McRobbie, 1991; Walker, 1987.

9 Apple and Weis, 1983; Giroux, 1983; Giroux and Simon, 1989; Pinar, 1999.

10 Christian-Smith, 1993; Clark, 1987; McRobbie, 1993; Roman and Christian-Smith, 1988.

11 Changes in how proms are organized, if implemented by agents of school, would most likely heighten the antagonism many students already feel toward school. Moreover, strategies that would call for a reorganization of the prom would do little to chip away at those structures of power that organize the space of the prom or sufficiently address why kids invest in proms in the first place. Eliminating the crowning of king and queen (a practice that clearly celebrates hierarchy), for example, would not erase the tyranny of heterosexuality or the hegemony of gender. Some schools, like Hudson, have stopped electing prom kings and queens entirely. But students at Hudson have resisted this decision; many feel they have been fundamentally denied the opportunity to experience the prom in a "traditional" way as others before them had. While I am not advocating that we simply give kids what they want, an important question educators need to ask is why young people have investments in such practices, even though they clearly gain little from them.

12 Giroux, 1992, 1997; Luke and Gore, 1992; McLaren, 1988, 1993.

13 I am referring here to the eroding opportunity structures for youth employment and upward mobility. The decline in educational funding and the general shift toward technocratic, skills-based schooling have undermined critical and liberatory pedagogies of change.

14 Daspit and Weaver, 1999; McLaren, 1993; Torres, 1998b; Voss, 1996.

15 Toward the end of my research I met with a group of high school teachers who teach sociology and have demonstrated an enormous concern with the social forces mediating kids' school lives. As I presented my analysis to them, they continually interjected, providing countless examples from their local schools of how proms are socially arranged. This sort of dialogue with teachers is precisely the form of pedagogy envisioned by critical educators.

16  Castells et al., 1999; Giroux and Simon, 1989; Pinar, 1998; Pruyn, 1999; Rivera and Poplin, 1995; Torres, 1998b; Unks, 1995.
17  Boler, 1999; Pinar, 1999; Simon and Giroux, 1989; Torres, 1998a.
18  Daspit and Weaver, 1999; Luke and Gore, 1992; Giroux and Simon, 1989; Steinberg and Kincheloe, 1998.
19  Rethinking educational politics with greater attention to multiculturalism and feminism—a central objective of critical pedagogy—underscores the necessity to understand how schools, and the spaces (classroom) and discourses (Eurocentrism) they privilege, are organized by a logic of domination.
20  Giroux and Simon, 1989: 3.
21  Fine et al., 1997; Giroux, 1992, 1995; McCarthy and Crichlow, 1993; Torres, 1999a.
22  West, 1993.
23  Castells, et al., 1999; McCarthy and Crichlow, 1993; McLaren, 1993.
24  hooks, 1992: 21.
25  This study has primarily focused on the organization of proms within urban and suburban schools. Of course, not all kids who attend proms attend them within these contexts. It would be useful to further expand our understanding of proms, school, youth, and commodity cultures by examining how proms are organized, experienced, and defined within other social settings. In particular, consideration of rural settings might yield a more complex analysis of how class, race, and gender as "everyday phenomena" gain meaning through various prom rituals and practices. Rural settings stand somewhat outside the commercial world, whereas commodity culture seems to penetrate cities and even suburban areas in more succinct and encompassing ways. It would be valuable to examine how class, consumerism, race, and gender intersect in rural areas.

Additionally, a more in-depth look at how gay proms figure in the ongoing formation of a gay youth politics might also be valuable. This direction might better illuminate how popular cultural forms emerge as "strategic" sites of political disruption. Over the past several years, more and more gay youth programs have organized proms, but these proms seem quite different from those proms organized within schools. Looking at how these proms are structured would also provide insight, through comparison, into how proms are planned and experienced within school contexts.

## Appendix A

1  Narrative analysis relies heavily on memory, with characteristic obstacles and disadvantages (Thorne, 1993). I found that older students were more likely to adopt adult perspectives on the prom, often relegating it to a space of sophomoric insignificance. Notwithstanding, this strategy proved to be enormously useful. Memory, because it is structured by our social consciousness, offers itself as a space in which to examine how individuals and social groups internalize and incorporate cultural ideologies into their everyday patterns of thought (Althusser, 1971; Haug, 1987). Many students did write in detailed ways, providing rich descriptions of their proms. Their narratives provided a terrain in which to analyze connections among local ideologies, dominant ideologies, and everyday understandings of the social.

2   Smith, 1987.
3   The majority of students who wrote narratives defined themselves as middle-class, though most did distinguish between being middle-class, lower middle-class and upper-middle-class. Two defined themselves as working-class. Two students identified themselves as poor and another two defined themselves as lower-middle-class. As Barbara Ehrenreich (1985) argues, most people tend to define themselves as middle-class in the United States. While she argues that this has much to with the American myth of a classless society, she also suggests that self-reports on class are often inaccurate. Significantly, several students, although defining their race and sex did not record their class location. Some students interpreted class to mean their location within their high school ranking system. For instance, one male student defined himself as popular and a member of a varsity sport team. This also reflects the ambiguous place of social class and class differences within our collective consciousness.
4   Bourdieu, 1984; Halle, 1993; Illouz, 1997.
5   I make an analytical distinction between material class relations and class ideologies, although in actual life these are interconnected. The cultural dimensions of class (e.g., how individuals and social groups consume goods, services, and symbols) often operate to obscure the material organization of class relations. I begin with the understanding that class ideologies and symbols arise from and are often expressions of actual class relations (DeVault, 1992; Smith, 1987).
6   Frankenberg, 1993.
7   DeVault, 1995, 1996; Reisman, 1987.
8   Hall, 1997.
9   Archival research was conducted with the help of the New York Public Library's Picture Collection.
10  Burawoy et al., 1991.
11  Where interviews were conducted was decided by those I interviewed. Some students expressed a preference for conducting interviews in their schools instead of in their homes.
12  Carspecken and Cordiero, 1995; Mac an Ghaill, 1994.
13  Mac an Ghaill, 1994.
14  Bogdan and Taylor, 1984; Emerson, Fretz, and Shaw, 1995; Strauss, 1987.
15  DeVault, 1992.
16  Brunt, 1992; Grossberg, Nelson, and Treichler, 1992; Smith, 1987; Spender, 1980.
17  DeVault, 1995.
18  I sometimes experienced a sense of discomfort writing about the significance of race in my analysis that left me with a sort of analytical paralysis. Feminist ethnographers have pointed to the gap in the social realities between researchers and those studied and the race and class dynamics that give rise to these gaps (Mueller, 1995; Minh-ha, 1989; Reisman, 1987; Reinharz, 1992). The necessity to take seriously how power produces these gaps has become a significant topic in feminist methodological work. In my analysis of race and class I wanted to avoid conflating white practices with middle-class practices, although I found this task exceedingly difficult, as the historical construction of whiteness is entangled with the historical construction of the middle class (MacPherson,

1997). Sometimes I was unable to distinguish between the influence of students' racial identities and their class identities.

19   Friend, 1992; Unks, 1995; Woog, 1995.

20   This became especially apparent to me when I interviewed three young gay men connected no longer to school, but to a gay youth organization. They spoke openly, which I attribute to the fact that they were talking within a safe space not dominated by heterosexism. See Pinar, 1999, and Unks, 1995, for further discussion of this issues surrounding institutional heterosexism, schooling, and queer youth.

21   Hebdige, 1979; Ross and Rose, 1994; Skelton and Valentine, 1998; Whiteley, 1998.

22   Before I began this study I was required, as are most researchers, to submit a proposal to an institutional review board at my university for them to determine if my research could harm or affect, in egregious ways, the people I had chosen to study. With the exception of a few minor revisions, the committee determined that my research on the prom would not cause irreparable harm to my research subjects. I was granted approval on the condition that I receive signed consent forms not only from the kids I would be interviewing but also from a parent or guardian. Having little choice, I agreed to these terms set by the committee and began my interviews, making sure to collect signed consent forms. From the outset, collecting consent forms from parents presented a problem for the progress of my research. Routinely, I had to cancel and reschedule interviews because the kids had forgotten these forms, often leaving them at home. In almost all the interviews, kids asked me why I needed a parent's signature, and often expressed their irritation with and opposition to this requirement. Toward the end of my data collection, I had scheduled an interview with two girls from Hudson who had signed their own consent forms but had forgotten to have one of their parents sign the other. They both offered to sign for their mothers, swearing by their skills at forging their mothers' signatures. I remembered, as a high school student, once forging my own mother's signature (hers over my father's because my father's was too difficult to copy). I came to see the act of forging and even forgetting to bring consent forms as meaningful acts of foiling the power of school and contesting its authority over our lives. Permission slips are used widely in schools, operating as bridges between sites of parental and school control. Kids often forge their parent's signature as a way to manage the terms of their own surveillance in school. They evade the direct control of school over their lives by disrupting the communication between parents and school administrators.

This paradox forced me to question how I, as a researcher, sustained institutional dominance and control. While I was concerned, on the one hand, with uncovering how power orders kids' lives, I realized that the tools I deployed to do research contributed to and secured a culture of surveillance.

23   McRobbie, 1991.

24   There was a distinct sense that these girls were performing for me. Sometimes they spoke in highly dramatized ways and there was a certain degree of bravado when they shared stories with each other that reminded me of Paul Willis's (1977) account of working-class boys' street talk. In many ways, their talk

appeared to be a direct challenge to cultural prescriptions of femininity that expect a certain level of discretion from girls when they engage in these type of conversations.

25  See Gordon, 1995. Janice Radway's 1984 study *Reading the Romance: Women, Patriarchy and Popular Culture* is an example of a multimethod design. Through content analysis, interviewing, and observation, Radway explored popular romance novels and the women who read them.

26  Marlene Webber, in her 1991 study of Canada's street kids, also took full advantage of these informal conversations and found herself collecting valuable data during the most unexpected times.

27  When I first conducted interviews in the spring of 1996, I was deeply interested in what students had to say about their proms. The analysis I develop about Woodrow and Woodrow's prom weighs heavily on interviews, much more than my analysis of the three schools I studied the following year (which relied more on informal discussions and observations).

28  Kids were allowed to smoke at the prom, but most schools have strict rules about smoking at school.

29  I was met with a range of responses from the kids, mostly positive, when I told them about my research. I wanted to be honest with them. I felt more accountable to them than to the teachers and administrators. A number of students asked me, with astonishment and genuine interest, how I managed to "land a job" that let me go to proms; many wanted to know if I got paid for my work. While these comments at first struck me as amusing, they led me to reflect that their sense of what counted as work was limited and narrowly defined. For them, my work was fun, and this contradicted how they thought about work. I realized that many of them identify work with either schoolwork or with the occupational fields that they will later enter. It is important to note that these inquiries were rare at Stylone, which confirmed for me my initial observation that these kids generally have greater intellectual and cultural capital that shapes their relationship to work.

30  I make a distinction between schools, as an institution, and teachers. Many teachers' projects run counter to the objectives of schools. While schools are organizations of power, many teachers actively work to undermine the operation of power in schools, and relate to their students in very productive ways.

31  Thorne, 1993: 27.

32  Bowles and Klein, 1983; Harding, 1987; Nicholson and Fraser, 1990; Reinharz, 1992; Roberts, 1981.

33  Like these girls, I, too, care about my appearance and have spent time concerned with my hair, my weight, and how I dress.

34  Denzin, 1992.

# References

Allinson, Ewan. 1994. "Music and The Politics of Race: It's A Black Thing: Hearing How Whites Can't." *Cultural Studies* 8 (438–55).

Althusser, Louis. 1971. "Ideology and The State." *Lenin and Philosophy and Other Essays*. London: New Left Books.

Anyon, Jean. 1997. *Ghetto Schooling: A Political Economy of Urban Educational Reform*. New York: Teachers College Press, Columbia University.

Apple, Michael W. 1997. "Consuming The Other: Whiteness, Education and Cheap French Fries." *Off White: Readings on Race, Power and Society*, ed. Michelle Fine, Lois Weis, Linda C. Powell, and L. Mun Wong. New York: Routledge.

Apple, Michael W. and Lois Weis. 1983. *Ideology and Practice in Schooling*. Philadelphia: Temple University Press.

Barthes, Roland. 1983. *The Fashion System*. New York: Hill and Wang.

Benstock, Shari and Suzanne Ferriss, eds. 1994. *On Fashion*. New Jersey: Rutgers University Press.

Berger, John. 1977. *Ways of Seeing*. London: Penguin.

Bernstein, Jonathan. 1997. *Pretty in Pink: The Golden Age of Teenage Movies*. New York: St. Martin's/Griffin.

Biklen, Sari Knopp. 1995. *School Work: Gender and the Cultural Construction of Teaching*. New York: Teachers College Press, Columbia University.

Blackman, Shane J. 1998. "The School: 'Poxy Cupid!' An Ethnographic and Feminist Account of Resistant Female Youth Culture: The New Wave Girls." *Cool Places: Geographies of Youth Cultures,* ed. Tracey Skelton and Gill Valentine. London: Routledge.

Bloom, John. 1998. "Rolling with the Punches: Boxing, Youth Culture, and Ethnic Identity at a Federal Indian Boarding School during the 1930's." *Generations of Youth: Youth Cultures and History in Twentieth-Century America*, ed. Joe Austin and Michael Nevin Willard. New York: New York University Press.

Bogdan, Robert and Steven Taylor. 1984. *Introduction to Qualitative Methods: The Search For Meaning*. New York: Wiley/Interscience.

Boler, Megan. 1999. *Feeling Power: Emotions and Education*. New York: Routledge.

Bordo, Susan. 1993. *Unbearable Weight: Feminism, Western Culture and the Body*. Berkeley and Los Angeles: University of California Press.

Bornstein, Kate. 1994. *Gender Outlaw*. New York: Vintage House Press.

Bourdieu, Pierre. 1984. *Distinction: A Social Critique of the Judgment of Taste*. Cambridge, MA: Harvard University Press.

Bowles, Gloria and Renate Duelli Klien. 1983. *Theories of Women's Studies*. London: Routledge & Kegan Paul.

Bowles, Samuel and Herbert Gintis. 1976. *Schooling in Capitalist America*. New York: Basic Books.

Brake, Michael. 1985. *Comparative Youth Culture: The Sociology of Youth Culture and Youth Subculture in America, Britain and Canada*. London: Routledge & Kegan Paul.

Brumberg, Joan Jacobs. 1997. *The Body Project: An Intimate History of American Girls*. New York: Random House.

Brunt, Rosalind. 1992. "Engaging with the Popular: Audiences for Mass Culture and What to Say about Them." *Cultural Studies*, ed. Lawrence Grossberg, Cary Nelson, and Paula Treichler. New York: Routledge.

Burawoy, Michael et al. 1991. *Ethnography Unbound: Power and Resistance in the Modern Metropolis*. Berkeley: University of California Press.

Butler, Judith. 1990. *Gender Trouble: Feminism and the Subversion of Identity*. New York: Routledge.

Cancian, Francesca. 1987. *Love in America: Gender and Self-Development*. Cambridge: Cambridge University Press.

Carrington, Kerry. 1989. "Girls and Graffiti." *Cultural Studies* 3 (89–100).

Carspeken, Phil and Paula Cordiero. 1995. "Being, Doing, Becoming: Textual Interpretations of Social Identity and a Case Study." *Qualitative Inquiry* 1:1 (87–109).

Castells, Manuel, et al. 1999. *Critical Education in The New Information Age*. Lanham, MD: Rowan & Littlefield.

Chalmers, Virginia. 1997. "White Out: Multicultural Performances in a Progressive School." *Off White: Readings on Race, Power, and Society*, ed. Michelle Fine, Lois Weis, Linda C. Powell, and L. Mun Wong. New York: Routledge.

Christian-Smith, Linda K. 1993. "Voices of Resistance: Young Women Readers of Romance Fiction." *Beyond Silenced Voices: Class, Race, and Gender in United States Schools*, ed. Michelle Fine and Lois Weis. Albany: State University of New York Press.

Clark, Ann K. 1987. "The Girl: A Rhetoric of Desire." *Cultural Studies* 1 (195–203).

Clifford, James. 1983. "On Ethnographic Authority." *Representations* 1:2 (118–46).

Cohen, Colleen Ballerino, Richard Wilk, and Beverly Stoeltje, eds. 1996. *Beauty Queens on the Global Stage: Gender, Contests and Power*. New York: Routledge.

Cohen, Jody. 1993. "Constructing Race at an Urban High School: In Their Minds, Their Mouths, Their Hearts." *Beyond Silenced Voices: Class, Race, and Gender in United States Schools*, ed. Michelle Fine and Lois Weis. Albany: State University of New York Press.

Collins, Patricia Hill. 1990. *Black Feminist Thought: Knowledge, Consciousness and the Politics of Empowerment*. New York: Routledge.

Collins, Randall. 1986. *Weberian Sociological Theory*. Cambridge: Cambridge University Press.

Connell, R. W. 1995. *Masculinities*. Berkeley: University of California Press.

———. 1987. *Gender and Power: Society, The Person and Sexual Politics*. Stanford, CA: Stanford University Press.

Connell, R. W., D. J. Ashenden, S. Kessler, and G. W. Dowsett. 1982. *Making the Difference: Schools, Families and Social Divisions*. London: Allen & Unwin.

Coward, Rosalind. 1985. *Female Desires*. New York: Grove Press.

Craik, Jennifer. 1989. "'I Must Put My Face On': Making Up the Body and Marking Out the Feminine." *Cultural Studies* 3 (1–24).

Cummins, Jim. 1993. "Empowering Minority Students: A Framework For Intervention." *Beyond Silenced Voices: Class, Race, and Gender in United States Schools*, ed. Michelle Fine and Lois Weis. Albany: State University of New York Press.

Cunningham, Amy. 1992. "Not Just Another Prom Night." *Glamour.*

"Dance Fever." 1996. *People*, May 27, 42–52.

Daspit, Toby and John A. Weaver, eds. 1999. *Popular Culture and Critical Pedagogy: Reading, Constructing, Connecting*. New York: Garland.

Davies, L. 1992. "School, Power, Cultures Under Economic Contraint." *Educational Review* 43:2 (127–36.)

de Certeau, Michel. 1984. *The Practice of Everyday Life*, trans. Steven Rendall. Berkeley and Los Angeles: University of California Press.

Delgado, Richard and Jean Stefancic, eds. 1997. *Critical White Studies: Looking Behind the Mirror*. Philadelphia: Temple University Press.

Denzin, Norman K. 1992. *Symbolic Interactionism and Cultural Studies: The Politics of Interpretation*. Oxford: Blackwell.

DeVault, Marjorie. 1999. *Liberating Methods: Feminism and Social Research*. Philadelphia: Temple University Press.

———. 1996. "Talking Back to Sociology: Distinctive Contributions of Feminist Methodology." *Annual Review of Sociology, 22.*

———. 1995. "Ethnicity and Expertise: Racial Ethnic Knowledge in Sociological Research." *Gender and Society* 9:5 (612–31).

———. 1991. *Feeding The Family: The Social Organization of Caring As Gendered Work*. Chicago: University of Chicago Press.

———. 1990. "Talking and Listening From Women's Standpoint: Feminist Strategies For Interviewing and Analysis." *Social Problems* 37:1 (96–116).

Devine, John. 1996. *Maximum Security: The Culture of Violence in Inner-City Schools*. Chicago: University of Chicago Press.

Devlin, Rachel. 1998. "Female Juvenile Delinquency and the Problem of Sexual Authority in America, 1945–1960." *Delinquents and Debutantes: Twentieth Century American Girls' Culture*, ed. Sherrie A. Inness. New York: New York University Press.

Dilg, Mary. 1999. *Race and Culture in the Classroom: Teaching and Learning Through Multicultural Education*. New York: Teachers College Press, Columbia University.

Dwyer, Clarie. 1998. "Contested Identities: Challenging Dominant Representations of Young British Muslim Women." *Cool Places: Geographies of Youth Cultures*, ed. Tracey Skelton and Gill Valentine. London: Routledge.

Dyer, Michael Eric. 1993. "Be Like Mike? Michael Jordan and the Pedagogy of Desire." *Cultural Studies* 7 (64–72).

Eckert, Penelope. 1989. *Jocks and Burnouts: Social Categories and Identity in High School*. New York: Teachers College Press, Columbia University.

Eder, Donna, Catherine Colleen Evans, and Stephen Parker. 1995. *School Talk: Gender and Adolescent Culture*. New Brunswick, NJ: Rutgers University Press.

Ehrenreich, Barbara. 1985. *Fear of Falling: The Inner Life of the Middle Class*. New York: HarperCollins.

Emerson, Robert M., Rachel I. Fretz, and Linda L. Shaw. 1995. *Writing Ethnographic Fieldnotes*. Chicago: University of Chicago Press.

Enloe, Cynthia. 1990. *Bananas, Beaches and Bases: Making Feminist Sense of International Politics*. Berkeley and Los Angeles: University of California Press.

Farber, Paul, Eugene F. Provenzo, and Gunilla Holm. 1994. *Schooling in the Light of Popular Culture*. Albany: State University of New York Press.

Fine, Gary Alan. 1987. *With The Boys: Little League Baseball and Preadolescent Culture*. Chicago: University of Chicago Press.

Fine, Michelle. 1997. "Witnessing Whiteness." *Off White: Readings on Race, Power and Society*, ed. Michelle Fine, Lois Weis, Linda C. Powell, and L. Mun Wong. New York: Routledge.

———. 1993. "Sexuality, Schooling and Adolescent Females: The Missing Discourse of Desire." *Beyond Silenced Voices: Class, Race and Gender in United States Schools*, ed. Michelle Fine and Lois Weis. Albany: State University of New York Press.

Fine, Michelle and Lois Weis. 1998. *The Unknown City: The Lives of Poor and Working Class Young Adults*. Boston: Beacon Press

Fine, Michelle and Lois Weis, eds. 1993. *Beyond Silenced Voices: Class, Race and Gender in United States Schools*. Albany: State University of New York Press.

Fine, Michelle, Lois Weiss, Linda C. Powell, and L. Mun Wong, eds. 1997. *Off White: Readings on Race, Power and Society*. New York: Routledge.

Fiske, John. 1989a. *Understanding Popular Culture*. Boston: Unwin Hyman.

———. 1989b. *Reading The Popular*. Boston: Unwin Hyman.

Fiske, John, Bob Hodge, and Graeme Turner. 1987. *Myths of Oz: Reading Australian Popular Culture*. Boston: Allen & Unwin.

Foley, Douglas E. 1990. "The Great American Football Ritual: Reproducing Race, Class and Gender Inequality." *Sociology of Sport Journal* 7 (111–35).

Foucault, Michel. 1982. *Discipline and Punish*. London: Peregrine Books.

Frankenberg, Ruth. 1993. *White Women, Race Matters: The Social Construction of Whiteness*. Minneapolis: University of Minnesota Press.

Fricke, Aaron. 1981. *Reflections of A Rock Lobster: A Story About Growing Up Gay*. Boston: Alyson.

Friend, Richard A. 1993. "Choices, Not Closets: Heterosexism and Homophobia in Schools." *Beyond Silenced Voices: Class, Race, and Gender in United States Schools*, ed. Michelle Fine and Lois Weis. Albany: State University of New York Press.

Gaines, Donna. 1994. "Border Crossing in the U.S.A." *Microphone Fiends: Youth Music and Youth Culture*, ed. Andrew Ross and Tricia Rose. New York: Routledge.

———. 1990. *Teenage Wasteland: Suburbia's Dead End Kids*. Chicago: University of Chicago Press.

Gettis, Victoria. 1998. "Experts and Juvenile Delinquency, 1900–1935." *Generations of Youth: Youth Cultures and History in Twentieth-Century America*, ed. Joe Austin and Michael Nevin Willard. New York: New York University Press.

Gilbert, Pam and Sandra Taylor. 1991. *Fashioning the Feminine: Girls, Popular Culture and Schooling*. Sydney: Allen & Unwin.

Gimlin, Debra. 1996. "Pamela's Place: Power and Negotiation in the Hair Salon." *Gender and Society* 10:5 (505–26).

Giroux, Henry. 1997. *Channel Surfing: Race Talk and the Destruction of Today's Youth*. New York: St. Martin's Press

———. 1995. *Fugitive Cultures: Race, Violence and Youth*. New York: Routledge.

———. 1994. *Disturbing Pleasure: Learning Popular Culture*. New York: Routledge.

———. 1992. *Border Crossings: Cultural Workers and the Politics of Education*. London: Routledge.

———. 1983. *Theory and Resistance in Education: Pedagogy for the Opposition*. South Hadley, MA: Bergin & Garvey.

Giroux, Henry and Roger Simon, eds. 1989. *Popular Culture, Schooling and Everyday Life*. Granby, MA: Bergin & Garvey.

Glassner, Barry and Julia Loughlin. 1987. *Drugs in Adolescent Worlds: Burnouts to Straights*. New York: St. Martin's Press.

Goffman, Erving. 1959. *The Presentation of Self in Everyday Life*. New York: Doubleday.

Gordon, Deborah A. 1995. "Feminism and Cultural Studies." *Feminist Studies* 21:2 (363–76).

Graebner, William. 1990. *Coming of Age in Buffalo: Youth and Authority in the Postwar Era*. Philadelphia: Temple University Press.

Gray, Herman. 1993. "African-American Political Desire and the Seduction of Contemporary Cultural Politics." *Cultural Studies* 7 (364–72).

Griggers, Camilla. 1997. *Becoming Woman*. Minneapolis: University of Minnesota Press.

Grossberg, Lawrence, Cary Nelson, and Paula Treichler, eds. 1992. *Cultural Studies*. New York: Routledge.

Guillamine, Collette. 1995. *Racism, Sexism, Power and Ideology*. London: Routledge.

Hall, Stuart, ed. 1997. *Representation: Cultural Representations and Signifying Practices*. London: Open University Press.

———. 1981. "Notes on Deconstructing 'The Popular.'" *People's History and Socialist Theory*, ed. R. Samuel. London: Routledge & Kegan Paul.

Halle, David. 1993. *Inside Culture: Art and Class in the American Home*. Chicago: University of Chicago Press.

Harding, Sandra. 1987. *Feminism and Methodology: Social Science Issues*. Indianapolis: Indiana University Press.

Harrington, Lee and Denise D. Bielby. 1995. *Soap Fans: Pursuing Pleasure and Making Meaning in Everyday Life*. Philadelphia: Temple University Press.

Haug, Frigga et al. 1987. *Feminine Sexualisation: A Collective Work of Memory*. London: Verso.

Hebdige, Dick. 1979. *Subculture: The Meaning of Style*. London: Routledge.

Hirsch, Melanie. 1994. "A Night To Remember." *Herald American*, May 15, BB6–BB8.

Holland, Dorothy C. and Margaret A. Eisenhart. 1991. *Educated in Romance: Women, Achievement and College Culture*. Chicago: University of Chicago Press.

Hollander, Ann. 1975. *Seeing Through Clothes*. New York: Viking.

hooks, bell. 1995. *Reel to Real: Race, Sex and Class at the Movies*. New York: Routledge.

———. 1992. *Black Looks: Race and Representation*. Boston: South End Press.

———. 1989. *Talking Back: Thinking Feminist, Thinking Black*. Boston: South End Press.

Hudson, Barbara. 1984. "Femininity and Adolescence." *Gender and Generation*, ed. Angela McRobbie and Mica Nava. London: Macmillan.

Hughes, Walter. 1994. "In the Empire of the Beat: Discipline and Disco." *Microphone Fiends: Youth Music and Youth Culture*, ed. Andrew Ross and Tricia Rose. New York: Routledge.

Illouz, Eva. 1997. *Consuming the Romantic Utopia: Love and The Cultural Contradictions of Capitalism*. Berkeley and Los Angeles: University of California Press.

Ingraham, Chrys. 1999. *White Weddings: Romancing Heterosexuality in Popular Culture*. New York: Routledge.

Innes, Sherrie A., ed. 1998a. *Delinquents and Debutantes: Twentieth Century American Girls' Cultures*. New York: New York University Press.

———, ed. 1998b. *Millennium Girls*. New York: Rowan & Littlefield.

Irvine, Janice M, ed. 1994. *Sexual Cultures and the Construction of Adolescent Identities*. Philadelphia: Temple University Press.

Jennings, Kevin, ed. 1998. *Telling Tales Out Of School: Gays, Lesbians, and Bisexuals Revisit Their High School Days*. Los Angeles: Alyson Books.

Jones, Carol and Pat Mahoney. 1989. *Learning Our Lines: Sexuality and Social Control in Education*. London: The Women's Press.

Jones, Lisa. 1994. *Bulletproof Diva: Tales of Race, Sex and Hair*. New York: Anchor Books.

Kellner, Douglas. 1994. "Madonna, Fashion, and Identity." *On Fashion*, ed. Shari Benstock and Suzanne Ferriss. New Brunswick, NJ: Rutgers University Press.

Kett, Joseph F. 1977. *Rites of Passage: Adolescence in America, 1790 to the Present*. New York: Basic Books.

Kozol, Jonathon. 1991. *Savage Inequalities*. New York: Crown.

Krisman, Anne. 1987. "Radiator Girls: The Opinions and Experiences of Working Class Girls In An East London Comprehensive." *Cultural Studies* 1 (219–30).

Lavenda, Robert H. 1996. "'It's Not A Beauty Pageant!' Hybrid Ideology in Minnesota Community Queen Pageants." *Beauty Queens on The Global Stage: Gender, Contests and Power*, ed. Colleen Ballerino Cohen, Richard Wilk, and Beverly Stoeltje. New York: Routledge.

Leadbeater, Bonnie J. Ross and Niobe Way, eds. 1996. *Urban Girls: Resisting Stereotypes, Creating Identities*. New York: New York University Press.

Leahy, Terry. 1994. "Taking Up A Position: Discourse of Femininity and Adolescence in the Context of Man/Girl Relationships." *Gender and Society* 8:1 (48–72).

Lefkowitz, Bernard. 1998. *Our Guys: The Glen Ridge Rape and the Secret Life of the Perfect Suburb*. New York: Vintage Books.

Leonard, Marion. 1998. "Paper Planes: Traveling and the New Grrrl Geographies." *Cool Places: Geographies of Youth Cultures*, ed. Tracey Skelton and Gill Valentine. London: Routledge.

Lesko, Nancy. 1996. "Denaturalizing Adolescence: The Politics of Contemporary Representation." *Youth and Society* 28:2 (139–61).

———. 1988a. The Curriculum of the Body: Lessons from a Catholic High School." In *Becoming Feminine: The Politics of Popular Culture*, ed. Leslie G. Roman and Linda Christian-Smith. London: The Falmer Press.

———. 1988b. *Symbolizing Society: Stories, Rites, and Structure in a Catholic High School.* New York: Falmer Press.

Lewis, Jon. 1992. *The Road to Romance and Ruin: Teen Films and Youth Culture.* New York: Routledge.

Lipsitz, George. 1994. "We Know What Time It Is: Race, Class and Youth Culture in The Nineties." *Microphone Fiends: Youth Music and Youth Culture*, ed. Andrew Ross and Tricia Rose. New York: Routledge.

Lomawaima, K. Tsianina. 1994. *They Called it Prairie Light: The Story of a Chilocco Indian School.* Lincoln: University of Nebraska Press.

Lorber, Judith. 1994. *Paradoxes of Gender.* New Haven, CT: Yale University Press.

Luke, Carmen, ed. 1996. *Feminisms and Pedagogies of Everyday Life.* Albany: State University of New York Press.

Luke, Carmen and Jennifer Gore, eds. 1992. *Feminisms and Critical Pedagogy.* New York: Routledge.

Mac an Ghaill, Mairtin. 1994. *The Making of Men: Masculinities, Sexualities and Schooling.* Buckingham, England: Open University Press.

MacLeod, Jay. 1995. *Ain't No Making It: Aspirations and Attainment in a Low-Income Neighborhood.* Boulder, CO: Westview Press.

MacPherson, Pat. 1997. "The Revolution Of Little Girls." *Off White: Readings on Race, Power and Society*, ed. Michelle Fine, Lois Weis, Linda C. Powell, and L. Mun Wong. New York: Routledge.

"May we have this dance? Queer Teens Don't Ask, They Cut in . . . and Make Their Own Rules at a Northern California Prom Just for Them." *Inside Out: The Essential Queer Youth Magazine* 9 (20).

McCarthy, Cameron and Warren Crichlow, eds. 1993. *Race Identity and Representation in Education.* New York: Routledge.

McCarthy, Cameron and Alicia Rodriguez. 1997. "Race, Suburban Resentment, and the Representation of the Inner City in Contemporary Film and Television." *Off White: Readings on Race, Power and Society*, ed. Michelle Fine, Lois Weis, Linda C. Powell, and L. Mun Wong. New York: Routledge.

McCoy, Liz. 1995. "Activating the Photographic Text." *Knowledge, Experience and Ruling Relations: Studies in the Social Organization of Knowledge*, ed. Marie Campbell and Ann Manicom. Toronto: University of Toronto Press.

McDowell, Linda. 1999. *Gender, Identity and Place: Understanding Feminist Geographies.* Minneapolis: University of Minnesota Press.

McLaren, Peter. 1993. "Multiculturalism and the Postmodern Critique: Towards a Pedagogy of Resistance and Transformation." *Cultural Studies* 7 (118–43).

———. 1988. "On Ideology and Education: Critical Pedagogy and The Politics of Empowerment." *Social Text* 19:20 (153–81).

McRobbie, Angela. 1994. *Postmodernism and Popular Culture.* London: Routledge.

———. 1993. "Shut Up and Dance: Youth Culture and Changing Modes of Femininity." *Cultural Studies* 7 (406–26).

————, ed. 1991. *Feminism and Youth Culture: From Jackie to Just Seventeen.* Boston: Unwin Hyman.

McRobbie, Angela and Jennifer Garber. 1981. "Girls and Subcultures." *Feminism and Youth Culture: From Jackie to Just Seventeen*, ed. Angela McRobbie. Boston: Unwin Hyman.

Mercer, Kobena. 1990. "Hair and Politics." *Out There: Marginalization in Contemporary Culture*, ed. Russell Ferguson, Martha Gerver, Trinh T. Minh-ha, and Cornel West. Cambridge, MA: MIT Press.

Messner, Michael A. 1997. *Politics of Masculinities: Men in Movements.* London: Sage Publications.

————. 1992. *Power At Play: Sports and The Problem of Masculinity.* Boston: Beacon Press.

Miceli, Melinda. 1997. "Delayed Adolescence of Accelerated Adulthood? Gay Youth, Culture and Identity Formation." Conference paper presented at the American Sociological Association Meetings.

Minh-ha, Trinh T. 1989. *Women, Native, Other: Writing Postcoloniality and Feminism.* Bloomington: Indiana University Press.

Mitchell, Sally. 1995. *The New Girl: Girls' Culture in England 1880–1915.* New York: Columbia University Press.

Molner, Alex. 1996. *Giving Kids the Business: The Commercialization of America's Schools.* Boulder, CO: Westview Press.

Montgomery, Maureen E. 1998. *Displaying Women: Spectacles of Leisure in Edith Wharton's New York.* New York: Routledge.

Morgan, David. 1996. "Learning To Be a Man: Dilemmas and Contradictions of Masculine Experience." *Feminisms and Pedagogies of Everyday Life*, ed. Carmen Luke. Albany: State University of New York Press.

Mueller, Adele. 1995. "Beginning in the Standpoint of Women: An Investigation of the Gap between Cholas and 'Women in Peru.'" *Knowledge, Experience and Ruling Relations: Studies in the Social Organization of Knowledge*, ed. Marie Campbell and Ann Manicom. Toronto: University of Toronto Press.

Nava, Mica. 1991. "Consumerism Reconsidered: Buying and Power." *Cultural Studies* 51 (57–172).

————. 1987. " Consumerism and Its Contradictions." *Cultural Studies* 1 (204–10).

Neal, Mark Anthony. 1999. *What The Music Said: Black Popular Music and Black Public Culture.* New York: Routledge.

Nicholson, Linda and Nancy Fraser, eds. 1990. *Feminism and Postmodernism.* New York: Routledge.

Odem, Mary E. 1998. "Teenage Girls, Sexuality, and Working Class Parents in Early Twentieth-Century California." *Generations of Youth: Youth Cultures and History in Twentieth-Century America*, ed. Joe Austin and Michael Nevin Willard. New York: New York University Press.

————. 1995. *Delinquent Daughters: Protecting and Policing Adolescent Female Sexuality in The United States, 1885–1920.* Chapel Hill: The University of North Carolina Press.

Palladino, Grace. 1996. *Teenagers: An American History.* New York: Basic Books.

Phillips, Jayne Anne. 1998. "Home After Dark: A Funeral for Three Girls In Kentucky." *Harper's*, November, 73–83.

Pinar, William F., ed. 1998. *Queer Theory in Education*. Mahwah, NJ: Lawrence Erlbaum.

Poster, Mark. 1988. *Jean Baudrillard: Selected Writings*. Stanford, CA.: Stanford University Press.

Proweller, Amira. 1998. *Constructing Female Identities: Meaning Making in an Upper Middle Class Youth Culture*. Albany: State University of New York Press.

Pruyn, Marc. 1999. *Discourse Wars in Gotham-West: A Latino Immigrant Urban Tale of Resistance and Agency*. Boulder, CO: Westview Press.

Rabinow, Paul, ed. 1984. *The Foucault Reader*. New York: Pantheon Books.

Radner, Hillary. 1995. *Shopping Around: Feminine Culture and The Pursuit of Pleasure*. New York: Routledge.

———. 1989. "'This Time's For Me': Making Up and Feminine Practice." *Cultural Studies* 3 (301–21).

Radway, Janice. 1984. *Reading the Romance: Women, Patriarchy and Popular Literature*. Chapel Hill: University of North Carolina Press.

Reinharz, Shulamit. 1992. *Feminist Methods in Social Research*. New York: Oxford University Press.

Reisman, Catherine Kohler. 1987. "When Gender Is Not Enough: Women Interviewing Women." *Gender and Society* 1:2 (172–207).

Roberts, Helen. 1981. *Doing Feminist Research*. London: Routledge & Kegan Paul.

Rodriquez, Nelson. 1998. "(Queer) Youth as Political and Pedagogical." *Queer Theory in Education*, ed. William F. Pinar. Mahwah, NJ: Lawrence Erlbaum.

Roman, Leslie G. and Linda Christian-Smith, eds. 1988. *Becoming Feminine: The Politics of Popular Culture*. London: The Falmer Press.

Rose, Tricia. 1994. "A Style Nobody Can Deal With: Politics, Style and The Post-Industrial City in Hip Hop." *Microphone Fiends: Youth Music and Youth Culture*, ed. Andrew Ross and Tricia Rose. New York: Routledge.

Ross, Andrew and Tricia Rose, eds. 1994. *Microphone Fiends: Youth Music and Youth Culture*. New York: Routledge.

Sadker, Myra and David Sadker. 1994. *Failing At Fairness: How America's Schools Cheat Girls*. New York: Charles Scribner's Sons.

Salinger, Rickie. 1995. *Wake Up Little Susie: Single Pregnancy and Race Before Roe v. Wade*. New York: Routledge.

Sapon-Shevin, Mara. 1993. "Gifted Education and The Protection of Privilege: Breaking the Silence, Opening the Discourse." *Beyond Silenced Voices: Class, Race, and Gender in United States Schools*, ed. Michelle Fine and Lois Weis. Albany: State University of New York Press.

Sato, Rika Sakuma. 1998. "What Are Girls Made of? Exploring the Symbolic Boundaries of Femininity in Two Cultures." *Millennium Girls*, ed. Sherrie Inness. New York: Rowan & Littlefield.

Schofield, Janet Ward. 1989. *Black and White In School: Trust, Tension or Tolerance?* New York: Teachers College Press, Columbia University.

Schrum, Kelly. 1998. "'Teena Means Business'": Teenage Girls' Culture and *Seventeen* Magazine, 1944–1950." *Delinquents and Debutantes: Twentieth Century American Girls' Culture*, ed. Sherrie A. Inness. New York: New York University Press.

Scott, Joan C. 1992. "Experience." *Feminist Theorizing the Political*, ed. Judith Butler and Joan C. Scott. New York: Routledge.

Sears, James T. 1998. "Growing Up as a Jewish Lesbian in South Florida: Queer Teen Life in the Fifties." *Generations of Youth: Youth Cultures and History in Twentieth-Century America*, ed. Joe Austin and Michael Novin Willard. New York: New York University Press.

Seidman, Steven. 1992. "Postmodern Social Theory as Narrative with a Moral Intent." *Postmodernism and Social Theory*, ed. Steven Seidman and David G. Wagner. Cambridge, MA: Blackwell.

Seidman, Steven and David G. Wagner, eds. 1992. *Postmodernism and Social Theory*. Cambridge, MA: Blackwell.

Sennet, Richard and Jonathan Cobb. 1972. *The Hidden Injuries of Class*. New York: Random House.

Shepard, Jean. 1971. *Wanda Hickey's Night of Golden Memories and Other Disasters*. New York: Doubleday.

Sikes, Gini. 1997. *8 Ball Chicks: A Year in the Violent World of Girl Gangsters*. New York: Anchor Books.

Silverstone, Roger, ed. 1997. *Visions of Suburbia*. New York: Routledge.

Simon, Roger I. 1993. "Forms of Insurgency in the Production of Popular Memories: The Columbus Quincentenary and the Pedagogy of Counter Commemoration." *Cultural Studies* 7 (73–87).

Skelton, Tracey and Gill Valentine, eds. 1998. *Cool Places: Geographies of Youth Culture*. London: Routledge.

Smith, Dorothy E. 1990a. *Texts, Facts and Femininity: Exploring the Relations of Ruling*. New York: Routledge.

———. 1990b. *The Conceptual Practices of Power: A Feminist Sociology of Knowledge*. Boston: Northeastern University Press.

———. 1987. *The Everyday World As Problematic. A Feminist Method*. Boston: Northeastern University Press.

Spender, Dale. 1980. *Man Made Language*. London: Routledge & Kegan Paul.

Spring, Joel. 1994. *The American School: 1642–1993*, 3rd ed. New York: McGraw Hill.

Steinberg, Shirley and Joe L. Kincheloe, eds. 1997. *Kinder-Culture: The Corporate Construction of Childhood*. Boulder, CO: Westview Press.

Stoeltje, Beverly. 1996. "The Snake Charmer Queen: Ritual Competition and Signification in American Festival." *Beauty Queens On The Global Stage: Gender, Contests and Power*, ed. Colleen Ballerino Cohen, Richard Wilk, and Beverly Stoeltje. New York: Routledge.

Strauss, Anselm L. 1987. *Qualitative Analysis for Social Scientists*. Cambridge: Cambridge University Press.

Swaminathan, Rajewari. 1997. "The Charming Sideshow: Cheerleading, Girls' Culture, and Schooling." Unpublished Ph.D. dissertation, Syracuse University.

Thomas, Helen, ed. 1993. *Dance, Gender and Culture*. New York: St. Martin's Press.

Thompson, Becky and Sangeeta Tyagi, eds. 1996. *Names We Call Home: Autobiography on Racial Identity*. New York: Routledge.

Thompson, Sharon. 1995. *Going All The Way: Teenage Girls' Tales of Sex, Romance and Pregnancy*. New York: Hill and Wang.

Thorne, Barrie. 1993. *Gender Play: Girls and Boys in School*. New Jersey: Rutgers University Press.

Tolman, Deborah L. 1994. "Doing Desire: Adolescent Girls' Struggle for/with Sexuality." *Gender and Society* 8:3 (324–42).

Torres, Carlos Alberto. 1998a. *Education, Power and Personal Biography: Dialogues with Critical Educators*. New York: Routledge.

———. 1998b. *Democracy, Education and Multiculturalism: Dilemmas of Citizenship in a Global World*. Lanham, MD: Rowan & Littlefield.

Tozer, Steven E., Paul C. Violas, and Guy Senese. 1993. *School and Society: Educational Practice as Social Expression*. New York: McGraw Hill.

Trend, David. 1995. *The Crisis of Meaning in Culture and Education*. Minneapolis: University of Minnesota Press.

Twitchell, James B. 1992. *Carnival Culture: The Trashing of Taste in America*. New York: Columbia University Press

Unks, Gerald, ed. 1995. *The Gay Teen: Educational Practice and Theory for Lesbian, Gay and Bisexual Adolescents*. New York: Routledge.

Vinitzky-Seroussi, Vered. 1998. *After Pomp and Circumstance: High School Reunion as an Autobiographical Occasion*. Chicago: University of Chicago Press.

Voss, Margaret M. 1996. *Hidden Literacies: Children Learning at Home and at School*. Portsmouth, NH: Heinemann.

Walcott, Rinaldo. 1998. "Queer Texts and Performativity: Zora, Rap and Community." *Queer Theory in Education*, ed. William F. Pinar. Mahwah, NJ: Lawrence Erlbaum.

Walker, J. C. 1987. *Louts and Legends: Male Youth Culture in an Inner-City School*. London: Allen & Unwin.

Walkerdine, Valerie. 1990. *Schoolgirl Fictions*. London: Verso.

Webber, Marlene. 1991. *Street Kids: The Tragedy of Canada's Runaways*. Toronto: University of Toronto Press.

West, Candice and Sarah Fenstermaker. 1995. "Doing Difference." *Gender and Society* 9:1 (8–37).

West, Candice and Don Zimmerman. 1987. "Doing Gender." *Gender and Society* 1 (125–51).

West, Cornel. 1993. "The New Cultural Politics of Difference." *Race Identity and Representation in Education*, ed. Cameron McCarthy and Warren Crichlow. New York: Routledge.

Whiteley, Sheila, ed. 1997. *Sexing the Groove: Popular Music and Gender*. London: Routledge.

Willis, Paul. 1977. *Learning to Labour*. Aldershot, England: Saxon House.

Willis, Susan. 1996. "Play For Profit." *Feminisms and Pedagogies of Everyday Life*, ed. Carmen Luke. Albany: State University of New York Press.

Woog, Dan. 1995. *School's Out: The Impact of Gay and Lesbian Issues on America's Schools*. Boston: Alyson.

Wray, Matt and Annalee Newitz, eds. 1997. *White Trash: Race and Class in America*. New York: Routledge.

Young, Iris Marion. 1994. "Women Recovering Our Clothes." *On Fashion*, ed. Shari Benstock and Suzanne Ferriss. New Brunswick, NJ: Rutgers University Press.

# Index